# Survival Skills
# for College

Mary C. Starke

*Ramapo College*

# Survival Skills for College

Prentice Hall, Englewood Cliffs, New Jersey 07632

Library of Congress Cataloging-in-Publication Data

Starke, Mary C.
    Survival skills for college / Mary C. Starke.
        p.   cm.
    Includes bibliographical references.
    ISBN 0-13-879008-6
    1. College student orientation.  2. Study, Method of.  3. College
students--Conduct of life.  4. College students--Health and hygiene.
5. College students--Time management.   I. Title.
LB2343.3.S74  1990
378.1'98--dc20                                            89-38990
                                                          CIP

Editorial/production supervision and
    interior design: WordCrafters Editorial Services, Inc.
Cover photo: Gabe Palmer
                The Stock Market
Cover design: Bruce Kenselaar
Manufacturing buyer: M. Woerner

 ©1990 by Prentice-Hall, Inc.
A Division of Simon & Schuster
Englewood Cliffs, New Jersey 07632

Printed in the United States of America

10  9  8  7  6  5  4  3

ISBN 0-13-879008-6

Prentice-Hall International (UK) Limited, *London*
Prentice-Hall of Australia Pty. Limited, *Sydney*
Prentice-Hall Canada Inc., *Toronto*
Prentice-Hall Hispanoamericana, S.A., *Mexico*
Prentice-Hall of India Private Limited, *New Delhi*
Prentice-Hall of Japan, Inc., *Tokyo*
Simon & Schuster Asia Pte. Ltd., *Singapore*
Editora Prentice-Hall Do Brasil, Ltda., *Rio de Janeiro*

*I dedicate this book to my parents, Eva and David Celnik, who taught me the value of survival, and to my husband, Charles Starke, and children, Katherine and Robert, who make survival worthwhile. I thank them for their support and understanding and apologize for all those pizza dinners, postponed birthday parties, nocturnal printing sessions, and missed vacations.*

# Contents

# Preface

The college experience! It is an exciting time: a time of dreams, hopes, and fears, of great joys, major adjustments, and some disappointments. It is a time to grow, to develop intellectual and emotional competencies, to learn about oneself and others, and to develop academic and interpersonal skills.

The freshman year is the gateway to this experience. It is the year in which you will acquire the skills and knowledge that will lay the foundation for the balance of your college career.

When I went to college in the sixties, students were expected to learn these types of skills and knowledge on their own. Many did learn them and they became successful college graduates. Others did not, and they dropped out of college.

College students today come from a broader variety of backgrounds. We have more students who are members of minority groups, more students who have interrupted their educations to work or to raise families, more students who need help with basic academic skills, more students who have physical or learning challenges of various sorts, and more students who are the first members of their families to attend college. Life is also more complex these days; there are greater pressures, more anxieties, and more choices to make.

As a result of the broader mixture of student backgrounds and the greater complexities in life choices, many educators feel that college students today can benefit from a course that teaches them survival skills and helps them make the transition from high school or work to the college environment.

Let me say a few words about the goals for this text and the type of course—sometimes known as the freshman seminar. Some of the goals are academic. The text will help you improve your writing, reasoning, and research skills; you will, therefore, find numerous writing assignments in this text. You will learn through these assignments to relate your own experiences to readings from assigned texts and to materials from the library.

The text will also help you improve your verbal skills and feel more comfortable when you speak in front of a group. For this reason, this text asks you to complete several oral assignments.

You will find yourself participating in units on study skills, note-taking skills, library skills, reading skills, test-taking skills, and time management skills. These chapters contain notes in the margins that highlight important concepts, guidelines, and key terms. Review these notes after you have read the chapter. This review will help you remember the most important points. These margin notes will also serve as models for the kinds of notes you should be making in your other textbooks to help you study more effectively. This text will help you to become a successful student who gets the most from your college education!

This text also has a number of personal and interpersonal goals. For one, that you will come to understand and like yourself better and that you will also come to understand others better and be more accepting of their differences, whether these differences are based on race, ethnic group, gender, or physical challenges. To this end you will have readings, exercises, and films on values and communication.

If you are to succeed in college, you must take care of your physical and mental ''plant.'' This text will help you to lead a healthier lifestyle; it includes units on stress, relaxation, nutrition, and drug and alcohol abuse. To succeed in college, you must also acquire or reaffirm responsible values regarding interpersonal relationships. For this purpose, you will explore issues in communication, intimacy, and sexuality.

This text should help to make you feel secure in your college environment. It will do this by familiarizing you with campus support services and policies, by having you participate in campus activities, by letting you know what you may expect from a college education, and also by giving you an idea of what the faculty and staff expect from you as a college student. The faculty and staff will offer you academic advisement so that you may make informed choices about courses, majors, and careers.

The exercises in the text will help make learning an active, participatory experience for you, as research shows that students feel better about themselves and their colleges when they are actively involved in campus activities. Students not only feel better, they also perform better and are less likely to drop out of school! The purpose of the text is to help you graduate with the best possible education. That will happen only if you take advantage of both extracurricular opportunities and academic opportunities offered at your college.

The text will also help you maximize your participation in class. You will experience relatively little lecturing in this course; rather you will find yourself writing about your research, giving oral reports about your experiences, interacting with guest speakers, participating in exercises and small group discussions, reacting critically to controversial films, keeping journals, and occasionally attending events with your class.

The text has several goals in promoting all of this activity: students learn better when they participate actively in the learning process. In addition, students gain a better understanding of themselves and others when they are involved in these sorts of exercises and discussions. Finally, students learn to interact more comfortably and competently with both faculty and students through this process.

Welcome to the freshman seminar, a course that will help you grow and become a successful college student. I do hope that you will make the most of your valuable college experience!

## A WORD TO THE PROFESSIONAL

This preface presents the goals and rationale for this text. The text forms the basis for a freshman seminar course that is meant to help students acquire the academic and personal skills that will ensure their success in college. The idea for such a course is not new; the first-known course of this type offered for credit was given at Reed College in 1911.[1] What *is* new today is the increasing number of institutions that offer such a course. A survey by the American Council on Education revealed that almost 78 percent of American institutions of higher learning offer a course in coping with the college experience and that the percentage of institutions is increasing.[2]

The increasing popularity of such courses is not surprising. Longitudinal studies at a growing number of institutions show that students who have enrolled in freshman seminar courses persist in college in greater numbers than students who have not taken such a course. The difference in retention rates varies among institutions, but the rates consistently favor students who have taken freshman seminar courses.[3]

It may well be that the various bonds these seminar students establish at their colleges are responsible for their higher persistence rates. For example, surveys at many institutions reveal that freshmen who enroll in these freshman seminar courses attend more events on campus, belong to more extracurricular organizations, are more familiar with campus services, feel more comfortable approaching faculty if they have a problem, and speak with faculty more frequently outside of class than freshmen who have not taken such a course.[4]

Students appreciate the value of this seminar. In one survey, for example, 78 percent of the freshmen who had taken the seminar recommended that it be given to freshmen in the future.[5] Other data indicate that seminar students see more of an improvement in their study habits and use the library more frequently than students who have not enrolled in the seminar.[6] A number of studies also find evidence of higher grade point averages among seminar enrollees than among students who have not taken the freshman seminar.[7]

This text offers both readings and exercises for the freshman seminar course. Researchers have found that students learn better by *doing* than by just reading or hearing material. The format of readings interspersed with exercises is also more likely than the traditional format to hold the students' attention.

The text contains many different types of exercises. You may not have time to use all of them in class. Tailor the exercises to fit your course. For example, you may wish to assign some exercises to be completed by students on their own outside of class. Other assignments may be completed outside of class and submitted as written assignments to the instructor. You may choose to have students write and discuss some exercises in class. The Instructor's Manual offers chapter-by-chapter guidelines to help you diversify your classes and make them successful. I have found that variety is the key to maintaining the students' interest and motivation.

The text is particularly detailed in the sections dealing with birth control, sexually transmitted diseases, substance abuse, nutrition, health, and exercise. This detail is included as backup for instructors who may not be comfortable or familiar in teaching these topics to students. Many colleges do not offer courses in these areas, yet knowledge about these topics can make the difference between a successful student and one who is forced to withdraw from college. The students' knowledge about sexually transmitted diseases and alcohol/substance abuse may literally mean the difference between life and death. If you do not wish to cover this material in class, you might consider assigning it solely as outside reading. The sections are complete enough so that students can learn this important information on their own.

The text is complete in itself; the course, however, can be improved by using films. For example "A Class Divided"[8] is an excellent aid to spurring discussion in the unit on minorities. Guest speakers from organizations such as Planned Parenthood, local suicide hotlines, and substance abuse programs also add diversity and stimulation. The Instructor's Manual offers additional suggestions along these lines.

Faculty across the nation are reporting that the freshman seminar helps them see the college experience from a new perspective. They also find themselves forming closer relationships with their students as they teach this course. A survey at Ramapo College revealed that 95 percent of the instructors who had taught freshman seminar were interested in teaching it again. I hope that you will become as enthusiastic about this text and learning experience as we have.

## NOTES

1. V.N. Gordon and T.J. Grites, "The Freshman Seminar Course: Helping Students Succeed." *Journal of College Student Personnel,* July 1984, pp. 315–320.

2. E. El-Kawas, ed., "Campus Trends, 1984: A Survey of the American Council on Education," *Higher Education Report* No. 65 (Washington, D.C.: American Council on Education, 1985): 9.

3. M.C. Starke, "Retention and Bonding: The Effectiveness of the Freshman Seminar at Ramapo College" (Paper presented at the Seventh Annual Conference of the Freshman Year Experience, White Plains, N.Y., April 1988); P.P. Fidler, "Evidence of the Effectiveness of the Freshman Seminar," in *Enhancing the Success of the First Year Students· The Freshman Experience,* ed. J.N. Gardner and M.L. Upcraft (San Francisco: Jossey-Bass, forthcoming), Chap. 15; L. Dunphy et al, in *Increasing Retention: Academic and Affairs Administrators in Partnership. New Directions for Higher Education,* ed. M.M. Stodt and W.M. Klepper (San Francisco: Jossey-Bass, 1987).

4. M.C. Starke, "Retention and Bonding: The Effectiveness of the Freshman Seminar at Ramapo College" (Paper presented at the Seventh Annual Conference of the Freshman Year Experience, White Plains, N.Y., April 1988); P.P. Fidler, "Evidence of the Effectiveness of the Freshman Seminar," in *Enhancing the Success of the First Year Students: The Freshman Experience,* ed. J.N. Gardner and M.L. Upcraft (San Francisco: Jossey-Bass, forthcoming), Chap. 15.

5. M. Harth, personal communication (1987).

6. M.C. Starke, "Retention and Bonding: The Effectiveness of the Freshman Seminar at Ramapo College" (Paper presented at the Seventh Annual Conference of the Freshman Year Experience, White Plains, N.Y., April 1988).

7. P.P. Fidler, "Evidence of the Effectiveness of the Freshman Seminar," in *Enhancing the Success of the First Year Students: The Freshman Experience,* ed. J.N. Gardner and M.L. Upcraft (San Francisco: Jossey-Bass, forthcoming), Chap. 15.

8. "A Class Divided" is available for rental or purchase from Public Broadcasting Services in Alexandria, VA: 800–424–7963.

# Acknowledgments

I am grateful to Charles Starke for his loving support and encouragement. I thank Charles Starke and Gordon Bear for editorial assistance, ideas, and support that were heroically and cheerfully given against a background of forbidding deadlines.

I am pleased to acknowledge the following faculty and staff who read chapters or suggested materials to be included in this book and helped me with the research: Kay Collins, David Greene, Marshall Harth, Karen Janus, Arnold Jones, Ellen Kaiden, Celia O'Brien, Linda Padley, Phyllis Pickens, Eileen Quaglino, Karen Rosenschein, and Linda Sadlock.

I also offer thanks to the editorial staff at Prentice Hall, especially Phil Miller, to Ann Mohan at WordCrafters, and to the reviewers of earlier drafts of this manuscript: Marshall S. Harth, Ramapo College of New Jersey; Margaret Anne Langer, University of the Pacific; Sara Lee Sanderson, Miami-Dade Community College; Robert Spier, Hartnell College; and Phyllis N. Weatherly, Southern College of Technology.

# Chapter 1

---

# Benefits and Goals of a College Education

According to the Bureau of the Census, over 12 million students are enrolled in college degree programs in the United States. More than 2.5 million of these students are freshmen; so take heart, you have lots of company![1]

## REASONS FOR ATTENDING COLLEGE

Why are so many people willing to spend considerable amounts of time, effort, and money to attain a college education? For many students, the goals of a college education are career related; for others, the benefits of college involve personal satisfactions such as developing one's mind, undertaking an exciting challenge, learning new skills or acquiring knowledge, and meeting new people. The advantages of a college degree run the gamut from higher salaries to better health, from happier marriages to greater satisfaction with careers, from higher self-esteem to better parenting skills. The more you know about what college can offer you and the clearer you are about your goals for your own college experience, the more likely it is that you will get the most from that experience.

EXERCISE:
REFLECTING ON
YOUR REASONS
FOR ATTENDING
COLLEGE

The list that follows presents many of the reasons students commonly give for attending college. Look over the list, then put a 1 next to the item that represents your main reason for enrolling in college, a 2 next to the item that comes next in importance for you, and a 3 next to the item that describes your third most-important reason for attending college. Then go back and put a 13, a 14, and a 15 next to the three items that were least important in influencing your decision to enroll in college.

1

I enrolled in college to

_____ prepare for a job or profession

_____ find a spouse or mate

_____ gain knowledge

_____ get a degree

_____ learn problem-solving skills

__14__ learn how to learn

_____ have something to do

__13__ please my parents

_____ make friends

__15__ raise my economic prospects

__1__ gain security

__3__ gain prestige or status

_____ become more mature

__2__ have fun

_____ become a more productive member of society

We know that many jobs are open only to individuals who have earned college degrees. We also know that a college degree means a higher starting salary and a greater probability of promotion in many companies. For example, a thirty-year study of managers at AT&T revealed that just earning a college degree has a strong influence on whether employees move up the management ladder.[2] The average professional earns $3,188 more each month than the average high school dropout, a difference of $1.75 million over the course of his or her working lifetime. The average monthly income for a college graduate is $1,841 compared to only $1,045 for the average high school graduate.[3] This represents $430,000 more in earned income over the course of a career.

Other vocational benefits associated with a college degree may be even more important than the financial ones. College graduates tend to get jobs that are more stimulating and challenging, that offer them greater safety from physical hazards, and that give them greater responsibility and freedom to prove their talents.

## CHOOSING A CAREER DIRECTION

Once you have decided to earn a college degree, your next question is, "What type of education should I pursue?" Many students these days are choosing majors in technical fields such as engineering, business, and computer science, where demand and starting salaries are high. Students feel more secure about these majors, as they seem to directly prepare them for a particular job after college. Yet studies show that very few people stay in the same line of work over the course of their working lives. The average freshman may well make four career changes during his or her lifetime, in addition to several job changes within each career.

No one can predict accurately which particular job skills will be in demand in ten years, much less in twenty or thirty years. As you change jobs, the best preparation for career success will be the knowledge of how to learn new skills and the willingness to undertake that learning. An education that emphasizes critical thinking skills will provide the key to success. A course of study is necessary that teaches you the ability to understand and interpret complex relationships and to analyze and question basic assumptions about how things are done. These are not necessarily fostered by a course of education that teaches technical skills designed to fit you for a particular job. These are abilities traditionally fostered by a liberal arts education—majors in history, literature, psychology, economics, philosophy, and political science, to name a few.

Perhaps this is the reason that a survey of two thousand graduates from the University of Virginia revealed that 91 percent of them recommend a liberal arts major.[4] Graduates holding varied positions, such as bank vice president, assistant district attorney, physician, editorial producer, and systems analyst, all felt that the liberal arts prepared them for the most-successful careers. Although these students often ended up in jobs that seem far removed from their undergraduate majors, they felt that the liberal arts background gave them the thinking, research, and communications skills to ensure flexibility and, therefore, success in a broad range of career shifts dictated by changes in their interests or in the economy's needs.

An informal survey by Lynne Cheney revealed that the communications world is dominated by liberal arts majors.[5] For example, Thomas H. Wyman, chairman of CBS, and Cathleen Black, publisher of *USA Today,* both majored in English. William Raspberry, columnist for the *Washington Post,* studied history, and NBC news anchorman, Tom Brokaw, specialized in political science.

A few phone calls around Capitol Hill revealed that an impressive number of the top positions in government are also held by liberal arts majors: both President George Bush and his economic advisor, Michael Boskin, majored in economics. Vice President Quayle and Secretary of Labor Elizabeth Dole both specialized in political science. Secretary of the Treasury Nicholas Brady pursued a degree in the liberal arts at Yale University, and Secretary of State James Baker III specialized in history and the classics at Princeton University. Secretary of Housing and Urban Development Jack Kemp received degrees in physical education and public affairs, while Manuel Lujan, Secretary of the Interior, majored in liberal arts. Secretary of Education Lauro Cavazos specialized in zoology, and U.S. Trade Representative Carla Hills received a degree in history.

Former president Ronald Reagan's government revealed a similar predisposition towards liberal arts majors. Reagan majored in economics and sociology. His communications director, Pat Buchanan, specialized in English and philosophy. Chief of Staff and former Secretary of the Treasury Donald Regan, majored in English before embarking on a highly successful career at the head of Merrill Lynch. Secretary of Commerce Malcolm Baldrige, who headed Scoville Manufacturing, was also an English major. Vice President George Bush, Secretary of State George Schultz, and Secretary of Energy John Herrington all majored in economics. Secretary of the Treasury James Baker specialized in history with a minor in classics, while Interior Secretary Donald Hodel found his niche in a government major. Transportation Secretary Elizabeth Dole chose political science, and Secretary of Education William Bennett majored in philosophy.[6]

Executives like Donald Regan, who headed Merrill Lynch, and Malcolm Baldrige, who steered Scoville Manufacturing before entering government service, are not unusual in their liberal arts backgrounds. A recent report in *Fortune* magazine revealed that 38 percent of the current chief executive officers majored in the liberal arts.[7] *The New York Times*[8] reports that nine of the top thirteen executives at IBM were liberal arts majors, and the AT&T study mentioned earlier found that humanities and social science majors were more successful in the managerial ranks of that company than engineering and business majors. A study by Northwestern University reports that many large companies plan to increase their hiring of liberal arts majors. They are looking for students with strengths in broader skills. They will then give these successful graduates the technical training they need for specific jobs.[9]

These surveys are not mentioned here to dissuade you from pursuing a major in business, engineering, or computer science. The starting salaries in these fields are higher than those in the liberal arts, and there are currently many job openings available in these areas. The more technical fields may be particularly appropriate for nontraditional students whose previous background in college or in the workplace gives them very focused career objectives. By all means, enroll in these courses if you enjoy them. I do mention these surveys in the hopes of dissuading you from pursuing a major that does not interest you just because it seems to offer initial job security. Most students in the late 1980s reported that career advancement was one of their major reasons for attending college. I have, unfortunately, seen many students try to cram themselves into a mold that doesn't suit them. It is not a strategy that is likely to breed success or happiness.

It might be a better investment of your college time to major in a field that interests you rather than to force yourself through courses that are boring just for the sake of improving your prospects for that first job. If you are interested in your courses, you will be motivated to study and get the best education you can in college. This will give you a better edge in the job market than you would receive from specific training in a field that you do not enjoy and that may not be in demand by the time you graduate. If you are interested in your job, you are less likely to "burn out" quickly and more likely to put in the long hours and effort that will ensure success and satisfaction.

Use your college years to expand your horizons, to broaden and strengthen your mind, to follow your intellectual curiosity, and to enjoy the stimulation of your instructors and peers. Even if this does not lead directly to the field with the highest starting salary immediately after graduation, it may well be the course that leads to ultimate career success in both financial and personal terms.

## EXTRACURRICULAR ACTIVITIES

In addition to your major and the actual courses you take, you will find that college offers you exposure to a wealth of experiences outside the classroom. Many of these experiences are organized in the extracurricular programs of the college. If you enjoy writing, there is the college newspaper or literary magazine. If you are interested in government or politics, there is the student government structure, where you can work actively to influence the quality of campus life; there are also local political campaigns where you can volunteer your services and learn about the electoral process. If you enjoy music, you may wish to join the college choir or learn to play an instrument.

There are opportunities to work on and off campus in cooperative education, internships, and research positions related to your studies. These activities offer you the chance to develop leadership skills, to work as part of a team, to initiate, organize, and implement programs, and to learn skills that cannot be taught in a classroom. Both a University of Virginia study and an AT&T study found that extracurricular activities and other kinds of experiential learning (internships, summer jobs, and cooperative education), along with personal initiative, were highly correlated with success in a chosen career.[10] So take advantage of these opportunities to develop your abilities and your career prospects.

**EXERCISE: DETERMINING YOUR COLLEGE GOALS**

This exercise is meant to help you clarify your goals for a college education, meet the other members of your class, and practice some public speaking skills.

1. Sit next to someone you do not know and discuss the questions below. Record each other's answers, as you will be introducing this person to the rest of the class when you have finished talking with each other.

Name: _____

Home town: _____

Favorite activities, hobbies, interests: _____

_____

_____

_____

_____

_____

If you could be anyone else in the world, who would you choose to be?

_____

Reasons for attending college: _____

_____

_____

_____

Reasons for attending this particular college: _____

_____

_____

_____

Two most memorable experiences (good or bad) that you have experienced at college so far: _____

_____

_____

_____

Probable major(s) or career: (Don't be afraid to say "undecided.") _____

_____

2.  When you have completed your individual conversations, your instructor will go around the room and ask each of you to introduce your partner to the class.

## NOTES

1.  "College Enrollment, Degree Credit Only," *Statistical Abstracts of the United States 1989* (Washington, D.C.: U.S. Department of Commerce, Bureau of the Census, 1989), p. 127.

2.  G. Dessler, "Just Earning College Degree Is Important," *Bergen County (N.J.) Record,* 8 September 1986.

3.  "What Value Education? Counting the Whys," *New York Times,* 3 October 1987, p. 29.

4.  S. T. Hitchcock and R. Benner, in "Life after Liberal Arts," by W. Raspberry, *The Bergen County (N.J.) Record,* 19 June 1986.

5.  L. Cheney, "Students of Success," *Newsweek,* 1 September 1986, p. 7.

6.  Ibid.

7.  Ibid.

8.  "What Value Education? Counting the Whys," p. 29.

9.  Ibid.

10.  S. T. Hitchcock and R. Benner, in "Life After Liberal Arts," by W. Raspberry.

# Chapter 2

## The College Structure

### THE COLLEGE CATALOG

A college, like any other organization, has a structure and a set of rules by which it functions. In order to succeed in this organization, you must know its rules and you must know where to go when you need help. The most-complete source for much of this information is the college catalog. It includes a wealth of information such as course descriptions, tuition fees, beginning and ending session dates, final withdrawal date, minimum grade point average, faculty and administrative titles and departments, grading policies, and requirements for majors. As you look through the college catalog, you may find some interesting fields of learning you did not know existed. The following exercise will help you familiarize yourself with your college's catalog and rules.

**EXERCISE: USING YOUR COLLEGE CATALOG**

Read the general information section of your college catalog and the program descriptions for two majors that might interest you in order to find the answers to the questions.

**The Academic Calendar**

1. During what dates will the college be closed for holidays this semester?

_____

_____

_____

2. What is the last date on which you may add or drop courses?

_____

_____

3. What is the last date on which you may withdraw from a course and still receive a partial refund on your tuition?

_____

_____

4. On what dates will registration for next semester take place?

_____

_____

5. If your school offers you the option of taking a grade of "incomplete," what is the last date to request this grade?

_____

_____

6. What is the last date on which you can withdraw from a course?

_____

7. When is final exam week scheduled?

_____

8. What is the last day of classes?

_____

9. What is the first day of classes next semester?

_____

**General Background Information**

1. When was your college founded?

_____

2. Does your college have any particular mission, focus, or area of specialization? If so, what is it?

_____

_____

_____

3. Is your college accredited by any national organization(s)? Which one(s)?

_____

_____

4. How many students are enrolled in the college?

_____

**Your College's Organizational Structure**

1. How is your institution organized (colleges, schools, divisions, departments)?

_____

_____

2. List three examples of departments or majors within your institution.

_____

_____

_____

3. Does your institution offer graduate or professional programs? List three programs.

_____

_____

_____

**Financial Information**

1. What is the annual tuition that applies to you at your college? (At most public institutions, state or county residents pay lower tuition than out-of-state residents.)

_____

2. What types of financial aid programs are available (scholarships, work/study programs, loans)?

_____

_____

_____

3. Where would you go to find more information about financial aid?

_____

_____

**Academic Policies and Grades**

1. Does your college offer credit for advanced courses taken in high school?

_____

2. Does your college accept transfer credits from other institutions?

_____

3. Does your college give credit for certain types of life experience outside the classroom?

_____

4. What is the grading system? (List the grades that may be given by instructors.)

_____

_____

_____

5. Explain the following grade options if your college offers them:

Incomplete

_____

_____

_____

_____

Pass/Fail

_____

_____

_____

_____

Repeat (If a course is taken a second time)

_____

_____

_____

_____

Audit

_____

_____

Withdrawal

_____

_____

_____

6. List any other special grade options offered by your college.

_____

_____

_____

_____

_____

7. What is the minimum grade point average that a student may earn and still remain in satisfactory academic standing?

_____

8. What happens if your grade point average falls below the minimum required for satisfactory academic standing?

_____

_____

_____

9. How does your institution deal with the following violations of academic integrity?

Cheating

_____

_____

_____

_____

Plagiarism

_____

_____

_____

_____

Other academic misconduct

_____

_____

_____

_____

**Special Programs**

1. If your college offers an honors program or programs, what are the eligibility criteria?

_____

_____

_____

_____

2. Does your college offer any other forms of recognition for academic excellence while you are working toward your degree (e.g., dean's list, scholarships, assistantships)? List several.

_____

_____

_____

_____

3. If your college offers a program to study abroad, what are the prerequisites for participation?

_____

_____

_____

4. If your college offers cooperative education or internship programs, what are the prerequisites for participation? (Cooperative education programs allow students to work off campus for pay while earning credits toward their degrees.)

_____

_____

_____

_____

5. Describe any other special programs your college offers that might interest you.

_____

_____

_____

**Graduation Requirements**

1. What are the requirements for graduation other than completing a major?

_____

_____

_____

_____

2. What is the minimum grade point average required for graduation?

_____

3. What is the minimum grade point average in your major required for graduation?

_____

4. Is it possible to graduate with more than one major?

_____

5. Does your college offer minors or concentrations?

_____

6. What honors or awards does your college extend to graduating seniors who have shown evidence of academic excellence?

_____

_____

_____

_____

**Academic Programs**

1. Skim the list of majors offered by your college. How many are there?

_____

2. Skim the list of minors offered by your college. How many are there?

_____

3. What major interests you?

_____

How many credits are required to complete this major?

_____

What particular courses are required for this major?

_____

_____

_____

_____

Must courses be taken in a certain sequence for this major? Are some courses prerequisites for others? Are some courses restricted to the junior or senior years? If so, give examples.

_____

_____

_____

_____

_____

4. What other major interests you?

_____

How many credits are required to complete this major?

_____

What particular courses are required for this major?

_____

_____

_____

_____

Must courses be taken in a certain sequence for this major? Are some courses prerequisites for others? Are some courses restricted to the junior or senior years? If so, give examples.

_____

_____

_____

_____

_____

5. Can you combine two majors or create your own major at your college?

_____

6. What minor interests you?

_____

How many credits are required to complete this minor?

_____

What particular courses are required for this minor?

_____

_____

_____

_____

Must courses be taken in a certain sequence? Are some of the courses prerequisites for others? Are some of the courses restricted to the junior or senior year? If so, give examples.

_____

_____

_____

_____

_____

## GRADE POINT AVERAGES (GPAs)

A recent survey of grading systems used in colleges across the United States reveals a considerable variety of practices.[1] Most colleges, however, use some variation of the alphabetic system (i.e., *A, B, C, D, F*), and there is a growing tendency to include plus and minus modifiers along with the letter grades (e.g., *B+* or *C−*).

The calculation of grade point average (GPA) described here is based on the most-common alphabetic grading system and a numerical scale ranging from 0.0 to 4.0 grade quality points. If your college uses a different system, familiarize yourself with it by checking the college catalog or asking your academic advisor about it.

Each letter is associated with a certain number of grade points. The particular numbers and letters will vary from college to college, but the following system is the most common.

> *A* = 4.0
>
> *B* = 3.0
>
> *C* = 2.0
>
> *D* = 1.0
>
> *F* = 0.0

Intermediate letters like *A−* or *B+* have intermediate values depending on the college's system, so that an *A−* might equal 3.5 or 3.67 grade points.

Figure 1 shows a sample grade report for a student enrolled in 16 credits of coursework. This report demonstrates how to calculate a GPA for the semester.

This student's GPA for the semester is 2.0, which is equivalent to a *C*. You will notice that courses worth more credits affect your GPA more than courses worth fewer credits. If your only consideration is your GPA, it pays to put more work into a 5-credit course so that the higher grade will be multiplied by 5 (for a 4-credit course, the grade will be multiplied only by 4, etc.). Rarely, however, is the GPA the only consideration. Some courses may be more important to you because they are in your major or because of your vocational goals. At other times, you may wish to do better in a course because the material interests you or is more meaningful to you. Grades should not be the primary considerations that guide your college studies.

You will also notice that a grade of *F* really brings your whole average down. Although an *F* results in 0.0 grade points earned, the grade still counts against you when your average is calculated because the number of course credits in the denominator is not balanced out by the 0.0 in the numerator. In some cases, you may wish to withdraw from a course if you believe that you will not

| Course Title | Number of Credits | Grade Earned | Grade Points Earned |
|---|---|---|---|
| Introduction to Accounting | 3 | C | 2.0 × 3 credits = 6 |
| Freshman English | 3 | B | 3.0 × 3 credits = 9 |
| Biology | 5 | D | 1.0 × 5 credits = 5 |
| Introduction to Psychology | 3 | A | 4.0 × 3 credits = 12 |
| Music Appreciation | 2 | F | 0.0 × 2 credits = 0 |
| *Total number of credits attempted* | = 16 | *Total of grade points earned* | = 32 |
| *Total grade points earned divided by total number of credits attempted* | | | = 32/16 = 2.0 GPA |

FIGURE 1. CALCULATION OF A GPA

be able to pass it. You may then enroll in the course at a future date when your chances of learning the material are better.

**EXERCISE: COMPUTING YOUR GPA**

Read the section of your college catalog that describes the grading system used in your institution. Using Figure 1 as a guide, complete the following exercise. First, write down the courses you are taking this semester and make a hypothetical list of grades that you might receive at the end of the semester. Do not give yourself all As; use a broad range of possible grades. Then compute your hypothetical GPA.

| Course Title | Number of Credits | Grade Earned | Grade Points Earned |
|---|---|---|---|
| _____ | _____ | _____ | _____ |
| _____ | _____ | _____ | _____ |
| _____ | _____ | _____ | _____ |
| _____ | _____ | _____ | _____ |
| _____ | _____ | _____ | _____ |
| _____ | _____ | _____ | _____ |
| _____ | _____ | _____ | _____ |
| *Total number of credits attempted* | = _____ | *Total grade = _____ points earned* | |

GPA earned for the semester _____

## SURVIVING IN THE SYSTEM

Your college is a large organization. As happens in many large organizations, there may come a time when you run afoul of the organization's rules or structures. This may happen if you receive a lower grade on a paper than you expected, if the computer loses the record of your tuition payment, or if the registrar's office misplaces your application for graduation. By the time most students become seniors, they have learned how to thread their way through the college's structural maze quite effectively.

The system is a little more confusing for freshmen; a few hints may help you to achieve a fair resolution of your problem. These suggestions will also stand you in good stead during other life experiences when you have to tackle large organizations such as the credit bureau that gives you an unfair credit evaluation, the bank that loses the record of your mortgage payment, or the car company that refuses to honor the warranty on the "lemon" you bought.

### Creating a File for College Documents

Early in your college career, begin a file in which to save important documents. Place in it a copy of the catalog that was issued the year you entered your college. Most schools will allow you to graduate under the policies that were in effect when you entered, even if regulations change after you have enrolled. If you have a copy of that catalog, you can readily produce it in your senior year to prove that you need only one laboratory course rather than the two that may be currently required for graduation. The same advice holds true for any prerequisites or requirements that may be waived for you on an individual basis. Ask the dean or advisor who is waiving the requirement to put the special exception in writing, and keep a copy in your file. When you are ready to graduate, that person may no longer be working at the college, and there may be no other way to confirm the dispensation that he or she made for you.

You should also keep records and receipts of all your financial dealings with the college (tuition receipts, bookstore receipts, library fine receipts, etc.). In these days of high-tech computer billing, errors are all too frequent. Many colleges will hold up your grade report or refuse to mail out a transcript for an application to graduate school until all bills have been paid. Errors in this area are easily resolved if you can produce a receipt or canceled check proving that you have paid the charges.

### Seeking a Grade Adjustment

Keep a copy of all papers you submit for course work until you have received your grade report for that semester. Although most professors try to be conscientious people, it is possible that a paper might be lost or that a grade might be incorrectly entered in an instructor's grade book. For this reason, you should also keep copies of exams that are returned to you until you receive the grade report at the end of the semester. You cannot depend on your professor to remember that your paper was one of the 125 handed in or that you received a 92 percent on an exam if the records show otherwise. If, on the other hand, you can produce a copy of the document in question, the problem is easily resolved.

If you feel that you have been graded unfairly on a paper or in a course, you should make an appointment to speak to your instructor about it before going any further. Professors enjoy the right of academic freedom, which means that any administrator will be reluctant to interfere with an instructor's way of teaching or with his or her grading policies. You will not gain anything by going to the chair of the department and complaining about the situation before speaking with your instructor. The first question you will be asked is whether you have discussed the problem with your professor. If you indicate that you are reluctant to complain to the instructor for fear that future grades might be jeopardized, the department chair will reply that there is nothing he or she can do to help you. A complaint that identifies the involved parties and describes the situation must be put in writing before a department chair or any other administrator can act on it.

In most cases, a professor will not become prejudiced against you if you question his or her grading policies or teaching methods. College instructors generally are fair people who enjoy the give and take of discussions even when their points of view are being questioned. Do not attack your instructor in front of a whole roomful of students, since he or she will naturally feel defensive under those conditions. Make an office appointment to see your instructor, and present your case as diplomatically and persuasively as you can. If the situation affects other students as well, you might wish to bring with you to the meeting a few tactful students who share your view.

If you cannot resolve the problem with your instructor and still feel that you have been treated unfairly, you must take the next step up the ladder. The procedures for pursuing a grievance vary from one college to another. In most institutions, the next step is to make an appointment with the department chair. The chair will ask you to describe the problem. If he or she feels you have some basis for complaint, you will probably have to submit a written account of the situation. Putting the problem in writing allows all parties involved to be sure that they are responding to the same facts. It also gives the professor a chance to defend his or her position. The department chair will then follow up with the instructor and try to mediate between the two of you.

If you do not receive satisfaction from the department chair, you will have to repeat the process with the dean or the vice president. As I have said, most professors try to treat their students fairly. Cases do exist, however, where disagreements must be mediated between students and faculty and where students are within their rights to complain about grading practices, teaching methods, or sexual harassment. If you control your temper, state your case clearly, and follow the appropriate steps, you can succeed in achieving a fair resolution of your problem.

Read about the procedure for a grade dispute that exists on your campus. List the steps you would take if you disagreed with an instructor about the grade for a course. In each case, list the title of the administrator to whom you would make your appeal.

## STUDENT SUPPORT SERVICES

Most schools offer services that are helpful to students throughout their college careers. You should become familiar with the nonacademic support services that are available so that you know where to turn for help when you need it. One of the best sources for this information is the student handbook. If your college does not publish a handbook, consult the dean of students or the student services office for a listing of the services available on your campus. The goal of the following exercise is to familiarize you with the many support services your college offers.

**EXERCISE:
USING STUDENT
SUPPORT
SERVICES**

Pair up with another member of your seminar. (Choose someone in the class you do not know; one goal of this exercise is to help you learn to work with new people.) Choose one of the following listed support services that your college offers. Call the person in charge of that service and request a brief interview so that you and your partner may learn what services are offered by that office. You should take notes on the types of services available, the days and hours when the office is open, the special restrictions regarding

### LIST OF SUPPORT SERVICES

| | Room Number | Telephone Number | Person in Charge |
|---|---|---|---|
| Dean of Students | _____ | _____ | _____ |
| Residence Life | _____ | _____ | _____ |
| Specialized Services | _____ | _____ | _____ |
| Health Services | _____ | _____ | _____ |
| Athletics | _____ | _____ | _____ |
| Counseling Center | _____ | _____ | _____ |
| Office of Orientation | _____ | _____ | _____ |
| Student Activities | _____ | _____ | _____ |
| Child Care Center | _____ | _____ | _____ |
| Career Planning | _____ | _____ | _____ |
| Cooperative Education | _____ | _____ | _____ |
| International Students | _____ | _____ | _____ |
| Registrar | _____ | _____ | _____ |
| Campus Security | _____ | _____ | _____ |
| Student Newspaper | _____ | _____ | _____ |
| Women's Center | _____ | _____ | _____ |
| Academic Affairs | _____ | _____ | _____ |
| Educational Opportunity Program | _____ | _____ | _____ |
| Financial Aid | _____ | _____ | _____ |
| Academic Advisement Center | _____ | _____ | _____ |
| Academic Skills Center | _____ | _____ | _____ |
| Student Government | _____ | _____ | _____ |
| Student Radio Station | _____ | _____ | _____ |
| Other | _____ | _____ | _____ |

eligibility for services, and the location and phone number of the office. Request a sample of the office's literature so that you may pass it around in class (e.g., a schedule of games from the athletics department, a brochure from the child care center, a pamphlet about birth control from the health services department, etc.). Prepare a presentation for the class with your partner. Report on the service you have researched so that your classmates may learn what is available at that office. Fill in the location and phone extension of each service on the list of services (p. 19) as it is presented in class.

## SUPPLEMENTING YOUR EDUCATION THROUGH EXTRACURRICULAR ACTIVITIES

Many campuses offer a wide variety of extracurricular activities. Clubs may focus on hobbies, such as photography or cycling, on majors, such as psychology or history, on vocations, such as accounting or law, or on a particular religion. Other extracurricular activities are more directly involved with services to the campus such as the student government, the newspaper, or the campus radio station. Many athletic departments sponsor a variety of teams that offer a good physical workout and a focus for campus spirit. Sororities and fraternities serve mainly social functions while other organizations may be organized around community services such as a food cooperative, a recycling project, or a political campaign.

Participation in these activities can offer relief from academic pressure, entertainment, and educational experiences. Extracurricular activities can help you to develop social and leadership skills. They can also introduce you to students with interests similar to yours, help you explore closer and less formal relationships with faculty, and give you valuable information about careers and majors.

Many employers look closely at the extracurricular activities of job applicants because these employers value the initiative, leadership, and social skills that the activities foster. Students who have been active in extracurricular activities are more likely to be well-rounded people who will make good members of a company team. These students may have had direct organizational experience that will be helpful in the vocational setting; they probably know how to cooperate with others on a group project; and they are more likely to follow up on interests and translate them into concrete products.

Graduate and professional program administrators are likely to have similar views about students who participate in extracurricular activities related to their majors. Like employers, these program administrators value initiative, organizational experience, and commitment to a specific area of interest. Do not view extracurricular activities as a luxury that must take a back seat to academic assignments and job-related pressures. Consider these activities as a valuable part of the college learning experience and as a way to enjoy yourself.

**EXERCISE: GETTING INVOLVED IN EXTRACURRICULAR ACTIVITIES**

1. This exercise will encourage you to get involved in extracurricular activities on campus. Choose at least five organizations or campus events that you will attend over the course of the semester. Listings of organizations and events are usually available in the student handbook, the student activities office, a campus bulletin, or the student newspaper. Make one of your choices a club meeting, a second, a student government meeting, a

third, an athletic event, a fourth, a community service organization meeting, and a fifth, some type of cultural campus event.

2. Attend the meeting or event, and write a brief summary. Include the date, the location, the name of the organization or event, the principal people involved (e.g., the names of the performing group or speaker, the club's president and faculty advisor, the teams involved, etc.), a brief summary of the main events, and your reaction to the event.

Your instructor may choose to collect this as a homework assignment or may ask you to share one or two events with the class so that you can benefit from each others' experiences.

## NOTE

1. M. C. Starke and G. Bear, "Grading in Higher Education: A Survey of American Systems and Practices," *Journal of Research and Development in Education* 21 (1988), 4:62–68.

# Chapter 3

## The Faculty as Resource

### COLLEGE TEACHERS

You will get a better education if you understand your instructors and the expectations they hold for college students. You will find that their expectations differ in important ways from those of your high school teachers. College faculty expect you to take greater responsibility for your education, to independently manage your assignments and time, to analyze and criticize the ideas of experts, to develop your own ideas, and to support those ideas with research.

Most instructors teach at the college level because they are enthusiastic about their disciplines and wish to pass on their enthusiasm and knowledge to others. They welcome your interest and participation in the course. As a matter of fact, many of them specifically apportion part of the student's grade for quality of class participation. Do not be afraid to interact with your instructors!

You should be aware, however, that your instructors are expected to perform many tasks in addition to teaching. Significant portions of their time must be spent on research, administrative work, and advisement. In order to fulfill all of their obligations, they must manage their time efficiently. This is the reason that instructors schedule office hours. If you have questions about a course or wish to talk with your instructor about other matters, go to his or her office during office hours or make an appointment for another mutually convenient time. If you wish to contact your instructor at some other time, leave a message and your phone number with the departmental secretary and your instructor will get back to you.

**EXERCISE: INTERVIEWING A FACULTY MEMBER**

This exercise is meant to acquaint you with at least one of your instructors, give you practice in arranging an appointment with a faculty member, familiarize you with faculty expectations, and give you practice in public speaking or in writing.

22

Choose one of the instructors at your college and make an appointment for a ten- to fifteen-minute interview at his or her office. (You may wish to choose an instructor who teaches courses in a major that interests you.) Bring your questions with you, and write down the answers so that you may share them with the other members of your class or with your freshman seminar instructor if this is to be a written assignment. The following exercise gives you some suggested interview questions. You may wish to add others.

**General Questions**

Professor's name: _____

Department in which the professor teaches: _____

Discipline: _____

Reasons the professor chose to teach in his or her particular discipline:

_____

_____

_____

_____

Type(s) of work the professor has performed other than college teaching:

_____

_____

_____

_____

Reasons the professor chose to teach at the college level: _____

_____

_____

_____

Reasons the professor chose to teach at your particular college: _____

_____

_____

_____

Expectations the professor has for the ideal student: _____

_____

_____

_____

Characteristics of a poor student (what bothers the professor most about

students today): _____

_____

_____

_____

**Optional Questions**

Institutions where the professor received undergraduate and graduate degrees; the degrees obtained: _____

_____

_____

The professor's area of research or specialization: _____

_____

_____

_____

The professor's interests or hobbies: _____

_____

_____

_____

## ACADEMIC ADVISEMENT

Academic advisement is an important part of your college experience. When you meet with your advisor, he or she will check to see that you are fulfilling college requirements for graduation. Your advisor may also help you to decide among several electives or courses in your major, make recommendations about the best sequence in which to take certain courses, or suggest changes in your overall course load or scheduling. Your advisor can also serve as a resource person if you are experiencing difficulty at the college. If you do not take advantage of advisement, you may find that you must postpone graduation because you have not fulfilled the appropriate requirements.

During your first two years at college, you may have a general advisor who will mainly work with you on courses required of all students at the college, regardless of major. Later in your college career, you will find it helpful to have an advisor who specializes in your major as you may have questions about graduate programs or career opportunities in your field.

### Advisement Documents

The faculty at the college consider you an adult. Therefore, they expect you to take on adult responsibilities for keeping advisement appointments, planning your program, and holding onto copies of your academic records. As mentioned earlier in this text, it is helpful to keep a copy of the college catalog that was issued the year you enrolled. College requirements change, but the college will usually allow you to graduate according to the requirements in place when you first enrolled. If an advisor or an administrator tells you that you are exempt from a certain course requirement, have that person put the exemption in writing and keep a copy of this document in your file of academic papers. It could make the difference between graduating and spending an extra semester at the college!

If you keep a cumulative record of the courses you have completed that fulfill various requirements, you will find that advisement and registration go more smoothly. Many schools have several categories of requirements for graduation. For example, you may have to take certain courses to fulfill general education requirements, other courses to fulfill requirements in your major, and still other courses to fulfill requirements for your department or school. Within each of these categories, you may be able to choose among several courses that fulfill a particular requirement.

The best way to keep track of which requirements you have fulfilled and which courses you still have to take is to make a master sheet that lists all the required categories. When you meet with your academic advisor each semester, write down each course in which you are enrolling next to the category of requirement it fulfills. Keep a separate list at the end of the required categories for elective courses. In this way, when you reach your senior year and you are trying to figure out whether you fulfilled the "Sophomore Level General Education" requirement in "Culture and Civilization," you will know that that requirement was the reason you enrolled in "History 215, Affluence and Anxiety in the Twentieth Century."

In summary, keep a copy of the college catalog, or other document that describes your major program, along with a list of any other courses that you are required to take over the course of your college career; keep these things with the master list of courses you have taken. You will then be ready to face each semester's registration period with confidence about the courses you need to take in order to progress toward graduation.

# Chapter 4

---

# Time Management

The efficient management of time is vital for success in any career. Learn to manage your time effectively now, and you will not only survive your first year at college, but you will also acquire a skill that becomes increasingly important as your life grows more complex and as you take on a larger number of roles. If you find that you must juggle commitments to your career, spouse, children, other family members, friends, community or charitable organizations, and weekly softball, bridge, or poker games, you will really appreciate the time management skills you learned in college!

As you begin college, you will find that time is not structured for you the way it was in high school. Courses will not meet every day as they do in many high schools. Most instructors will not take attendance in class, and the school will certainly not send a note home to your parents when you are absent. Study halls will not be scheduled for you. Instructors will not collect daily homework assignments to make sure that you have read or studied a particular chapter. Parents will not ask you whether you finished your homework before you run out the door to a movie.

College instructors expect you to behave in an adult manner with regard to time management. If responsibilities are met, then you will succeed; if they are not, then it is your own problem. Many freshmen fail and drop out of college after the first year because they have not developed an effective time management system. If you do not keep up with college assignments on a regular basis, these assignments accumulate until you are overwhelmed by due dates for exams, papers, and projects. If, on the other hand, you use your time efficiently, you will be rewarded. You will have leisure time to use as you please; you will enjoy yourself without feeling guilty because you are not studying; you will have better health because you are getting enough sleep; and you will undergo less stress because you do not have to cram for an exam or write a paper the night before it is due.

## SETTING TASK PRIORITIES

The effective management of time requires decision making and planning. You must decide on your priorities: What is most important to you? What must you accomplish today? Tomorrow? Next week? There is never enough time to do everything you must do in addition to everything that you want to do. Should you stay up late and party with your friends or get a good night's sleep before that important physics exam tomorrow? Should you go to work or finish the English paper that is due the next day? Should you go home and visit with your family this weekend or catch up on the reading for your anthropology course? Establish your priorities on a general basis so that you do not have to agonize over daily decisions that cause conflict and waste precious time. The exercises below will help you determine how much time you need for course work and for other obligations so you can make decisions about the best way to use your time.

**EXERCISE: KEEPING A TIME JOURNAL**

### Using the Time Journal

The time journal shown on pages 29–33 is designed to help you determine exactly how you spend your time. Many of us think we know where our time goes. When we actually write down what we do minute by minute, however, we are surprised by all the little interruptions and time wasters we encounter and by the amount of time we actually spend on various activities.

Keep a time journal for at least three weekdays. During the evening, before you begin recording in the journal, make a list of things you have to do the next day. Assign each item a priority number based on the total number of items on your list. For instance, your rating scale will extend from most important (1) to least important (7) if there are seven items on your list. Your list might look like the following example.

---

PRIORITIZE DAILY ACTIVITIES

4   Attend biology class

3   Attend computer class

5   Attend basketball practice

1   Study for economics exam (scheduled tomorrow)

2   Drive sister to work

6   Review biology notes

7   Prepare draft of English paper (due in three weeks)

---

Carry the time journal with you. As the day goes on, record each activity, the time it began, and the amount of time used for the activity. If you wait to record your activities until the end of the day, you will forget many of the fifteen-minute interruptions (phone calls, brief chats, daydreaming lapses) that may actually eat up so much of your time.

At the end of the day, evaluate how you have used your time. Did you accomplish everything that had to get done? Did you waste time that could have been put to better use? Did you finish high-priority items before taking time for activities that were not essential? Make comments in the last column of your time journal, with an eye to improving your time management (e.g., to study at desk instead of in bed, move an item to the end of the day, use break between classes for study in library, avoid scheduling social activities the night before an important exam, eliminate specific time wasters, avoid watching television during the day, etc.).

EXERCISE:
KEEPING A
WEEKLY
SCHEDULE

Now that you have made some improvements in the day-to-day use of your time, do a little arithmetic to set your priorities and improve your weekly planning. Make a photocopy of the weekly schedule form on page 35 to write out a typical schedule for your week. Write in the hours that you should be in class, that you spend at your job, that you commit to any regularly scheduled family or household obligations, and that you spend commuting. Then calculate and record, on the weekly expenditure of time form on the top of page 39 the number of hours you spend on activities. In recording time for meals, don't automatically put down an hour for each meal; calculate the time you need based on the actual amount of time you spent eating when you were keeping the time journals.

Add up the total number of hours you spend for classes, work, and personal needs. Subtract that number from 168, the total number of hours in a week. This gives you the number of hours you have available for study and leisure.

On the form for weekly expenditure of time in study at the bottom of page 39, list your courses and estimate the number of study hours you are willing to devote to each course in order to achieve the grade you want. Remember that the traditional rule of thumb suggests that you spend two or three hours of study and preparation time outside of class for every hour you spend in class. This rule will vary, of course, depending on how good a student you are, how difficult a particular course is for you, and how heavy the work load (reading assignments, papers, exams) is for that particular course over the span of the semester. You will have a better idea of how much time each course requires once the first two weeks of the semester have passed. Up to a certain point, the greater the number of hours you are willing to devote to a course, the higher your grade in that course should be.

Add weekly study time to the total number of hours you have calculated for classes, work, and personal needs, and subtract that number from 168. The answer is the number of hours you have available per week for leisure. You should schedule at least some relaxation time or leisure activity each day.

**The Time Journal Form**

Name _____     Day/Date _____

Priority Rating: 1 = Most Important ................................................. 7 = Least Important

Goals for Today:

1. _____     5. _____

2. _____     6. _____

3. _____     7. _____

4. _____

| Time | Activity | Amount Time Used | Priority Rating | Comments |
|------|----------|------------------|-----------------|----------|
|  |  |  |  |  |
|  |  |  |  |  |
|  |  |  |  |  |
|  |  |  |  |  |
|  |  |  |  |  |
|  |  |  |  |  |
|  |  |  |  |  |
|  |  |  |  |  |
|  |  |  |  |  |
|  |  |  |  |  |
|  |  |  |  |  |
|  |  |  |  |  |
|  |  |  |  |  |
|  |  |  |  |  |
|  |  |  |  |  |
|  |  |  |  |  |
|  |  |  |  |  |
|  |  |  |  |  |
|  |  |  |  |  |
|  |  |  |  |  |
|  |  |  |  |  |
|  |  |  |  |  |
|  |  |  |  |  |
|  |  |  |  |  |

**The Time Journal Form**

Name _____  Day/Date _____

Priority Rating: 1 = Most Important ................................................................ 7 = Least Important

Goals for Today:

1. _____   5. _____

2. _____   6. _____

3. _____   7. _____

4. _____

| Time | Activity | Amount Time Used | Priority Rating | Comments |
|------|----------|------------------|-----------------|----------|
|      |          |                  |                 |          |
|      |          |                  |                 |          |
|      |          |                  |                 |          |
|      |          |                  |                 |          |
|      |          |                  |                 |          |
|      |          |                  |                 |          |
|      |          |                  |                 |          |
|      |          |                  |                 |          |
|      |          |                  |                 |          |
|      |          |                  |                 |          |
|      |          |                  |                 |          |
|      |          |                  |                 |          |
|      |          |                  |                 |          |
|      |          |                  |                 |          |
|      |          |                  |                 |          |
|      |          |                  |                 |          |
|      |          |                  |                 |          |
|      |          |                  |                 |          |
|      |          |                  |                 |          |
|      |          |                  |                 |          |
|      |          |                  |                 |          |
|      |          |                  |                 |          |
|      |          |                  |                 |          |

# THE WEEKLY SCHEDULE FORM

| | A.M. | | | | | | | | | | | | | | P.M. | | | | | | |
|---|---|---|---|---|---|---|---|---|---|---|---|---|---|---|---|---|---|---|---|---|---|
| | 5 | 6 | 7 | 8 | 9 | 10 | 11 | 12 | 1 | 2 | 3 | 4 | 5 | 6 | 7 | 8 | 9 | 10 | 11 | 12 | 1 | 2 |
| MON | | | | | | | | | | | | | | | | | | | | | | |
| TUES | | | | | | | | | | | | | | | | | | | | | | |
| WED | | | | | | | | | | | | | | | | | | | | | | |
| THURS | | | | | | | | | | | | | | | | | | | | | | |
| FRI | | | | | | | | | | | | | | | | | | | | | | |
| SAT | | | | | | | | | | | | | | | | | | | | | | |
| SUN | | | | | | | | | | | | | | | | | | | | | | |

Form Designed by Kay Collins, Ramapo College

## THE WEEKLY SCHEDULE FORM

Form Designed by Kay Collins, Ramapo College

---

**WEEKLY EXPENDITURE OF TIME FOR CLASS, WORK, AND PERSONAL NEEDS**

| | |
|---|---|
| Number of hours per week you need to sleep | *40 hrs.* |
| Number of hours per week used for meals | *8 hrs.* |
| Number of hours per week used for personal grooming | *10 hrs.* |
| Number of hours per week spent on fixed family and household duties (laundry, child care, meal preparation, cleaning) | *4 hrs.* |
| Number of hours per week spent in class | *14 hrs.* |
| Number of hours per week spent at work, if you are employed | *—* |
| Number of hours per week spent commuting (between school, home, and work, or among classes) | *2 hrs.* |
| Total number of hours: | *78 hrs.* |
| Number of hours available for study and leisure: | *40 hrs.* |

*including*
*sleep 80 hrs*

$$168$$
$$-78$$
$$\overline{\phantom{0}80}$$
*sleep* $-40$
$$\overline{\phantom{0}40}$$

$$168$$
$$-104$$
$$\overline{\phantom{0}64}$$
$$-24$$
$$\overline{\phantom{0}24}$$

---

**FORM FOR WEEKLY EXPENDITURE OF TIME IN STUDY**
**(READING, EXAMS, PAPERS, ETC.)**

Course 1

*GSU 120*     *4 hrs.*

Course 2

*Psy.*     *12 hrs.*

Course 3

*Art in Life*     *8 hrs.*

Course 4

*Tennis*     *—*

Course 5

Total number of study hours per week *24 hrs.*

Number of hours available for leisure *24 hrs.*

*(not including sleep)*

## LEISURE ACTIVITIES

If you work more than twenty hours per week, carry significant family obligations, enroll in difficult courses, or read slowly, you may find that you have little leisure time. You may have to reevaluate your priorities in order to make time for leisure activities. Decrease the number of hours you spend on meals, personal needs, family and household obligations, or work. If this is not possible, you may have to drop a course or adjust the goals you have set for grades in your courses. It is generally better to drop a course than to plan on scraping by just to receive a passing grade. Pick up the course again during a summer session or a less harried semester when work or family commitments decrease. No ironclad rule says you must graduate in four years. As a matter of fact, more than half of all college students take longer to complete their bachelor's degree.

## HINTS FOR EFFECTIVE TIME MANAGEMENT

*Schedule High Priority Activities for Peak Energy Times*

After you have given some thought to your priorities and weekly schedule, incorporate the following suggestions to help you use your time more effectively. Identify your peak efficiency times during the day—when you are most alert and energetic and when you do your best work. For most people, these are the morning hours. Use these peak times to schedule classes, study periods, and other high-priority items that must be completed. Be realistic about scheduling study times. Sunday morning is not a good time to schedule study time if you stay out late Saturday night or enjoy sleeping in on weekends.

*Schedule Most Difficult Activities for Peak Times and Do Them First*

Tackle your most difficult assignments during your peak energy times, and leave other more mechanical tasks for times when you are tired. For example, composing a paper, reading a difficult assignment, or studying for an exam should be done during your peak efficiency hours. Copying a lab report, typing a paper, alphabetizing the sources for your bibliography, going through your mail, or straightening up your room can be left for other time periods when you are not working at peak efficiency. Make a habit of starting your study period with the most-difficult task for the day. The beginning of a study period is when your mind is most alert and rested. Leave short, trivial, or routine tasks for the end of your study period.

*Make Weekly Schedule*

Make up a schedule for each week. Sunday evening is a good time to do this. Include classes, meals, time at your job, meetings and appointments (social, medical, school related, etc.), exercise and *study time*. Add items to your schedule as they come up during the week, and check your schedule each morning so that you leave your room with all the materials you need for that day. It does not pay to get to the library, planning to read a chapter in your psychology text, only to find that you have left the textbook at home.

*Check Schedule Daily*

*Schedule Study Time Close to Class Time*

Try to schedule study time for each particular course in a time period soon before or after that class meets. This will allow you to relate reading assignments to class lectures more easily, help you to participate in class discussions more readily, and prime you to review class notes while they are still fresh in your mind. It will also keep you from having to carry an extra book as you will already have the notebook or text with you for a course when you attend class.

*Schedule Specific Study Assignments*

When you schedule study time, write down specifically what you are going to study. For example, instead of writing just "study biology," write "read Chapter 6 for biology," "proofread history paper," or "review psychology class notes." The more specific you make your commitment on your schedule, the more likely it is that you will be "psyched" to start your study period on time.

Do not waste valuable study time hunting through your syllabus for the next assignment or rummaging through your desk to find the draft of the history paper. When you see a specific item listed on your schedule for the day, use the previous night to prepare whatever materials you need; or, you can prepare in the morning before you leave your room.

*Establish a Regular Study Schedule*

Once you schedule study time, be sure to use that time to study. Do not wait until you feel like studying. It is too easy to put it off or to hang out with a friend if you wait until you are in the right mood. If you regularly schedule certain times and places for study, you can condition yourself to study under those circumstances. Your mind will automatically prepare itself, and it will become easier for you to get to work once you have established a regular routine. If you consistently associate certain stimuli with studying, you can even condition yourself so that those stimuli trigger a frame of mind conducive to studying. You might even wish to prompt yourself with a certain piece of music, specific lighting, certain clothes, or a particular place that you use only for study.

*Change Study Subjects Frequently*

You should be studying approximately 2 to 3 hours for every hour that you spend in class. Spread out your study time for any particular course into several sessions over the week rather than in one long marathon session. Your mind will remain more alert if you change subjects every 45 to 55 minutes. This advice does not apply if you are really into the groove of writing a paper or if you have to catch up for an exam that is scheduled for the next day. Plan to take a short break (approximately 10 minutes) after studying for 45 to 55 minutes, regardless of whether you are changing subjects. This will refresh your mind, maintain your concentration, improve retention of the material, and reward you for sticking with the study schedule.

*Take Breaks*

Take advantage of odd hours to catch up on study time. You might be able to review course notes during the time you spend waiting for an appointment with a doctor or a professor. If lines in your supermarket are long, bring your English book and complete part of your reading assignment. While you are walking to your math class, practice reciting formulas that must be memorized. You will get your work done sooner and have more time for leisure.

*Use Odd Hours for Study*

Schedule study time with a friend if this helps motivate you, but choose your study partner wisely. This strategy can backfire if you spend the time socializing instead of studying. Choose your study area carefully so that you are not tempted by distractions and do not waste valuable time traveling to the study area. It is not easy to study in the cafeteria if all your friends are hanging out there. Use an empty classroom to review notes between classes if the library is located all the way across campus. Do not return to your room after classes if you know that you will be tempted to take a nap or turn on the television. Instead, schedule this study session in the library or in a quiet lounge.

*Study with a Partner*

*Choose Study Area Carefully*

Use some operant conditioning on yourself, and reward yourself *after* you have studied. Do not allow yourself to go through your mail, call your friend, read the newspaper, or watch a television program until you have completed a scheduled study activity. Take that candy or soda break *after* you have written the laboratory report. Allow yourself ten or fifteen minutes to socialize in the lounge *after* you have finished the marketing assignment. Schedule leisure and social activities when possible, so that they occur after work periods. Many of these leisure activities should be scheduled in the more relaxing evening hours unless this is your peak efficiency time. Write the leisure activities down on your schedule so that you can motivate yourself to study and earn them. Reward yourself for sticking to your study schedule by going to a party or a movie. You will find it easier to settle down to study if you apply this rule consistently. Do not allow yourself to attend the event if you have "goofed off."

*Condition Yourself*

*Reward Yourself After Study*

Schedule your leisure time so that you can look forward to activities you

*Write Leisure
Activities on
Schedule*

really enjoy; do not fritter away time just because you have nothing better to do. Seeing enjoyable items on your schedule will help you avoid the temptation to socialize or daydream during times that you have scheduled for study. You may have to learn to be more assertive (see Chapter 11, ''Relationships'') so that you can say *No* to friends who ask you to socialize or to a parent who invites you to go shopping during a time slot that you have scheduled for study. If you stick to your schedule, you will be able to enjoy your leisure time without guilt or anxiety, knowing that your work will get done during the scheduled work time. Be sure that you do schedule some physical exercise or recreation every day.

*Avoid Partying During
Week*

*Get Enough Sleep*

Avoid heavy partying on week nights. You need that time to study or to get enough sleep so that you can function efficiently the next day. Schedule extra study time during peak work times, such as midterms and finals weeks, so that you can avoid late-night cramming. Try not to meet your study needs by cutting back on your need for sleep. You will pay for it in the long run through lowered efficiency the next day or by getting sick because your resistance to infection is decreased.

*List and Prioritize
Daily Goals*

*Keep and Check
Long-range Schedule*

Establish the habit of listing, in the evening, the things you have to do the following day; prioritize those things so that the most important ones are completed first. Be sure to check your list in the morning before you leave your room. Carry your weekly schedule with you so that you can refer to it during the day to keep yourself on target and add appointments or assignments as they come up. You should also keep a yearly schedule so that you can make note of long-range due dates over the course of the semester. You should check this schedule every Sunday when you are writing out your weekly schedule, so that you can plan ahead for the extra study sessions before an exam or a project deadline. Most stationery stores sell appointment books that are useful for writing down daily, weekly and long-term schedules. If you cannot find one that fits your needs, duplicate the weekly schedule form on pages 35 and 37. Make up a monthly chart for longer-range scheduling.

## A SAMPLE WEEKLY SCHEDULE

You are now ready to plan your schedule for the week. Make a copy for future use of the blank weekly schedule form that appears on page 45. Use the sample weekly schedule in figure 2 as a guide and fill in the blank weekly schedule form with your own schedule. Remember to use the suggestions for effective time management when you design your schedule.

**A.M.** 5 6 7 8 9 10 11 12 1 2 3 4 5 6 **P.M.** 7 8 9 10 11 12 1 2

**MON**
- Sleep (5–7)
- Breakfast and Grooming
- Biology class
- Review Bio. Notes / study for Bio. Quiz
- History Class
- Read History Text ch 4 — Library / Write Lab Report – Bio. / Review Hist. Notes
- Lunch
- Rev. Soc. Notes
- Soc. Class
- Ski Club Meeting
- Prepare outline + Draft for Hist. paper — Library
- Dinner
- Work and Commuting Time
- Hang Out in Lounge
- Sleep

**TUES**
- Sleep (5–7)
- Breakfast and Grooming
- Listen to Music Assignment and Write Analysis
- Read Ch 3 Marketing Text
- Marketing Class
- Lunch / Rev. Marketing Notes
- Rev. Music Notes
- Music Class
- Basketball Practice
- Work and Commuting Time
- Dinner
- Study for Bio. Quiz
- Read Hist. Ch. 5
- T.V.
- Sleep

**WED**
- Sleep
- Rev. Bio Notes for Quiz
- Breakfast and Grooming
- Bio Class
- Rev Bio Notes / Finish Hist Ch 5
- Hist Class
- Write Hist. Paper / Read Soc. Ch 7
- Lunch / Rev Soc Notes
- Soc Class
- Prepare Oral Presentation for Soc. / Rewrite Hist Paper
- Dinner
- Work and Commuting Time
- Work-out in Gym
- Hang out in Lounge
- Sleep

**THURS**
- Sleep (5–7)
- Breakfast and Grooming
- Read Bio Ch 3
- Read Marketing Ch 4 / Rev Notes
- Marketing class
- Begin Research for Marketing Class in Library / Lunch
- Music Class
- Basketball Practice
- Rev Bio. Ch 3
- Type History Paper / Dinner
- Type History Paper
- Proofread History Paper
- Arrange Bibliography for Hist. Paper / Type + Proofread
- T.V.
- Sleep

**FRI**
- Sleep
- Rev Procedure for Bio Lab
- Breakfast and Grooming
- Bio Class
- Rev Bio Notes / Read Ch 4
- Hist Class
- Rev Hist Notes / Lunch
- Prepare Oral Presentation for Soc
- Soc Class Cont. Rev.
- Library: Read Soc ch 8 / Research for Marketing Paper / Bio Ch 2 & 3
- Dinner
- Movie with Jane
- Snack Socializing
- Sleep

**SAT**
- Sleep and Relax
- Brunch
- Work and Commuting Time
- Draft Marketing Paper
- Laundry and chores
- Dinner
- Party at Jim's
- Sleep

**SUN**
- Sleep and Relax
- Work-out in Gym
- Rewrite Marketing Paper
- Listen to Music Assignment Write Analysis
- Work and Commuting Time
- Dinner
- Read Ch 4 Bio
- TV Relax Socialize
- Make up Schedule for Next Week

**FIGURE 2. SAMPLE WEEKLY SCHEDULE**

# Chapter 5

## College Lectures

### *Listening and Taking Notes*

**IMPROVING YOUR LISTENING SKILLS**

Many college professors lecture. Therefore, if you wish to learn the information they are teaching, you must know how to listen. The bad news is that listening for the purpose of learning is not a natural, passive process; it is not the same as hearing or even paying attention. It is an active process in which you convert the material you hear so that it becomes meaningful to your mind. You organize it, you relate it to your experiences, and you make it part of yourself. The good news is that you can learn to listen effectively.

*Identify Purpose of Lecture*

One aspect of effective listening involves figuring out the professor's purpose in lecturing. Is it to help you solve a particular problem, to discuss and raise questions, to demonstrate certain trends, or to show you how the course material relates to your own life? The professor often states his or her purpose at the beginning of the lecture. If this is not done, go over your notes after class and see if you can determine the purpose.

*Identify Main Point or Points*

Identify your professor's main point or points. Is he or she explaining how individual citizens' private debts lead to inflation? Is the professor stating that the American Revolution was primarily caused by economic considerations and not by patriotic factors? Is he or she contending that corporal punishment and tougher discipline will increase learning in the schools?

*Examine Supporting Evidence*

Once you have decided what your teacher's main point is, examine how the main idea is supported. Do the presented statistics demonstrate a correlation between balances on individuals' MasterCard accounts and inflation? Does a relationship exist over the years between increasing interest payments and spiraling prices? Are the theories of famous economists used to support the main point?

Identifying the main points and supporting details of the lecture will help you to understand and learn the material more easily. Deciphering your pro-

*Note the
Organizational Plan*

fessor's organizational plan will also help you to remember and to study more effectively. Is the professor using a chronological organization, telling you about events that happened early in the course of the American Revolution and then tracing the sequence of later events? Is the lecture organized by comparison and contrast, explaining how the American Revolution was similar to the French and Latin American Revolutions, but then going on to note the differences among them?

Is the presentation based on cause and effect, showing you what led up to the Boston Tea Party or the Boston Massacre and then explaining the consequences these events had for later developments on the road to the revolution? Is the professor presenting one main idea and then going on to give you many examples that support that idea? For example, he or she may contend that the revolution was based on economics and then discuss the stamp tax, the trade restrictions, and the billeting of soldiers as examples of English actions that hurt the colonists' pocketbooks. If you can follow the lecture's organization, you will find yourself understanding and remembering the material better.

As you listen to the lectures in your classes, you should also try to evaluate what you are hearing. Do not just accept ideas at face value. Question, criticize,

*Evaluate What You
Hear*

and compare them to your own experiences and to material you have read or heard from other sources. Is it a fact that tougher discipline will help children in schools to develop better learning skills, or is it an opinion? What types of data support the statement? Does your professor offer results from surveys of educators or parents? Does he or she compare test scores from schools that allow corporal punishment with those that do not allow it? Is your professor biased in regard to this question based on his or her own experiences or values? If you question and listen critically, you will become actively involved with the material. You will find yourself learning better and more easily!

## EXERCISE: LISTENING TO A SAMPLE LECTURE

This exercise is part of a lecture on the history of mental illness. Your instructor may choose to read the lecture to you in class so that you can practice listening for the purpose, main points, and organizational structure. If your instructor assigns this exercise as homework, ask a friend to read the lecture to you. Before you have your friend read you the lecture, look over the questions that follow it so that you know what information to listen for. Think critically about the lecture. How does it relate to your experience or readings? Is the lecturer biased? Is sound support offered for the main thesis?

### A Sample Lecture

Today we will take a historical look at the concept of mental illness. We will examine how, during various time periods, people have explained the causes of mental illness. We will also examine how these views have affected the treatment of emotionally disturbed individuals. By the end of the lecture, you will appreciate the very different approaches society has taken in dealing with the mentally ill and how these approaches are linked to the greater values and belief systems espoused by a society.

It seems that ancient people believed that many illnesses, including mental illnesses, were caused by spirits or demons. We have evidence of this belief in the art, writings, and skulls that remain from this period. For example, paleontologists have collected numerous skulls from Stone Age people that show evidence of trephination, a primitive surgical procedure during which a hole was made in the patient's skull so that the evil spirits would be free to depart. Subsequent healing tells us that many of these early patients survived the surgery. Patients may even have benefited from the procedure in cases where fluid was putting pressure on the brain and resulting in disordered behavior.

Another treatment method associated with the demon possession theory was used by ancient Greeks, Hebrews, and Chinese: exorcism. Praying, noisemaking, and in some cultures, starvation and beating were used to drive the evil spirits out of the afflicted individual. Societies and subcultures still exist in America today where root doctors and shamans engage in a variety of rituals to drive demons from the bodies of unfortunate victims.

A change in the views of mental illness occurred around 2,500 years ago when a number of Greek physicians and philosophers espoused naturalistic, rather than supernatural, explanations of mental illness. They believed that emotionally disturbed behavior was caused by disease of the brain or by imbalances in the body's vital fluids. Hippocrates, for example, recommended a peaceful environment, moderate exercise, abstinence from sexual activity, and a balanced diet in treating melancholia, a condition associated with symptoms of depression. Although many of the specific explanations and treatments recommended by the Greeks are no longer followed today, the general view of natural, rather than supernatural, causation of mental illness is currently widely held.

As society entered the Dark and Middle Ages (approximately A.D. 400–1500), the naturalistic beliefs of the Greeks and Romans gave way to the ancient superstitious views of mental illness. People believed that illness was God's punishment for wrongdoing. Bands of flagellants traveled from town to town, whipping themselves to achieve forgiveness and a state of ecstasy. Fear often afflicted large groups of people so that they danced and writhed madly in the streets, raving and, finally, collapsing in convulsions. This form of mass hysteria was called *tarantism*, and it spread from Italy to the rest of Europe.

As the feudal structure collapsed and war, famine, and bubonic plague killed large numbers of people, panic spread throughout Europe. People looked to the church for guidance, and the church reinforced the spreading belief that demons and witches were responsible for these catastrophes. Torture was sanctioned as an acceptable means of obtaining confessions from suspected witches. People who were seen as peculiar or different, such as many of the emotionally disturbed, were particularly vulnerable to accusations of witchcraft. Sometimes their own delusions or feelings of guilt caused them to confess to associations with the devil. At other times, torture was used to extract the desired confession. Society believed that associations with the devil or other demons explained these individuals' strange behavior. The usual "treatment" was torture and death.

As the Middle Ages came to an end, there was a resurgence in the naturalistic beliefs espoused by the ancient Greeks. However, the mentally ill continued to be badly treated through the early nineteenth century. They were viewed as animals or criminals and incarcerated in dungeons, prisons, poorhouses, or asylums. They were beaten and chained, naked and starving, to be exhibited in cages to the public for a fee. It was not until Phillipe Pinel's daring experiment with moral therapy that the concept of humane treatment for the mentally ill became widely accepted.

By the twentieth century, medical explanations for mental illness became prevalent, and mental patients were treated by doctors in large mental hospitals located in rural areas. Patients continued to suffer abuse, however, in these large, isolated mental institutions where they were often warehoused for life under inhumane physical conditions with no hope for treatment.

By the 1960s, many professionals believed that emotional disorders were caused by problems in living and not by medical problems. The community mental health movement was inaugurated to keep the emotionally disturbed in their own communities where they would receive compassionate treatment and return to their families and jobs. Unfortunately, local facilities were not adequately staffed or funded. They were not able to cope with the large numbers of patients discharged from the mental hospitals. As our society continues to shun the emotionally disturbed, we are faced with a growing population of homeless people, many of whom suffer from the dual afflictions of emotional disturbance and poverty.

**Questions About the Lecture**

Answer the following questions about the lecture you have just heard.

1. What is the purpose of the lecture?

_____

_____

_____

_____

_____

2. What are the speaker's main points?

_____

_____

_____

_____

3. What types of supportive evidence does the speaker use to back up the main points?

_____

_____

_____

_____

4. What is the organizational structure of the lecture?

_____

_____

_____

_____

5. Evaluate the lecture. Is the speaker biased? Are the conclusions sound? How does the content of the lecture relate to your experience or knowledge of the subject?

_____

_____

_____

_____

_____

## IMPROVING YOUR NOTE TAKING SKILLS

Note taking is a major survival skill. Taking notes forces you to pay closer attention in the first place and to remember the material better at a future date. Studies have shown that you will remember up to 78 percent of the information you record. If you do not write it down, you will remember only 5 to 34 percent. Although you may understand the contents of a lecture while your professor is speaking, within two weeks you will probably forget 80 percent of what you hear. After four weeks, 95 percent of what you hear will be gone! Ideas that were clear and simple in class often seem hazy and complicated a few weeks later, and they may make no sense at all a month later when you are studying for an exam.

## Strategies for Note Taking

Professors go over the most important material in class. Many of them base tests solely or primarily on the information they present in class. This is true for information presented in the lecture as well as points raised by students during discussions. If you are going to succeed in college, you must learn that information, and the only way to guard against the insidious process of forgetting is to take notes immediately so that you can review the information later.

*Take Notes During Each Class*

*Date Each Set of Notes*

*Record Your Name and Phone Number in Your Notebook*

If you take more complete notes, you will do better on exams. Take notes during every class! Date each set of notes so that you can ask the instructor or a friend for help if your notes are not clear to you later when you are studying for the exam. If you miss a class, borrow a set of notes as soon as possible from a classmate who takes good notes. Put your name, address, and phone number on your notebook.

*Keep Course Notes Together*

*Leave Blank Pages*

*Use Full Size Paper*

Keep all your notes for a particular course together in one place so that you can review them more easily. A looseleaf notebook is convenient because you can insert the syllabus and any handouts right into the book along with your class notes for the course. Leave the back of each page of notes blank so that you can integrate summaries from your reading assignments next to the appropriate lecture notes. Use full size paper that is at least 8½ by 11 inches so that you can readily see the organization of the lecture. When notes are chopped up and spread over a large number of small pages, it is hard to see the relationships among different points.

*Read Ahead*

You will find it easier to take notes and you will take better notes if you come to class prepared. Read the assignment before class so that you are familiar with key words, concepts, and relationships. If you do not have time to complete the reading assignment before coming to class, at least scan the chapters so you have a general idea of the material's organization and the topics that will be discussed. This overview will help you to organize your class notes and to zero in on major points.

*Summarize Main Points*

Your class notes should provide a summary of the main points of the lecture and enough details and examples to trigger your memory several weeks later. Along with margin notes to summarize main ideas, you can use an outline format to show the relationships between ideas and to emphasize which points are most important. You should be able to accomplish these goals most effectively if your notes follow these general guidelines:

- Main ideas should be summarized in the margins of the page.

*Use Outline Format*

- Major subgroups in your outline should be indented.

• More subordinate examples or details in your outline should be indented even further.

Such an outline will allow you to see the organization and the relationships in the material without having to copy down the entire lecture. It is not practical to write down everything your professor says. Lecturers usually speak at 125 words per minute. Even the best shorthand system will not allow you to record everything. Furthermore, if you are constantly scrambling to get every word down, you will not have time to understand or think about what is being said, to see the relationships between ideas, or to realize which points are most important. Tape recording lectures is not a good idea because it is too time-consuming to play the tapes back. You can use that same study time more efficiently by reviewing the main points of the presentation.

*Note Organization and Relationships*

Summarize each major idea in a phrase or two, and try to write down a phrase for each detail that illustrates or explains the major point. If your instructor gives four or five examples, record two or three in your outline so that you will be able to understand the point and illustrate it several weeks later. Write "ex." in the margin next to the example so that you recognize the relationship between the concept and the example indented under it.

*Summarize Major Ideas and Examples*

Several types of information must be recorded. If your professor gives a definition, write it down. If he or she enumerates items, record them. For example, "There are five classes of occupation . . . ," can be written, "classes of occupation," with the five classes written in outline form under it. Instructors will often indicate that a particular item is important by repeating the item, slowing down their rate of speech as they present it, changing their tone of voice, or emphasizing the item. If your professor writes an item on the chalkboard, tells you that it is important, or relates it to previous material, write it down! You should also make a note to yourself in the margin next to that item (by writing an asterisk [*] or the word *important*), indicating that this material was emphasized by your instructor.

*Record Definitions and Enumerated Items*

*Record Chalkboard Items*

Develop a system of abbreviations so that you may write down as much information as necessary in the shortest period of time. A number of common abbreviations are listed in figure 3, but you can make up your own shorthand as long as you make a note of a particular abbreviation (e.g., "comp = comparison.") If you do not write down these abbreviations, you may have an unintelligible set of notes as you try to decide several weeks later whether *comp* means *comparison, computation,* or *completion.*

*Use Abbreviations*

If certain words come up repeatedly during a course or lecture, create your own abbreviations, but keep a key of these abbreviations at the front of your notebook. For example, it will save you considerable time to write "OD" instead of "organizational development," "rft" for "reinforcement," and "MB" in place of "management by objective."

*Keep a Key of Abbreviations*

If you miss information during the lecture, leave blank spaces and compare notes after class with a classmate or with your instructor. If your attention wanders during class, keep bringing it back. One way to help yourself concentrate is to sit in front of the class. You are less likely to nod off or to daydream if you are looking directly at your instructor and know that he or she is looking at you. Ask questions or think of relevant examples to keep yourself alert. Sitting in the front row also conveys a positive attitude of interest and motivation to your professor. Don't allow fatigue toward the end of class to slow down your note taking. Teachers sometimes mistime their lectures and have to cram important information into the last few minutes of class. This is not the time to nod off!

*Leave Blanks*

*Sit in Front*

*Participate*

*Stay Alert*

| Common Words | Abbreviations |
|---|---|
| with | w/ |
| and | & |
| definition | def |
| introduction | intro |
| example | ex |
| important | imp't |
| continued | cont'd |
| therefore | ∴ |
| leads to | → |
| organization | org |
| information | info |

**FIGURE 3. LIST OF COMMON ABBREVIATIONS**

*Review Notes*

Review your notes as soon after class as possible, while the lecture is still fresh in your mind. Fill in blank spaces with information that you remember. Clarify phrases that will not make sense in a week or two. Add any new abbreviations to the abbreviation key in the front of your notebook. Jot down notes in the margin that will help you study for an exam (e.g., "key concept," "important definition," etc.). Based on your notes, make up questions that might appear on your exam; write these questions in the margin. Each of the main themes and subtopics can be turned into a good exam question. Review these questions, and try to answer them at least once a week. Coordinate notes from your textbook readings by adding them to the backs of your class notes where appropriate. Note the relationships between the material covered in class and the material covered in assigned readings.

*Form Questions*

*Coordinate Notes with Readings*

**EXERCISE: TAKING NOTES FROM A SAMPLE LECTURE**

Your instructor may assign this exercise as homework or choose to have you do it in class. If you do the exercise in class, your instructor will read the lecture on cocaine to you so that you can practice taking notes. If the exercise is assigned for homework, have a friend read the practice lecture while you take notes on it. Then compare your notes with the sample notes that follow.

**A Sample Lecture**

COCAINE[1]

Today we will consider the crisis caused by cocaine in the United States. First we will take a brief look backward at the history of cocaine. Then we will examine the effects this drug is having on individuals and on our society as a whole.

Dr. Mark Gold, researcher and founder of 800-COCAINE, the national cocaine hotline, reports that twenty-five million Americans have used cocaine at least once. One million Americans report that they are so dependent on the drug that they cannot stop using it even though it is destroying their lives and those of their loved ones. Three thousand teenagers and adults try the drug for the first time every day.

Statistics like these, along with the increasing daily reports of murders, robberies, and assaults associated with the drug's use, have forced Americans to realize that we have a crisis on our hands. The long-term threat to our society is emphasized by events in South America where widespread corruption and terror caused by the drug's traffickers have reached the highest levels of the government and the law enforcement system. A look at cocaine's history and effects may place the seriousness of this problem in better perspective.

Experts believe that the coca plant, *erythroxylum coca,* has existed on this planet longer than people. It grows wild in South America, but careful cultivation has resulted in successful crops in Europe, Asia, and the United States. South America is by far the largest producer, with yields increasing dramatically over the past ten years. Bolivia, for example, produces three times as much cocaine now as it did a decade ago.

Native peoples in South America have chewed coca leaves for several thousand years. They believe that this practice gives them a number of benefits: increased energy, decreased appetite, greater tolerance for the effects of altitude, better digestion, and elevated mood. The plant played a role in religious ceremonies and in political control of the Inca. Indeed, coca leaves may have aided native survival in these inhospitable regions. One hundred grams of coca leaves satisfies the U.S. government's daily recommended allowance for vitamin A, vitamin B2, vitamin E, calcium, phosphorous, and iron. The same 100 grams of coca leaves also supplies 305 calories, 19 grams of protein, and 40 grams of carbohydrates.

Of the fourteen alkaloids present in coca leaves, only cocaine aroused the major interest of Europeans in the nineteenth century, and this interest was not based on its nutritional value. Europeans in the mid-nineteenth century touted cocaine for its medicinal and recreational properties. It was included as an ingredient in a number of popular elixirs, and Coca Cola became known as a health drink in the United States. Since the amount of cocaine contained in these drinks was small, overdoses and other medical complications did not constitute a major problem.

Sigmund Freud was one of the early advocates of cocaine, recommending it as a cure for asthma, morphine addiction, and digestive disorders and also as a local anaesthetic. He described its pleasurable stimulatory properties based on his own personal experimentation. Cocaine became widely used as a local anaesthetic; it was touted by medical communities on both sides of the Atlantic as a cure for everything from seasickness to masturbation to head colds. We know now that cocaine is not an effective treatment for any of these disorders, and other drugs have replaced it as an anaesthetic. By the beginning of the twentieth century, the medical community's love affair with the drug had ended, based on disastrous case reports and on its highly addictive properties.

It is these negative properties of cocaine that concern us today. The most dramatic attention has been given to sudden, unexplained deaths in healthy individuals who have experimented with cocaine. These deaths have occurred in chronic users, but they have also been reported in individuals with little or no previous experience with cocaine.

These deaths might occur because cocaine has dramatic stimulatory effects on electrical and chemical activity in the brain and on heart rate, blood pressure, and breathing. It is difficult to predict the precise effects cocaine may have on any given individual because these effects depend on the dose and purity of the drug, the mode of administration, and the individual's personal physical make-up. Some individuals cannot metabolize the drug, and this can lead to an overdose from small quantities. The "Casey Jones" reaction immortalized in a song by the Grateful Dead can result in failure of the body's major systems leading to convulsions and death within a few minutes.

Cocaine can result in mild to life-threatening symptoms in the respiratory system. Any of the following four symptoms are grounds for an immediate trip to the hospital emergency room: gasping for breath, irregular breathing, accumulation of fluid in the lungs, and failure to breathe. Freebasing also leads to symptoms usually associated with smoking cigarettes: bronchitis, hoarseness, and coughing. Symptoms frequently experienced by individuals who snort cocaine are asthma, chronic respiratory infections, rhinitis (clogged, inflamed, swollen, runny, and bleeding nose), and damage to the vessels or septum of the nose.

Cocaine's effects on the cardiovascular system also run the gamut from uncomfortable to deadly. Any of the following four symptoms require emergency medical attention: irregular heart rate; sudden, rapid decrease in blood pressure; weak or irregular pulse; blue or gray skin color resulting from lack of oxygen.

Malnutrition and severe vitamin deficiency are common in chronic cocaine users. These disorders lower the individual's resistance and open him or her to infection and disease by any of the organisms commonly found in the environment. Sleep disorders, digestive disorders, hallucinations, and seizures are all disturbing symptoms frequently reported by cocaine users.

The question remains as to why the drug has become so popular despite the dangers and discomforts described above. The answer seems to be the cocaine high. Users report that they feel confident, competent, energetic, alert, powerful, and in total control. Many users feel that cocaine helps them to perform better socially and on the job. Unfortunately, the feelings of euphoria are short-lived, and then the crash occurs. The feelings of enhanced competence are mostly illusory, particularly at higher levels of cocaine.

And cocaine users do go on to higher levels. Very few individuals can control a cocaine habit for long. The brief high is followed by a severe slump, and addicted users feel that the only way out of the depression is through another dose. Larger and larger doses are required to reach the high, and the time between doses becomes shorter and shorter. These reports are in keeping with definitions of addiction where users become habituated so that larger doses become necessary to achieve the drug's effect. Additional evidence of dependency involves the fact that users' lives become centered around the drug, and they cannot function without it. It is horrifying to read reports, from successful individuals in every age group, that describe how cocaine has taken over their lives.

Successful doctors, students, engineers, athletes, business executives, songwriters, and lawyers have all reported the same result: cocaine destroyed their lives. It is a powerfully addictive drug, and many are not able to give it up. They lose their families, careers, fortunes, and self-respect, and they also lose the values that formed the foundations of their lives. Devoted sons steal from their mothers, successful models prostitute themselves, devoted fathers leave their children hungry and penniless, ethical lawyers steal from their clients; they do these things to finance a habit that grows more and more expensive until it consumes their lives and the lives of their loved ones.

Cocaine is a drug that poses a serious threat to our society. It attacks the health of individuals, breaks down the relationships that bind people together, threatens our moral fiber and values, and costs us dearly in terms of increased crime and law enforcement, medical treatment, and loss of job productivity. It is a problem for which we must find a solution if we are to survive as a nation.

Now compare the notes you took with the sample notes that begin on page 56.

## NOTE

1. Much of the material in this sample lecture is summarized from Mark S. Gold, *800-Cocaine,* 6th printing, (New York: Bantam Books, 1985).

**Sample Notes on Cocaine Lecture**

*Cocaine*

I. Amer. Crisis
   A. 25 mil. Amers. used cocaine at least once
   B. 1 mil. Amers. dependt on drug
      1. Can't stop using it
   C. 3000 new users try it every day
   D. corruptn + terror in S. Amer. gov'ts + legal sys.

II. Hist.
   A. native S. Amer plant — grows wild
      1. predates man
      2. natives chew leaves — many benefits
        a. incrsd energy
        b. decrsd appetite
        c. betr tolerance of altitude
      3. impt to Inca
        a. relig rites
        b. politicl contrl

*origin + prodctn: S. Amer.*

   B. 19th cent. Europe + Amer.
      1. medicl + recreatl propers
        a. populr elixirs
        b. Coca Cola = health drink
      c. Freud
        1. cure for asthma, morphine addictn + oth. disords.
        d. useful aneasthetic
        f. no medicl uses now
      2. by 1900, doctors against cocaine
        a. bad cases
        b. addictive

*pop in 19th century — medical uses*

*popularity declined in 20th cent.*

III. Negative Propers
   A. Sudden Unexplained Deaths
      1. in healthy people
      2. in users + first timers
      3. Casey Jones reactn
        a. sudden death from convulsns.
      4. affects brain, heart, + breathg
   B. Respirtry Damage
      1. warning signs — Emergncy Rm.
        a. failure to breathe
        b. irreg. breathg/gaspg

*affect brain, heart + breathg*
*→ sud. death*
*respiratry*

*Abbreviations*
*HR = heart rate*
*B-P = blood pressure*

damage &
disords.              c. fluid in lungs          $O_2$ = oxygen
          ex.   2. bronchitis
          ex.   3. asthma
          ex.   4. rhinitis = inflamed, runny, bleedg nose
      C. Cardiovasclr Damage
          1. warng signs → Emergcy Rm.
              a. irreg H-R
heart +           b. sudn fall in B-P
circulatn         c. weak/irreg pulse
damage +          d. blue/gray skin — not enuf $O_2$
disords.    D. Malnutrition
              1. → infection or illness
          E. Oth. Disords.
susceptbl.      1. sleep
to infectn  ex.  2. hallucinats.
& illnss    ex.  3. seizures
            ex.
          F. Warnings
**important:      1. to peop. susceptbl. to heart or circulatory probs.
written on        2.   "    "    "    "   "  diabetes
blackboard        3.   "    "    "    "   "  epilepsy or seizures
                  4.   "    "    "    "   "  asthma


    IV.  Why is it Popular?

        A. "High" = Euphoria

          ex.      1. alert
          ex.      2. powerful
          ex.      3. energetic
high → low    B. "High" → "Low"
              1. nd. anothr dose to get out of depressn.
              2. nd. bigger & bigger doses mo. often
dy. of        3. life centered ar. drug
addctn


main pt.  V.  Dangers to Socty

indiv.      A. Ruin lives - even most successfl peop.
tragedies     1. lose families, jobs, $, self-respect, & health
crime       B. Incr. Crime
            C. Expensive
              1. law enforcemt
costs to      2. medicl costs
society       3. prodctvty & jobs

# Chapter 6

# Textbooks
*Reading, Studying,
and Underlining*

## MAKING THE MOST
## OF YOUR TEXTBOOKS

Just as listening to a college lecture is not the same as listening to a friend's account of a football game, reading a textbook is not the same as reading for pleasure. When you read a textbook, you are reading to acquire information. It is not enough just to read the material; you must study and learn it so that you can apply the information to future tasks in class, on exams, or at work. Research has shown that one of the best ways to study is the SQ3R system.

## THE SQ3R SYSTEM: SURVEY,
## QUESTION, READ, RECITE, REVIEW

The SQ3R system is a reading and study system based on information-processing theory developed by Francis P. Robinson in 1941. It is the most widely used and the most-effective way to study. The system works for several reasons.

1. It gives you an overview of your reading assignment.
2. It helps you learn the organization of the chapter so that you have a framework into which you can connect the many loose pieces of new information.
3. It helps you focus on the reading; you form questions and search for particular answers rather than plod aimlessly through the paragraphs.
4. It provides you with the repetition and rehearsal that are necessary to ensure learning.

# The Basic Steps in SQ3R

*Survey, or Preread, Assignment Title, Introduction, Section Headings, Figures, Summary, Questions*

The first step in using the SQ3R system is to survey, or preread, the assignment in your textbook. Read the title and the introduction of your assignment. If the introduction is very long, read only the first paragraph of the introduction. Now you know the general content and purpose of your assignment. Next read each of the section headings (they are usually printed in bold-faced type) and the first sentence after each heading. These will tell you more about the content and organization of your chapter. Examine any graphs, tables, and pictures. Finally, read the chapter summary or last paragraph and review the study questions at the beginning or end of the chapter.

Prereading takes only a few minutes. You will make up for that time by being able to read faster because you are familiar with the material and the organization of the chapter. Your survey will motivate you to go on to the reading, and it will help you to relate your assignment to information you already know about the topic. Prereading also provides an extra review of the most-important points in the assignment, and review is vital to learning and remembering the material. Students who survey their assignments understand and remember the material better than students who do not use this technique.

*Form Questions as You Read*

The second step of the SQ3R system is to form questions as you read. Turn each section heading into a question. For a section with the title "Memory Storage," you might ask, "How are memories stored?" If a heading is titled "The Process Approach," you might ask, "Why should you use the process approach?" If you see a heading titled "Advantages of Capitalism," you can ask a question like, "What are the advantages of capitalism?" Jot down your questions in the margin of the text. You will find these questions helpful when you review the material. If the text you are reading does not have section headings, turn the first sentence of each paragraph into a question.

*Ask How? Why? What?*

You will find that questions beginning with the words *how, why,* or *what* are most useful. A heading such as "World War II" can be transformed into questions like "What caused World War II?" or "Why did World War II happen?" or "How did World War II come about?" These questions require more thought and deeper reading than questions such as "When did World War II begin?" or "Where did World War II begin?" or "Who started World War II?" When you ask questions that require more thought and deeper processing, you will discover that you are learning more.

*Read and Find Answers*

As you transform section headings into questions, you will find yourself setting goals for your reading, which is the third step of the SQ3R system. You will read to find answers to your questions. It will be useful for you to underline key ideas as you read; the next section will give you some helpful hints about underlining. It is also useful for you to get actively involved while you are reading. Evaluate the material. Is it true or false? Is the author biased? How does the material relate to what you know? How does this information make a difference in your life? When you are actively involved in your reading, you will find yourself learning better.

*Get Actively Involved*

*Recite*

Now that you have surveyed the reading, asked questions for each section, and read each section, it is time for you to go to the fourth step of SQ3R: recitation. Before you leave a section to go to the next part of an assignment, be sure that you can answer the question you posed for that section. Look away from the text for a few moments, and say the important points in your own words. This is a form of rehearsal or practice. As you may remember from grade school, "practice makes perfect." This step is important in helping you remember the material better.

The final stage of the SQ3R system involves reviewing. When you have

*Review Each Section*

*Answer Each Question*

completed the entire assignment, go back to each section heading and answer each question you posed. If you cannot answer the question, review the section again until you find the answer. The recitation and reviewing steps encourage you to evaluate the material and to identify the most-important points. Narrow down the amount of material that you have to remember, and then review the major points. Rehearsal or review is the most-effective technique for remembering information. You may find it helpful to write down the answers to your questions. You will then have an excellent set of study notes for class discussions or exams.

When you complete an assignment using the SQ3R system, you will have an overview of the subject, you will understand the relationships among the topics, you will have read the material carefully, and you will have reviewed the main points at least four times. You will learn better, you will remember better, and you will not have to cram for exams!

## EXERCISE: USING SQ3R WITH A SAMPLE TEXT

### SQ3R System Techniques

Use the SQ3R system techniques in the following list to study the "Managers and Management" sample reading selection in this exercise.

1. Use a highlighter to mark the sections that you would read during your survey.

2. Turn each section heading and bold-faced term into a question; write the question in the margin.

3. Read each section.

4. Answer the question(s) you have posed for each section as you finish reading it.

5. Review the entire selection by going back to the beginning and answering all the questions you have posed. Write your answer in the margin underneath your question. If you are unable to answer a question for a particular section, read that part again until you find your answer.

### A Sample Textbook Selection

LEARNING OBJECTIVES

After reading this chapter, you should be able to:

1. Define an organization.
2. Define management.
3. Describe what managers do.

CHAPTER I   MANAGERS AND MANAGEMENT

This book is about managers and management. In this chapter we want to introduce you to managers and management by answering, or at least beginning to answer, these questions: *Who* are managers? *What* is management and *what* do managers do? And *why* should you spend your time studying management?

---

Stephen Robbins, MANAGEMENT, 2/E, © 1988, pp. 3–8. Reprinted by permission of Prentice-Hall, Inc., Englewood Cliffs, N.J.

## Who Are Managers?

Managers work in a place we call an organization. Therefore, before we can identify who managers are, it is important to clarify what we mean by the term *organization.*

An *organization* is a systematic arrangement of people to accomplish some specific purpose. Your college or university is an organization. So are fraternities, government agencies, churches, the Xerox Corporation, your neighborhood gas station . . . and the United Way. These are all organizations because they all have three common characteristics. First, each has a distinct purpose. This is typically expressed in terms of a goal or set of goals. Second, each is composed of people. Third, all organizations develop a systematic structure that defines and limits the behavior of its members.

Managers work in organizations, but not everyone in an organization is a manager. For simplicity's sake, we can divide organizational members into two categories: operatives or managers. *Operatives* are those who work directly on a job or task and have *no* responsibility for overseeing the work of others. In contrast, *managers* direct the activities of other people.

## What Is Management and What Do Managers Do?

Just as organizations have common characteristics, so do managers. In this section, we define management; present the classical functions of management; review recent research on managerial roles; and consider the universal applicability of managerial concepts.

*Defining Management*   The term *management* refers to the process of getting activities completed efficiently with and through people. The process represents the functions or primary activities engaged in by managers. These functions are typically labeled planning, organizing, leading, and controlling. We elaborate on these functions in the next section.

*Management Functions*   In the early part of this century, a French industrialist by the name of Henri Fayol wrote that all managers perform five management functions: they plan, organize, command, coordinate, and control. The most popular textbooks (and this one is no exception) still continue to be organized around *management functions,* though these have generally been condensed down to the basic four: planning, organizing, leading, and controlling. Let's briefly define what each of these functions encompasses.

If you don't know where you're going, any road will get you there. Since organizations exist to achieve some purpose, someone has to define that purpose and the means for its achievement. Management is that someone. The *planning* function encompasses defining an organization's goals, establishing an overall strategy for achieving these goals, and developing a comprehensive hierarchy of plans to integrate and coordinate activities.

Managers are also responsible for designing an organization's structure. We call this function *organizing.* It includes the determination of what tasks are to be done, who is to do them, how the tasks are to be grouped, who reports to whom, and where decisions are to be made.

## Summary

An organization is a systematic arrangement of people to accomplish some specific purpose. It has a distinct purpose, includes people or members, and contains some type of systematic structure. Management is defined as the process of getting activities completed efficiently with and through other people. Managers work in an organization and direct the activities of other people. They should perform four functions: planning, organizing, leading, and controlling.

How does your work compare with the markings on the selection that follows? The sections highlighted by bold-faced type are the ones that you should have read during your surveying, or prereading. Go back over your exercise; mark any items that you missed for the survey and any questions or answers you missed during the question, recitation, or review phases of your studying.

**Textbook Selection Marked for SQ3R**

LEARNING OBJECTIVES

After reading this chapter, *you should be able to:*

*1. Define an organization.*

*2. Define management.*

*3. Describe what managers do.*

### CHAPTER 1  MANAGERS AND MANAGEMENT

*This book is about managers and management. In this chapter we want to introduce you to managers and management by answering, or at least beginning to answer, these questions: Who are managers? What is management and what do managers do? And why should you spend your time studying management?*

**Who Are Managers?**

*What is an organizatn?*

*Managers work in a place we call an organization.* Therefore, before we can identify who managers are, it is important to clarify what we mean by the term *organization.*

*Arrangmt of peop w purp + syst struct.*

*An organization is a systematic arrangement of people to accomplish some specific purpose.* Your college or university is an organization. So are fraternities, government agencies, churches, the Xerox Corporation, your neighborhood gas station . . . and the United Way. These are all organizations because they all have three common characteristics. First, each has a distinct purpose. This is typically expressed in terms of a goal or set of goals. Second, each is composed of people. Third, all organizations develop a systematic structure that defines and limits the behavior of its members.

*Who is an operative? No resp. for supervisg.*

Managers work in organizations, but not everyone in an organization is a manager. For simplicity's sake, we can divide organizational members into two categories: operatives or managers. *Operatives* are those who work directly on a job and have *no* responsibility for overseeing the work of others. In contrast, *managers* direct the activities of other people.

*Who is a mngr? Directs others.*

**What Is Management and What Do Managers Do?**

*Just as organizations have common characteristics, so do managers. In this section, we define management; present the classical functions of management; review recent research on managerial roles;* and consider the universal applicability of managerial concepts.

*What is managmt? Gets activity done thr peop.*

**Defining Management**  *The term management refers to the process of getting activities completed efficiently with and through people.* The process represents the functions or primary activities engaged in by managers. These functions are typically labeled planning, organizing, leading, and controlling. We elaborate on these functions in the next section.

*What do mangrs do? 1. plan 2. lead 3. org 4 contr*

**Management Functions**  *In the early part of this century, a French industrialist by the name of Henri Fayol wrote that all managers perform five management functions: they plan, organize, command, coordinate, and control.* The most popular textbooks (and this one is no exception) still continue to be organized around *management functions,* though these have generally been condensed down to the basic four: planning, organizing, leading, and controlling. Let's briefly define what each of these functions encompasses.

*What is*
*planng?*

*1. def goals*
*2. est Stratgy*
*3. coord*
*   actvys*
*what is org?*
*Dtrmn*
*org's struct.*

If you don't know where you're going, any road will get you there. Since organizations exist to achieve some purpose, someone has to define that purpose and the means for its achievement. Management is that someone. The *planning* function encompasses defining an organization's goals, establishing an overall strategy for achieving these goals, and developing a comprehensive hierarchy of plans to integrate and coordinate activities.

Managers are also responsible for designing an organization's structure. We call this function *organizing*. It includes the determination of what tasks are to be done, who is to do them, how the tasks are to be grouped, who reports to whom, and where decisions are to be made.

### Summary

*An organization is a systematic arrangement of people to accomplish some specific purpose. It has a distinct purpose, includes people or members, and contains some type of systematic structure. Management is defined as the process of getting activities completed efficiently with and through other people. Managers work in an organization and direct the activities of other people. They should perform four functions: planning, organizing, leading, and controlling.*

## MARKING YOUR TEXTBOOK

*Underline Judiciously*

Underlining a textbook is the most-popular study technique used in college. When you highlight an item so that it stands out against its background, you will find it easier to remember that item. Underlining is effective, however, only if it is practiced judiciously. The most-common mistake students make is to underline too much. Many students read along mindlessly, underlining almost everything. This is almost no better than just reading passively. It does not force you to identify the major points in the text. It also means that you will have to reread practically the whole text when you study for an exam. Indiscriminate underlining is useless!

*First Read*

It is best to read a paragraph first, then go back and underline the important points. This allows you to identify the main points, and it also gives you an extra review of the key material. Use the section headings and the questions you pose in the SQ3R system to help you identify the main points in each paragraph.

*Then Underline Key Phrases*

Underline the parts of the paragraph that answer your questions. Do not underline complete sentences, but do underline complete thoughts so that the material will make sense when you reread just the underlined sections.

The sample paragraph in figure 4 is an example from a student who ha' underlined too little. The student will miss important information and will have to go back and reread the entire text because the underlinings are just unrelated words that don't make sense.

The paragraph in figure 5 is an example from a student who has underlined too much. This student has not distinguished key points from background material and will have to reread practically the entire text when reviewing the underlinings.

The final paragraph in figure 6 is an example of an appropriate approach to underlining. Key points are emphasized, and the underlined phrases make sense on their own.

*Underline About One-Third of Paragraph*

In general, you will find that underlining about one-third of each paragraph will allow you to highlight the important points. If you underline too much, you will not distinguish key points from background material, and you will find yourself rereading practically the entire text when you review your underlinings. If you underline too little, you will miss important information or

> Resources are scarce. Scarcity is a relationship between how much there is of something and how much it is wanted. Resources are scarce compared to all of the uses we have for them. If we want to use more than there is of an item, it is scarce. Note that this definition is different from the usual definition of scarce, which means "rarely found in nature." How are they different? Consider this example. Is water scarce? How could anyone argue that water is scarce in the usual sense? Water covers nearly two-thirds of the earth's surface. Yet an economist would say that water is scarce. Why? The reason is that there are so many competing uses for water that more water is needed than is available. If you find this hard to believe, ask farmers and ranchers in the West, where water rights are among the most jealously guarded properties. As soon as someone is willing to pay for a good, or a resource, it is scarce by the economist's definition.

**FIGURE 4. SAMPLE PARAGRAPH WITH TOO LITTLE UNDERLINING**

> Resources are scarce. Scarcity is a relationship between how much there is of something and how much it is wanted. Resources are scarce compared to all of the uses we have for them. If we want to use more than there is of an item, it is scarce. Note that this definition is different from the usual definition of scarce, which means "rarely found in nature." How are they different? Consider this example. Is water scarce? How could anyone argue that water is scarce in the usual sense? Water covers nearly two-thirds of the earth's surface. Yet an economist would say that water is scarce. Why? The reason is that there are so many competing uses for water that more water is needed than is available. If you find this hard to believe, ask farmers and ranchers in the West, where water rights are among the most jealously guarded properties. As soon as someone is willing to pay for a good, or a resource, it is scarce by the economist's definition.

**FIGURE 5. SAMPLE PARAGRAPH WITH TOO MUCH UNDERLINING**

> Resources are scarce. Scarcity is a relationship between how much there is of something and how much it is wanted. Resources are scarce compared to all of the uses we have for them. If we want to use more than there is of an item, it is scarce. Note that this definition is different from the usual definition of scarce, which means "rarely found in nature." How are they different? Consider this example. Is water scarce? How could anyone argue that water is scarce in the usual sense? Water covers nearly two-thirds of the earth's surface. Yet an economist would say that water is scarce. Why? The reason is that there are so many competing uses for water that more water is needed than is available. If you find this hard to believe, ask farmers and ranchers in the West, where water rights are among the most jealously guarded properties. As soon as someone is willing to pay for a good, or a resource, it is scarce by the economist's definition.

**FIGURE 6. SAMPLE PARAGRAPH WITH APPROPRIATE UNDERLINING**

Paragraphs in figures 4, 5, and 6 are excerpted from A. J. Hoag and J. H. Hoag, © 1986, IN-TRODUCTORY ECONOMICS, pp. 4–5. Reprinted by permission of Prentice-Hall, Inc., Englewood Cliffs, N.J.

have to reread the entire text because your underlinings are just unrelated words that don't make sense.

## Margin Notes

*Distinguish Main
Points from Support
Material*

It is helpful to distinguish main points from supporting details while you are underlining. You may wish to use two different colors of highlighter to make this distinction, or you may prefer to develop a system of notations in the margin that helps you to make this differentiation (e.g., an asterisk [*] for main points and a plus sign [+] for support material). Sometimes a sentence in your text will be too long or complicated to underline effectively. Summarize or paraphrase these difficult or lengthy points in brief phrases in the margin.

*Highlight Definitions,
Enumerations, and
Items for Review with
Margin Notes*

Margin notes are also helpful for marking definitions ("defs") and classifications or enumerations (e.g., "causes of trade deficits '#1,' '#2,' '#3,' etc.). You may draw arrows in the margins as a shorthand way to indicate causal relationships between the ideas you have highlighted. Circle words you do not understand so that you can look them up in the dictionary or glossary after you have finished reading. Use margin notes like "good test item," "reread," and "?" to flag items that need review or consultation with the instructor.

*Get Involved with the
Text*

Making these types of notes in the margin is an active process that forces you to evaluate the information. Both underlining and marking help you to concentrate by keeping you physically involved. They help focus your attention on the key points. They force you to see the organization of the material and the relationships between ideas. They encourage you to evaluate these ideas. They highlight the main points and make it easier for you to remember them.

*Outline Underlined
Sections and Add to
Class Notes*

At the end of each week, take notes in outline form on the sections you have underlined. If you are using a looseleaf notebook, insert these notes next to the class lecture notes you have taken on the same subject. If you are using a spiral notebook, write the notes on the backs of the pages where you have written your lecture notes. Review your lecture notes at this time, and note the relationships between texts and lectures.

**EXERCISE:
UNDERLINING AND
MARKING YOUR
TEXTBOOKS**

Read the paragraph that follows and then underline the important points. Be sure that the phrases you underline make sense when read on their own. Make margin notes that distinguish the main idea from the support material. Add other margin notes to summarize ideas and highlight important points.

### A Sample Selection from a Textbook

CHAPTER I   THE MEANING OF ECONOMICS

The chapter starts with a definition of economics. In each of the remaining sections, one concept in the definition will be discussed. We must take the definition apart before it can be put together in a meaningful way.

*Economics* is a social science that studies how society chooses to allocate scarce resources, which have alternative uses, to provide goods and services for present and future consumption.

Excerpted with permission from A. J. Hoag and J. H. Hoag, © 1986, INTRODUCTORY ECONOMICS, pp. 4–5. Reprinted by permission of Prentice-Hall, Inc., Englewood Cliffs, NJ.

The definition starts "Economics is," and that is what is being defined. So the remaining words need to be understood to make sense of economics. Let us start with "goods and services."

*Goods and Services*

What exactly are goods and services? A *good* is anything that satisfies a want. That is the purpose of production—to provide goods that satisfy wants. Therefore goods are produced, and the consumption of those goods satisfies wants. Goods can be tangible or intangible. Tangible goods are physical items such as bulldozers or pizzas. Intangible goods such as medical care or education are called services. Both goods and services satisfy wants and therefore can be called goods.

*Resources*

The satisfaction of wants can only be accomplished by using up resources, the so-called factors of production or means of production. These resources can be classified as land, labor, and entrepreneurship.

Now compare your underlinings and margin notes with those in the following paragraph. Did you underline too much or too little? Are there markings in the margin that you might have added to help you focus and review?

**Selection from a Text with Underlining and Notes in the Margins**

CHAPTER I   THE MEANING OF ECONOMICS

The chapter starts with a definition of economics. In each of the remaining sections, one concept in the definition will be discussed. We must take the definition apart before it can be put together in a meaningful way.

*What is economics? def.*

*Economics* is a social science that studies how society chooses to allocate scarce resources, which have alternative uses, to provide goods and services for present and future consumption.

The definition starts "Economics is," and that is what is being defined. So the remaining words need to be understood to make sense of economics. Let us start with "goods and services."

*Goods and Services*

*What is a good? def.*

*2 class of goods #1 + #2 Def. them*

What exactly are goods and services? A *good* is anything that satisfies a want. That is the purpose of production—to provide goods that satisfy wants. Therefore goods are produced, and the consumption of those goods satisfies wants. Goods can be tangible or intangible. Tangible goods are physical items such as bulldozers or pizzas. Intangible goods such as medical care or education are called services. Both goods and services satisfy wants and therefore can be called goods.

*Resources*

*How are wants satisf? 3 class of res.*

The satisfaction of wants can only be accomplished by using up resources, the so-called factors of production or means of production. These resources can be classified as land, labor, and entrepreneurship.

# Chapter 7

# Examinations
## *Studying, Improving Your Memory, and Reducing Anxiety*

**THE PURPOSE OF EXAMS**

Exams have been with us since the first colleges and universities. Contrary to the opinion of many students, exams were not invented by sadistic instructors to torture hapless students. It may also interest you to know that most professors dislike making up and grading exams almost as much as you dislike taking them.

Exams actually serve a number of useful purposes. Test scores let professors know how well their teaching techniques are working and whether they need modification. They also give instructors feedback on how well students have mastered important skills and information. They can be helpful to administrators, admissions officers, and employers in making decisions about which students have mastered the material best. Tests give students and their parents feedback on how well they are doing. They are also useful in motivating students to learn; there is nothing like an upcoming exam to encourage students to hit the books. Finally, perhaps the best justification for examinations is that they serve as a learning experience; in reviewing and studying for a test, you are forced to learn the material better.

**EFFECTIVE EXAM PREPARATIONS**

For this reason, exams are likely to be with us for a long time to come. If you want to succeed in college, it is worth your while to learn how to study for exams effectively. Studying for exams involves organizing, reviewing, and learning the key material from your class lectures and reading assignments. If you practice the skills you have learned in the sections on listening, note taking, and reading and marking textbooks, this will be a piece of cake! If you use these techniques to keep up with your assignments and the weekly reviews of your class notes, you will never have to cram the night before an exam, and you will find that you already know most of the material.

*Avoid Cramming*

Last-minute cramming is never a good idea. Cramming the day before an exam is likely to tire you out and raise your anxiety level so that you will not think as clearly as you usually do on the day of the exam. You also will not remember the material as well as you would if you had learned it in smaller portions over a period of several weeks. Many studies have showed that break-

*Distribute Study Sessions*

ing up your study time results in more efficient learning. Three 2-hour study sessions are better than one 6-hour study session. Even better are 40- to 50-

*Take Breaks*

minute sessions separated by breaks. Your brain automatically reviews what you have been studying while you wash dishes, call your mother, or have a snack. The break gets your blood circulating, refreshes your mind, and keeps you from nodding off.

*Organize Study Area*

Organize your study area so that you get the most out of your study time. Reduce interference. Don't study near a tempting television or in a tempting bed. If music or roommates distract you, go to the library. Clear your desk. Don't leave that letter to your friend (the one you meant to answer last week) in plain sight when you have to study for an exam. Have your study area organized so that pens, paper, books, and other materials you need are at hand.

*Spread Out Your Study Time*

Spread your study time for a major exam over a one- to two-week period before the test date. Review your textbook underlinings and class notes. Summarize the notes and underlinings; organize them according to the topics outlined on your syllabus so that lecture topics and textbook topics are integrated. Condense and streamline these notes until you have three to five pages of key terms, ideas, and relationships. Include supporting details, examples, defini-

*Summarize and Condense Notes*

tions, graphs, and diagrams. You will want to review these notes several times before the exam. You should certainly review them the night before and the morning of the exam.

*Make Practice Tests*

Make practice tests with the questions you have posed in the margins of your text and lecture notes. Include questions that occur to you as you review your underlinings and notes. Add questions from the end-of-chapter exercises and from a student study guide if your text comes with these study aids. Brainstorm with a study group, and make up a collective list of test questions. Answer these questions and compare your answers with those of your study partners.

*Obtain Sample Tests*

Ask your instructor if he or she can provide you with copies of tests from previous years or with sample items like those that will be on the exam. Although past exams will not be identical to the one you will take, you will gain a better understanding of what information your professor thinks is important and how he or she tests for it.

Answering practice test questions is an effective study technique, and it also helps to reduce some of the anxiety you will experience when you take the exam. Ask your instructor about the format of the test so that you can study

*Ask About Test Format*

most effectively. Different study strategies are effective for essay as opposed to objective tests. Essay and fill-in questions rely on recall memory. You must be able to supply terms, definitions, and supporting details, and you must be able to organize the material. If your instructor is going to ask for it, you must be prepared to write out a word like *phenylketonuria* (which is a type of disease). For multiple choice and matching items, you need not reproduce the word itself, but you must be able to recognize the disorder, to distinguish it from other disorders, and to know about its causes, consequences, and treatment.

*Practice Solving Similar Problems*

Examinations in science, math, and many technical areas require that you know how to solve various types of problems. In order to do this, you may have to memorize certain formulas, tables, or values. You must understand and know how to apply certain problem-solving strategies. The best way to prepare for these exams is to practice solving similar problems.

*Prepare Answers*  Essay questions require well-organized replies. Prepare outlines for sample questions that synthesize your class notes with your reading notes. Plan out answers to possible questions ahead of time so that you can readily explain the major theories, compare and contrast several approaches, give advantages and disadvantages of different strategies, provide examples of various principles, and explain the causes and consequences of major events. Study those outlines before you come to the exam.

*Memorize Material*  Memorize enough material so that the answers to questions come quickly to mind. If you have difficulty with a practice question, go back and review the material in your text or notes until you can answer it satisfactorily. Take your practice test several times before the test day, and check your answers for accuracy and completeness. Review your practice test the night before the exam. *"Overlearn" Material*  Remember that "overlearning" the material will be beneficial in helping you to remember items when you are experiencing the tension of the exam situation.

## STRATEGIES FOR TAKING TESTS

We all know that some students test well; they perform better on exams than others even when they do not know the material as well. This ability is not related to luck or heredity. Many of these students have learned certain techniques for studying that, like the ones described in the preceding paragraphs, stand them in good stead. You can learn these, too.

## Multiple-Choice and True/False Items

The section below focuses on strategies that are helpful once you are taking the exam. These strategies apply to multiple-choice, true/false, and matching examinations, and you can use them when you are not sure which answer is correct. *These strategies are not a substitute for studying thoroughly or for reading the exam questions carefully, but they can be helpful when you are stuck and need to guess.*

*Choose Longest Answers*  Few generalizations about the world we live in can be stated in simple or black-and-white terms. For this reason, the longest or most complicated option in a multiple-choice question is more often the correct answer. It also happens to be true that instructors are less likely to place the correct answer as the first or last option. (This is not true for computer-generated exams. The computer *Choose Middle Answers*  randomly allocates correct responses to all possible positions.) If you have to guess, your choice of one of the middle options is more likely to be correct when your professor has made up the test. This is particularly true if the middle item is longer.

*Choose Qualified Answers*  Most truths are relative rather than absolute so that multiple-choice answers qualified by terms like *often, most,* and *generally* are more likely to be the correct choice. There are exceptions to almost every rule, especially in social sciences and humanities, so options that include absolute words like *always, Reject Absolute Answers  everyone,* and *never* are more often wrong. Advice to avoid absolute statements should be followed only after you have carefully read the question, since some questions do not follow this general rule. A true/false item like "Every monopoly has complete control," is true even though it includes absolute terms like *every* and *complete.*

*Use Process of
Elimination*

*Read all Answers*

If two multiple-choice items are opposite in meaning, it is likely that one of them is the correct answer. You may then be able to eliminate the other three choices and focus on which of these two opposite options is correct.

Read the instructions for each question. If your instructor asks for the *best* answer, you must read all choices carefully; several answers may be correct, but only one will be the best. This advice is particularly true for multiple-choice exams. Read all the options before choosing one; it doesn't pay to choose the first correct answer if the last option reads "all of the above," and indeed all of the answers are correct. Before you choose "none of the above" as your answer, be sure that *none* of the three or four options you have read is correct.

*Try Questions with
Answers*

If you have read all of the choices and cannot single out the correct one, try reading the question again and following it with the first option. Next read the question and try answering it with the second option. Continue doing this until you have tried all of the choices. It is often confusing to read four or five complicated choices one after the other; "hearing" the question next to each option may make your choice clearer.

*Narrow Down
Choices*

If you are dealing with matching items, read all the choices in both columns before you begin to answer the questions. An item in Column B may fit several items in Column A, but it may represent the *best* match for only one. Complete the easiest items first, to narrow the number of options you must deal with for the remaining questions. Check the directions, or ask your instructor whether you can use items for more than one match. If you may use an item only once, cross off each option as you use it. You may be able to get an item correct by using the process of elimination.

*Simplify the Question*

If your exam includes complicated true/false items, try to simplify the grammar. Remember, for example, that two negatives make a positive: "You won't be unprepared for tests if you make up practice questions for study," is equivalent to "You will be prepared for tests if you make up practice study questions." The second version of the statement is less likely to trip you up, so convert the original item by eliminating the negatives. As with multiple-choice items, statements that include absolute terms like *every* or *never* are less likely to be accurate; mark them "false." Items based on terms like *some* or *occasionally* are more likely to be true. Figure 7 gives some general hints for using test strategies.

1. Answers that have qualifying terms like *some, usually, probably,* and *many* are more likely to be correct.

2. Answers that have absolute terms like *none, never, always,* and *everyone* are less likely to be correct.

3. Long answers, particularly those that are qualified, are more likely to be correct than short, unqualified answers.

4. If your instructor made up the exam, options located in the middle position are more often correct than options in the first or last position.

5. If two multiple-choice options are opposite in meaning, one of them is likely to be the correct answer.

6. If you have difficulty choosing an option, read the question followed by each option in turn. Often grammatical agreement between question and answer can hint at the correct answer.

**FIGURE 7. HINTS FOR USING TEST STRATEGIES**

**EXERCISE:
APPLYING
STRATEGIES TO
OBJECTIVE TESTS**

Here is some practice in applying a number of strategies for taking objective tests. Read the test strategies shown in figure 7. Then answer the practice questions that follow. Choose the best answer, and then indicate why you chose that particular option. The correct answers follow the questions.

**Sample Test Items**

1. *True or false.* Many decision makers select information more for its accessibility than for its quality.

   Answer: _____

   Strategy number: _____

2. *True or false.* Organizational structures never influence solutions to problems.

   Answer: _____

   Strategy number: _____

3. *Choose the best answer.* The French Revolution was caused by

   a. economic forces

   b. ideological forces

   c. a combination of economic and ideological forces

   d. particular leaders

   e. the American Revolution

   Answer: _____

   Strategy number: _____

4. *Choose the best answer.* Antifederalists opposed ratification of the Constitution because they feared

   a. decentralization

   b. centralization

   c. the British

   d. the army

   Answer: _____

   Strategy number: _____

5. *Choose the best answer.* Parents who abused their children

   a. wants children but can't afford them

   b. hate children

   c. were themselves abused as children

   d. believe in discipline

   Answer: _____

   Strategy number: _____

### Answers to Sample Test Items

1. *true.*  Strategy 1: the term *many* is a qualifier.
2. *false.*  Strategy 2: the term *never* is an absolute.
3. *c.*  Strategies 3 and 4: *c* is longer, more complicated, and in the middle position.
4. *b.*  Strategy 5: the answer is one of two opposite choices.
5. *c.*  Strategies 6 and 4: for *c,* there is agreement between the noun in the question (*parents* = plural) and the verb in the correct answer (*were* = plural); for *c,* there is agreement between tense of the verb in the question (*abused* = past tense) and tense of the verb in the answer (*were* = past tense); and *c* is in a middle position.

## SUCCESS ON EXAM DAY

*Be Prepared*

One of the best ways to reduce exam anxiety is to be prepared: read and study the assignments, take good notes in class, and review both assignments and class notes. Test yourself on the key terms and definitions; go over the enumerations and review how they are related; review the items that you and your professor had flagged as important. It is normal to feel somewhat nervous when you take an exam; if you have prepared as well as you can, however, you are much less likely to panic and forget what you have studied.

*Review Notes and Go Directly to Bed*

Make a final review of your notes the night before the exam, then go directly to bed. Your brain will automatically continue to review the material as you drop off to sleep. If you get involved in television programs or heated debates with your roommates, it is possible that the content of these activities will interfere with the material you studied. This interference results from a phenomenon psychologists call retroactive inhibition, where new information coming into the brain interferes with the memory of other information that was previously learned. Get a solid night's sleep so that you will be functioning at your best when you take the exam.

*Get Enough Sleep*

*Review Notes*

Wake up a half hour earlier than necessary on the day of the exam, and review your notes again. Make sure that you bring all the materials you need with you (e.g., pens or pencils, calculator, and watch and text or notes, if these are allowed). Plan to arrive a little early for the exam. Being late raises your anxiety level and adds unnecessary time pressure while you are working on the test; it may also cause you to miss important last-minute instructions or hints that the instructor delivers. Take the opportunity to review your notes again while you are waiting for the exam to begin.

*Bring the Necessary Materials*

*Arrive Early*

*Read Instructions*

Listen to your professor's instructions and read over the instructions on the exam before you rush into it. Put your name on the answer sheet. Take a moment to scan the exam; note the number and extent of the questions so you can budget your time appropriately. If your instructor has included point allotments next to the questions, use these as guides to the length of your answers. You should spend roughly twice as much time on the question worth 30 points as you do on the question worth only 15 points.

*Scan Exam*

*Budget Time*

*Answer Easy Questions First*

Go through the exam and first answer the questions that come easily to you. Put asterisks (***) or some sort of notation next to the items you skip so that you remember to come back to them. This instills confidence as you realize that you do in fact know a lot of the material. It also ensures that you will have time to complete the questions you know while leaving yourself the maximum amount of time to go back and work on the difficult items. Part of your mind will continue to work on the difficult questions, and you may find yourself remembering the answers when you return to these items later. This strategy is also useful because you may find that later test items give you hints or information that you can use to answer earlier ones that you missed.

*Read Instructions Carefully*

Read the instructions for each question carefully. Underline key words in the questions such as the verb (e.g., *compare, contrast, define, give an example of*). Circle the number of items that you have to complete (e.g., ''Choose *two* of the following four essays.''). If your professor wants you to answer *A* or *B,* it does not pay to waste valuable time in answering both parts. If the question asks for two examples, you will receive only half the credit for the item if you give just one example.

*Answer All Questions*

Answer all the questions unless you are penalized for wrong answers. If you leave a question blank, you automatically get a zero for it. If you guess, particularly when you can eliminate one or two of the options, you have a chance of getting it right. Even if you can't answer an essay question, put down whatever you can think of that relates to the item. Your instructor may be able to give you partial credit for the information you put down.

*Outline Essay Response*

It always pays to outline your response to an essay question. This is especially true if it is to be a lengthy essay. An outline ensures that your response will be organized and that you will not forget to include information that you know because of the pressures of the exam situation. It is also more likely that you will remember to answer the question completely. (If the instructor asks you to compare and contrast, you will get only half the credit if you forget to contrast.) The outline may also be the only information you are able to get down if you run out of time. In that case, you will at least get partial credit for the item. After you've written your answer, reread the question to be sure that you have answered it correctly and completely.

*Ask the Professor for Clarification*

If you have difficulty understanding a question or if two answers seem correct, ask your professor to clarify the item or explain your difficulty to him or her. Your professor will not give you the answer but may be able to rephrase the question or give you some other type of helpful hint. If your instructor is not present during the exam or will not entertain questions, write a comment on the exam explaining the nature of the ambiguity. You may be able to get full credit even if you choose the wrong answer.

*Comment on Ambiguity*

*Check Exam*

After you have completed the exam, check it over to make sure that you have answered all items and the correct number of parts for essay questions. Again, unless there is a penalty for guessing, answer every question even if you are unsure of the answer. Read over your answers to check that they are complete. If you have time, review the objective items to be sure that you have answered them correctly. Often information that you receive from later items may cause you to correctly reevaluate an earlier answer.

## IMPROVING YOUR MEMORY

If your studying is going to pay off on exam day, you will have to remember a great deal of what you read. For this reason, it is worth knowing a little about the human memory so that you can make the best use of your memory when you study. Psychologists believe that there are three kinds of memory: sensory memory, short-term memory, and long-term memory.

Sensory memory registers everything that makes an impression on one of your five senses at any moment. These memories are very short-lived unless you single them out as important in some way.

If the information is important, you then transfer it to your short-term memory system. You can keep limited amounts of information alive here for only a few moments unless you rehearse it. A good example is a new phone number that you can remember only long enough to dial unless you repeat it over and over or process it in some other way that ties it into information you already know. If you want the information to last more than a few minutes, you will have to do some more processing so that it can be transferred to long-term memory.

Once you transfer material to long-term memory, it is permanently stored, but retrieving it for use may be tricky unless you have processed it well. Information must be organized or hooked in with other information in your memory for you to be able to get at it. The more connections you make between the new material and the information you already know, the easier it is for you to remember or retrieve these new facts when you need them.

*Organize Material in a Meaningful Way*

It is always easier to remember information that is organized in some meaningful way than to memorize random facts. As an example, how easy do you think it would be for you to memorize the number 149,162,536,496,481 and retrieve it for an exam two months later? If you organized that number in a different way, however, and fit it in with information you already know, you would have no difficulty remembering it ten years from now. Remembering the numbers 1 4 9 16 25 36 49 64 81 (the squares of 1, 2, 3 . . . 9) as a specific series is much easier than remembering 149,162,536,496,481. This is the reason that you should try to follow the organization of a lecture or a chapter: you will find it easier to learn the information. This is also the reason that you should relate the new material to information that is already familiar. You will be able to remember it more easily.

*Connect Material with Other Information*

*"Overlearn" Material*

It is also much easier to retrieve information if it has been "overlearned." Many studies have demonstrated that continuing to rehearse material past the point where you have gotten it perfect the first time will result in better scores when you are tested. Continued drill or practice is the most-effective technique for learning information so that you can retrieve it later. This is the reason that you should use the SQ3R system; it involves at least four opportunities to review the most important aspects of an assignment.

## Strategies for Improving Your Memory

1. Study over a period of time—do not cram.
2. Organize the material and relate it to what you already know.
3. Review and rehearse until you have overlearned the material.
4. Use the mnemonic devices described below.

## Mnemonic Devices

*Use Mnemonics*

There will be times when you have to memorize information. Mnemonic devices can be very helpful at these times because they build on material that is already familiar to you. I learned a sentence in fourth grade that helped me to remember the order of the planets of our solar system according to their distance from the sun. Although I never used this information after fourth grade, I remembered it twenty-eight years later when I had to help my seven-year-old son with his science project!

### Mnemonic for Planets in the Solar System

**Man   Very   Early   Made   Jars   Serve   Useful   Needs (Period)**
**Mercury, Venus, Earth, Mars, Jupiter, Saturn, Uranus, Neptune, Pluto.**

The name "ROY G. BIV" has helped thousands of students through their physics courses when they had to memorize the order of colors in the light spectrum. (You can also use this mnemonic to show off your knowledge about rainbows.)

## *Mnemonic for Colors in the Light Spectrum*

**R      O      Y      G.      B      I      V**
**Red, Orange, Yellow, Green, Blue, Indigo, Violet**

Do you need to memorize the reciprocal of pi for a math course?

## *Mnemonic for the Value of Pi*

**Can I remember the reciprocal?**

**Count the number of letters in each word of the sentence above and you will have your answer any time you need it.**

**The reciprocal of pi = .3 1 8 3 10.**

Is your zoology professor going to ask you whether a Bactrian camel has two humps or one? How about a dromedary?

## *Mnemonic for Bactrian Camel versus Dromedary*

**Place the *B*, for the Bactrian camel, on its back like this:** ⌒⌒
**How many "humps" do you see?**

**Place the *D*, for dromedary, on its back in the same way:** ⌒
**Count the "humps."**

Do you always forget how to spell the word *geography?* Try the following mnemonic:

## *Mnemonic for Spelling* Geography

**George Elliot's Old Grandfather Rode A Pig Home Yesterday.**
**G      E      O      G      R      A      P      H      Y**

We all realize how useful rhymes can be in helping us retrieve information like the number of days in each month:

## *Mnemonic for Number of Days in the Months*

**Thirty days hath September, April, June, and November.**

**All the rest have 31 except February which has 28 till leap year gives it 29.**

Do you have difficulty remembering the musical notes on the treble clef for your music exam? Here's a sentence that will help:

## *Mnemonic for Notes on Treble Clef*

Every Good Boy Does Fine
E      G      B      D      F

Mnemonic devices cannot guarantee *A*s on all your exams, as they can assist you only in recalling information. They cannot help you to understand it or to apply it. When an exam calls for memorizing certain facts, however, try a mnemonic to get you through.

**EXERCISE: MAKING UP MNEMONICS**

Here is a practice problem. Make up a sentence that will help you remember the following classifications in the order they are used in biology. The first word in your sentence should begin with a *k*, the second with a *p*, the third with a *c*, and so on. If you make the sentence vivid and unusual, you are more likely to remember it.

Kingdom    Phylum    Class    Order    Family    Genus    Species

_____

_____

## Imagery and the Method of Loci

Psychologists have found that imagery can be a powerful tool in boosting the efficiency of your memory. If you visualize information, you can expand the capacity of your memory. This is particularly true if you use startling or unusual images.

Greek and Roman orators who had to remember long speeches used the method of "loci" to trigger their memories. This was also one of the methods used by an amazing subject who was studied by the noted psychologist, Alexander Luria.[1] He was able to memorize books in foreign languages that he did not know and recite whole chapters of these books twenty years later!

**EXERCISE: USING THE METHOD OF LOCI**

*Use the Method of Loci*

*Create Dramatic Imagery*

1. In using the method of loci, visualize a room or route that is familiar to you. Then place each of the items you wish to remember in a location along that route and "pick it up" as you take a mental walk around that room. For example, if you wish to memorize the presidents of the United States in order, you might deposit a dramatic image of each president in strategic locations around your house.

Start in the front yard of your house, and visualize George Washington chopping down your favorite tree. Then, as you open your front door, you are greeted by John Adams whose Adam's apple is wildly bobbing up and down while he pumps your hand in greeting. You walk through the front hall into the living room to see a short "Mutt" and a tall "Jeff" sitting next to each other on the couch. Jeff's son (Jefferson) is sitting on his father's lap and shrieking at the top of his lungs because he wants some candy from the dish located on the lamp table next to the couch. You then see James *Mad*ison, hopping *mad*, jumping up and down next to the lamp table because Jeff's son has broken the lamp while trying to get at the candy dish.

Continue through the house "picking up" a president at each stop along your route. The more vivid and unusual you make the images, the easier it will be to remember your items. This method need not be used with only with the rooms in your house; any familiar route, such as a street with particular shops, will work as well.

2. Here is a list of the first ten presidents of the United States. Next to each name write an image that is associated with a room in your house or a stop along a route you know well. Read the list over twice after you have

completed it, imagining the scenes as clearly as possible. Then test yourself by writing down the names of the ten presidents in order. Check your
answers against this list.

George Washington          chopping down a cherry tree in the front yard
_____

John Adams                 _____
_____

Thomas Jefferson           _____
_____

James Madison              _____
_____

James Monroe               _____
_____

John Quincy Adams          _____
_____

Andrew Jackson             _____
_____

Martin Van Buren           _____
_____

William Henry Harrison     _____
_____

John Tyler                 _____
_____

## REDUCING EXAM ANXIETY

It is normal to feel somewhat nervous as you sit down to take an exam. Not
only is this anxiety normal, it is also helpful! If you feel totally calm and collected during a test, you may not perform as well as you could. A small amount
of anxiety, however, is helpful in arousing all your systems so that you are motivated to do your best.

On the other hand, too much anxiety is disruptive; it interferes with your
concentration. If you are worrying about your pumping heart, churning stomach, or sweaty palms, you will not be focusing on the test.

Psychologists have developed very successful techniques for lowering examination anxiety. Two of the most successful techniques are relaxation training
and systematic desensitization. Relaxation training is discussed in Chapter 15,
"Stress and How to Cope With It." Practice the exercises in that chapter, and
then try the systematic desensitization exercise that follows if you believe that
anxiety is interfering with your performance on exams.

# Systematic Desensitization to Exam Anxiety

If your anxiety level is not too high, relaxation exercises can help you to feel more comfortable during exams or other problematic situations. If, on the other hand, anxiety really interferes with your performance, you may wish to consider systematic desensitization in addition to the relaxation exercises.

When you use systematic desensitization, you actually condition yourself to replace anxiety with relaxation during the situations that are troublesome for you. Psychologists have demonstrated the effectiveness of systematic desensitization in thousands of studies. This method has proven successful with a wide range of fears from public speaking to exams to snakes. Ordinarily, the technique is conducted with the guidance of a psychologist; there is evidence, however, that individuals can develop effective programs for themselves.

Exam anxiety can offer a good example of how to set up a program of desensitization, but you can tailor a program to fit any inappropriate fear. Analyze your fear and break it down into the specific situations that make you anxious. Then place those situations in order from least to most anxiety-producing, and proceed with the following instructions. If you are not successful in reducing your anxiety on your own, consult a therapist in your college counseling center for additional guidance.

**EXERCISE:
LEARNING
SYSTEMATIC
DESENSITIZATION**

Systematic desensitization builds on relaxation exercises. After you have learned to relax, write down a list of the situations associated with tests that make you tense. You can then systematically pit these tension-producing situations against your relaxation skills, beginning with a situation that produces only a small amount of anxiety. You can gradually condition yourself to remain relatively relaxed in situations that used to cause you a great deal of discomfort.

1.  Review the following list of situations connected with exams. Make your descriptions specific and detailed. Use the following four examples of items that make many students nervous; you may, however, have different situations that are more relevant for you.

---

**Sample Items for Systematic Desensitization to Exam Anxiety**

- You are going over the markings you made in your biology text and realize that you do not understand a number of key concepts. The exam is one week away, and you are afraid that you will not get it together in time.

- It is the morning of the exam, and you have gotten up early so that you can review your final notes before the exam. Your head feels fuzzy, and the notes do not make sense to you. You feel as if you have forgotten most of what you studied.

- You are looking over the exam quickly to get an idea of its scope and length. You see a lot of tough questions that do not look familiar. You do not think you will make it through the exam.

- The instructor has announced that there are only five minutes left to go before the exam is over. You cannot possibly finish in that time.

---

2. Write down ten exam situations that create anxiety for you. Include some that cause a relatively small amount of anxiety, and work your way up to those that really make you tense. You may wish to use some situations from the list above; there may be other situations, however, that trigger greater anxiety for you. For example, you may find the sensation of initially walking into the exam room more upsetting than any of the listed examples. Perhaps trading questions and answers with your classmates before the exam starts causes you great anxiety. If test anxiety is not particularly a problem for you, choose another fear and break it down into ten situations that cause you to feel anxious.

Situation 1: _____

_____

_____

_____

Situation 2: _____

_____

_____

_____

Situation 3: _____

_____

_____

_____

Situation 4: _____

_____

_____

_____

Situation 5: _____

_____

_____

_____

Situation 6: _____

_____

_____

_____

_____

Situation 7: _____

_____

_____

_____

Situation 8: _____

_____

_____

_____

Situation 9: _____

_____

_____

_____

Situation 10: _____

_____

_____

_____

_____

3. When you have finished writing down your anxiety-producing situations, rank each one on a scale from 1 to 10. A rating of 1 is equal to complete relaxation, the way you might feel after a hot shower or while listening to your favorite music. A rating of 10 should equal the most tense you have ever been, the way you felt when you maneuvered your car out of a near-miss accident or when you were stopped by an officer for a speeding violation.

Place your situations in order from the least to the most anxiety-provoking. Your lowest item should be rated somewhere between 2 and 3, and it should elicit very little tension. You may need to add or change items so that they create more or less anxiety as you go through the desensitization process. You will go through these items systematically while practicing relaxation exercises. When you can imagine an item clearly and it no longer brings on feelings of anxiety, you are ready to go on to the next item. The following instructions will help you desensitize yourself.

4. Choose a quiet place where you will not be disturbed for at least fifteen minutes. Practice your relaxation exercises until you are thoroughly relaxed. Now imagine the first item in your list as clearly and vividly as you can. It is helpful at first to have the anxiety items recorded on tape after

the relaxation exercises so that hearing the description can help you visualize the situation.

Imagine the first scene until you begin to feel some anxiety. Then *stop imagining* the scene, continue your relaxation exercises, and imagine yourself coping successfully with the situation. Here is an example using the first item from the sample list of part 1 in this exercise.

*Item 1:* After you have gone through the relaxation exercises and are feeling very comfortable, imagine that it is one week before your biology exam. You are sitting in your room or in the library or wherever you typically study for an exam. Picture the room as clearly and vividly as you can. What do you see? What do you hear? What do you smell? Picture yourself sitting in your usual position. You are looking at the stack of texts and notes, and you do not want to study. How do you feel? You realize that you have only one week before the big day, you do not understand a number of key concepts, and you are worried that you will not get your studying done in time.

When you feel some tension beginning, *stop imagining* the scene and continue breathing deeply and regularly. Repeat some of the autogenic phrases to yourself: "I am very calm and comfortable," "My breathing is deeper and deeper," and "I am more and more relaxed."

*Item 1 with Coping Imagery:* Now imagine yourself in your study situation, again facing your books one week before the exam. You begin to worry about the material you do not understand, but this time you stop and tell yourself that one week is plenty of time to clarify the concepts you do not understand. You read the sections again, trying to paraphrase the concepts in your own words. You write down questions on the items that are still unclear so that you can get help from your instructor or a classmate. You plan out a schedule so that you can study two hours each day before your favorite television show. You will not let yourself watch that program until you have finished studying for the day. You promise that you will apply yourself and study efficiently up to the day of the exam. You will succeed in finishing on time.

If you feel no anxiety after imagining this scene for 45 to 60 seconds, then do some more relaxing and go on to the next item on your list. If you still feel some anxiety when you imagine the first item, repeat the item, using the relaxation exercises and coping suggestion, for 20 seconds. If you feel no anxiety after 20 seconds, increase the duration to 30 seconds. Whenever you feel anxiety, stop and do some breathing and relaxing. Continue to gradually increase the duration of the image to 60 seconds until you have desensitized yourself to it.

Continue from one item to the next on the list only after you have desensitized yourself to the previous item and feel no anxiety when imagining it. If you hit a stumbling block and cannot desensitize yourself to a particular item, try making up an additional item that is halfway, in terms of the amount of anxiety produced, between the one you have completed and the next one that is giving you difficulty.

**EXERCISE: DECREASING ANXIETY THROUGH COPING IMAGERY**

Make up coping suggestions for each of the items on your list. Here are some coping suggestions for situations from the list of sample items in part I of the previous exercise.

**Sample Items for Coping Imagery**

*Item 2:* It is the morning of the exam, and you have gotten up early so that you can review your final notes before the exam. Your head feels fuzzy, and the notes do not make sense to you. You feel as if you have forgotten most of what you studied.

*Item 2 with Coping Imagery:* You take a shower, have some coffee, do some deep breathing, and say some autogenic phrases to clear your head. You look at your notes slowly and concentrate on the key words. You know that what you need is stored in your long-term memory, which never loses information. You look at the key words that will help you get that information out of memory storage.

*Item 3:* You're looking over the exam quickly, to get an idea of its scope and length. You see a lot of tough questions that do not look familiar. You do not think you will make it through the exam.

*Item 3 with Coping Imagery:* You tell yourself not to worry. You probably know more than you think you do, and the information will come back to you when you really start to focus on it. Finish your survey of the exam, take a few deep breaths, and start on the easy questions.

*Item 4:* The instructor has announced that there are only five minutes left to go before the exam is over. You cannot possibly finish in that time.

*Item 4 with Coping Imagery:* You take a few deep breaths and outline the answers to the rest of the questions as quickly as you can. Look around to see whether other students are still in the room. Chances are that you are not the only one experiencing time pressure, and the professor will take this into account. Figure that the instructor will probably let you have some extra time if he or she sees that you are not finished. You can move through the material fairly quickly if you have to, and you should get partial credit at least.

Write down coping imagery for the ten anxiety-producing situations you created earlier in this chapter.

Situation 1: _____

_____

_____

_____

_____

Situation 2: _____

_____

_____

_____

Situation 3: _____

_____

_____

_____

Situation 4: _____

_____

_____

_____

_____

Situation 5: _____

_____

_____

_____

Situation 6: _____

_____

_____

_____

Situation 7: _____

_____

_____

_____

_____

Situation 8: _____

_____

_____

_____

_____

Situation 9: _____

_____

_____

_____

_____

Situation 10: _____

_____

_____

_____

_____

Desensitization is a gradual process. It will take you some time to learn and practice the relaxation exercises, then some more time to desensitize yourself to the anxiety-provoking situations. Work on these exercises ten to fifteen minutes at a time. If you practice once or twice a day, you should see significant improvement within a month or two. If you feel that the situation is not improving, get some additional help at the counseling center.

## NOTE

1. A. R. Luria, *Mind of a Mnemonist,* trans. L. Solotaroff (New York: Basic Books, 1968).

# Chapter 8

## Library Research

### RESEARCH SKILLS

One of the most important skills you can learn at college is how to find information. You will need research skills when you prepare term papers and oral reports. You will also find these skills useful once you graduate from college if you need to look up statistics for a business presentation, write an article for a newsletter, or decide which automobile to purchase. There has been a tremendous increase in the number of works published in the past decade. It is estimated that more than forty thousand books are published each year in the United States alone, and thousands of newspapers, magazines, and journals come out on a daily, weekly, or monthly basis to add to this information explosion.

*Become Familiar with the Library*

It is well worth your time to become familiar with the services and locations offered by your college library. Take a tour of the library, if your school offers one. Many colleges offer library orientation workshops or courses, pamphlets on library services, or videotapes to acquaint you with what is available and where to find it. The small amount of time you invest in becoming familiar with your library, at the beginning of your college career, will save you much time later when you are working under the gun of the due date for that important research paper.

*Ask the Reference Librarian for Help*

The reference librarian is your best ally in the time-consuming but ultimately rewarding search for information. Learn as much as you can about the library, but always check with a reference librarian if you are stuck about how or where to find the information you need. Even if you have done a thorough research job, the reference librarian may be able to help you locate additional or superior sources. The reference librarian's job is to help people use the library. Do not be afraid to ask for help, no matter how simple your question seems!

*Bring Assignment Guidelines with You*

In order to help you, however, the reference librarian needs certain information from you. Bring your syllabus and the guidelines for your assignment to the library with you in case the librarian has a question about the type of information you need for your assignment. Spend some time choosing a topic and narrowing it down before you approach the librarian. Know what types of sources your instructor expects you to use. For example, an encyclopedia may be fine for certain assignments, but totally inadequate for others; magazine articles may be appropriate for some courses, but only the more scholarly journal articles may be acceptable for others. Do not be afraid to ask for help. As your research skills improve, you will experience less frustration and greater rewards when you use the library.

If you have not used a research library before, you may feel overwhelmed by the size and complexity of your college library. A research library includes many types of services that are not found in your high school or neighborhood library. Although your local library may be simpler, it does not contain many of the resources that you will need for college-level work.

## LIBRARY SECTIONS AND SERVICES

*Familiarize Yourself with the Entire Library*

Familiarize yourself with the main section of the college library in your freshman year. You may in later years also need to become familiar with smaller or more specialized collections that are located in other campus buildings. The central library on a college campus usually includes a main desk where books are checked out, a reference section that contains specialized materials used in research, a card catalog where you may look up the location of books, the stacks where books are shelved, and a periodicals section where journals are housed.

*Be Able to Find the Tape Collection, Reserve Section, Vertical File, and Government Documents*

In addition to these areas, there may be audio and videotape collections, a section for reserve books set aside by instructors for certain courses, shelves where current newspapers and magazines are displayed, a vertical file containing clippings and pamphlets on topics of current interest, and a government documents collection. Most research libraries also include photocopy machines for duplicating materials, microfilm and microfiche machines for reading and duplicating materials printed on film rather than paper, typing areas, and study areas.

## THE REFERENCE SECTION

The reference section contains sources as diverse as handbooks, thesauri, dictionaries, encyclopedias, indexes, atlases, yearbooks, bibliographies, and directories to guide you with your research. These are usually expensive volumes, and they do not circulate. That means that you may use them in the library, but you may not take them home with you.

*Become Familiar with the Special Dictionaries*

You are familiar with dictionaries, but in addition to the general dictionaries that help you out with routine spelling and definitions, the reference section contains specialized dictionaries to answer technical questions in a particular field (e.g., *A Dictionary of Biological Sciences, Dictionary of Music and Musicians, Mathematical Dictionary,* and *Dictionary of Quotations*).

*Find the Special Encyclopedias*

The same is true of encyclopedias. In addition to the more general *Encyclopedia Britannica,* you may find more specialized encyclopedias such as the *Encyclopedia of Sports,* the *Encyclopedia of Banking and Finance,* and the *Encyclopedia of Bioethics.* You may not be able to use these as one of your major sources for a research paper, but they are often a good place to begin research. You may find them useful in giving you an overview of a particular topic, helping you to recognize the major subdivisions of an area, or guiding you when you have to narrow down a topic that is too broad.

*Use Indexes to Journals*

The reference section also houses the many indexes that will help you locate information published in newspapers, magazines, and journals. *Biological Index,* for example, lists by subject and by author all the articles published in biology for a given year. *Education Index* does the same for the field of education, as does *Sociological Abstracts* for sociology articles and *Historical Abstracts* for historical material. *Bibliographic Index* is an annual publication that lists published bibliographies by subject. As you take more advanced courses in your major, you will find these indexes to be invaluable guides to the information available in your field.

*Ask the Reference Librarian*

The most valuable resource in the reference section, however, is probably the reference librarian. This text can give you only a taste of the wide assortment of materials available in this area. Whether you need to know the batting average of a particular player, the birth date of a specific author, the address of a certain university, the approved subject heading for a particular topic, or the location of a government document, your reference librarian is your best guide to finding information.

## THE CARD CATALOG

The card catalog is your guide to what books your library owns and where to find them. The catalog may be arranged on individual cards, which are housed in wooden files familiar from your high school days. Or, as is becoming the case in more and more libraries, the card catalog may be a computerized listing.

*Check the Author File*

The card catalog is divided into three sections. Each book is listed in the author section, under the last name of the person who wrote it. It is also listed in the title section, by the first word in the book's title. (Leave out words like *The* or *A* if these are the first words in the book's title, and look up the book alphabetically by the second word.) In writing a research paper, however, you may find that the listing in the subject section is most useful to you.

*Check the Title File*

*Check the Subject File*

Books in the subject section are listed by the topic that they cover. Be aware, however, that the topic or subject that you choose may not be listed under the most obvious subject heading. If you do not find books under a particular heading, ask the reference librarian to show you the *Library of Congress Subject Headings,* a guide to official subject headings. You will find, for example, that books about fraternities are listed under "Greek letter societies," those that deal with teenagers are listed under "youth," and publications on the greenhouse effect are cataloged under "greenhouse atmospheric." Until recently, books about toilets were to be found under "water closets," and works dealing with nuclear power were filed under "atomic power." These last two subject headings were recently updated, so it pays to check the latest edition of *Library of Congress Subject Headings* if you are having difficulty finding your sources. The guide may also suggest additional headings that you might check to find information about your topic.

*Find the Library of Congress Subject Headings*

The sample cards in figures 8 to 10 show the listings in the library card catalog for a book entitled *The Jazz Age;* the listings are, respectively, in the subject, author, and title sections of the card catalog. Notice that the cards tell you the name of the publisher, the date, and the place of publication. If you ever misplace some of the bibliographical information you need for your list of references, you will not have to go back to the book itself to trace this infor-

*Note the Publisher, Date, and Place of Publication*

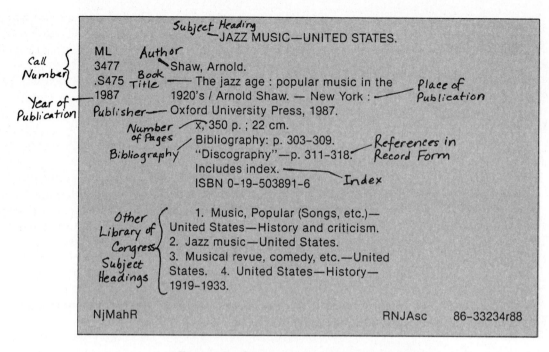

**FIGURE 8. CARD CATALOG LISTING BY SUBJECT**

mation. It can be found in the card catalog. The card also gives you helpful information about how many pages the book has and whether it includes illustrations, bibliography, and index. The subject headings under which the book is listed are printed at the bottom of the card. These subject headings offer good suggestions for additional categories that could yield more books on your topic. The most important information on the card is the call number, which tells you where to find the book. This number appears in the upper left hand corner of the card and on the spine of the book. Write it down carefully, as your library

*Check the Subject Headings*

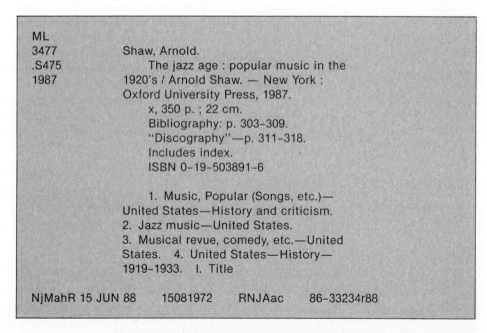

**FIGURE 9. CARD CATALOG LISTING BY AUTHOR**

FIGURE 10. CARD CATALOG LISTING BY BOOK TITLE

*Copy Call Number Carefully*

is a big place. If you copy even one of the letters or numbers incorrectly, you are not likely to find the book.

*Understand the Library of Congress Call Numbers*

Most research libraries use the Library of Congress system of call numbers that include letters and numbers. You will find, for example, that general history books are listed under *D* and *DX;* chemistry books are shelved under *QD.* Obtain a directory of the library from the main desk. If the library at your college is housed on more than one floor, copy down the floor numbers where books with various call numbers are shelved. You may find, for example, that *D* books are located on the third floor. If you are looking for *Revolutions and Dictatorships,* which is listed under call number D 720 .K6, go to the appropriate floor, locate the *D* section, and then look for books with call numbers in the 700s. Continue narrowing your search until you have used all the digits in the call number. Once you have found your book, you might take a moment to look at the books shelved next to it since these are likely to cover similar topics.

## PERIODICALS

Books are, of course, a fine source of information for a term paper. You may find, however, that many of your instructors prefer that you use periodicals rather than or in addition to books in conducting your research. Periodicals include newspapers, journals, and magazines. Magazines contain articles written for the general public, whereas journals consist of more specialized articles written for students and scholars with backgrounds in a particular field. These journals are published on daily, weekly, or monthly schedules and therefore include information that is more current than the information found in books. The information in periodicals also tends to be more focused and specialized than that found in most books.

## Indexes

You will find that your library subscribes to a number of indexes that will help you find journal articles on almost any topic. These indexes are published on a monthly and annual basis so that the 1977 volume of *Business Periodicals Index,* for example, will include all the articles published in that year by the business journals covered by that index. In general, you will wish to consult the most-recent editions of the indexes. Your instructor may suggest that you review research over the past ten or fifteen years to find articles on your topic.

The most general index is the *Reader's Guide to Periodical Literature.* It lists articles by author and subject that appear in more than one hundred popular magazines such as *Reader's Digest, Time,* and *Newsweek.* You will find that the index lists the periodicals it covers on a page near the front of the volume. If your instructor wants you to use magazines in your research, this is a good index to consult. Check the *Library of Congress Subject Headings* for the appropriate subject headings. You may find that articles about your topic are listed under several headings. Make a list of these headings and check each of them to compile a comprehensive list of sources.

*Consult the Readers' Guide to Periodical Literature*

*List and Check Subject Headings*

If you are doing a paper on marriage, for example, you will find that pages 1197 and 1198 of volume 47 in the 1987 edition of *The Readers' Guide to Periodical Literature* list more than eighty-five articles on this topic. The listing includes articles on marriage counseling, marriage law, marriage customs and rites, and marriage contracts. If, however, you are researching a paper on movie stars, you will find those articles listed under "motion picture actors and actresses" on page 1284. The sixth article on this topic is listed in a sample citation in figure 11.

The information about the article always appears in the same order, as would other citations from the *Readers' Guide to Periodical Literature:*

1. The subject heading for the article.

2. The title of the article.

*Copy Bibliographic Information Carefully*

3. The author's name (last name first, followed by initials). If there is more than one author, you will need the names and initials of all of them for your bibliography. In many cases, there is no author listed for the article.

4. Information about a bibliography or illustrations. Abbreviations for these (e.g., il., bibli.) are indicated if the article includes them.

5. The title of the magazine. You will have to check the list of magazines in the front of the index to interpret the abbreviations used. Please don't guess, as it will make it hard for you to find the magazine. "Psych" could stand for "psychological," "psychiatric," or "psychology." As many journals have similar titles, you could lose a great deal of time if you make a mistake about the periodical's title.

6. The volume number of the magazine.

7. The page numbers where the article appears.

---

How the stars make love on-screen [chemistry between couple]. M. Musto. il. *Mademoiselle* 93: 68 My '87

(This citation tells you that the title of the article is "How the Stars Make Love On-Screen." The author is M. Musto. The article is illustrated, and it appeared in *Mademoiselle* magazine, volume 93, on page 68, of the May 1987 edition.)

FIGURE 11. SAMPLE CITATION FROM *READERS' GUIDE TO PERIODICAL LITERATURE*

**8.** The date of the magazine in which the article was published. Check the list of abbreviations in the front of the index for the key. *Je,* for example, refers to June, and *Ja* stands for January.

**EXERCISE:
USING THE
READERS' GUIDE
TO PERIODICAL
LITERATURE**

As a practice exercise, fill in the bibliographical information for the following article that appears as the first listing under "marriage" on page 1197 of the 1987 edition of the *Readers' Guide to Periodical Literature.* You will need to include *all of this information* in the bibliography of your research papers. You will also need this information in order to find the article in the library's periodicals section. If you copy it down carefully, and hold onto it, you will save yourself a great deal of time and frustration!

10 ways to keep your marriage strong [excerpt from How to Honeymoon] C. Weston il. *Essence* 18: 65–66+ N '87.

Author's name: _____

Date of publication (month and year): _____

Title of article: _____

_____

Title of magazine: _____

_____

Volume number: _____

Page numbers: _____

*Check Abbreviations
in Front of Index*

*Copy Volume Number
and Page Number of
Index*

All abbreviations are listed in the front of the index, and you may have to keep checking these until you become accustomed to the systems used by the various indexes. If you are doing a large research project, you may find it helpful to write down the issue and page number of the *Readers' Guide to Periodical Literature* where you found the citation. In case you miscopied some of the bibliographical information, forgot to write some information down, or need to order a magazine through the interlibrary loan network, writing down the issue and page number will save you considerable time in searching through back issues of the *Readers' Guide to Periodical Literature.*

*Look Up Call Number
or Fill Out Call Slip*

Once you have copied down all the bibliographical information for the articles that interest you, you will have to see whether your library carries those magazines. It is likely that your library does subscribe to most of the magazines listed in the *Readers' Guide to Periodical Literature.* If the periodicals are shelved in open stacks, you must then look up the call number for the magazine you want and locate it in the same way you would locate a book. If the stacks are not open, you will need to fill out a call slip with the bibliographical information so that the librarian can retrieve the magazine for you. Please be careful to write down the bibliographical information correctly so that you don't have to go back to the *Reader's Guide* and check it again!

*Use Specialized
Indexes*

*Use Newspaper
Indexes*

You will find that other indexes work much like the *Readers' Guide to Periodical Literature* so that once you have mastered one, you can easily use others like the *Education Index, Art Index,* or *Engineering Index Monthly.* Many newspapers have indexes that catalog their articles. The *New York Times Index* and the *Wall Street Journal Index,* for example, list bibliographical information for articles that appear daily in those newspapers.

*Use Journals Instead of Magazines for More Scholarly Papers*

The *Social Science Index,* on the other hand, covers a broader territory by listing articles published in the more scholarly journals of the social sciences. The difference between a magazine and a journal is that a journal is written for a more specialized, professional audience. It tends to be more scholarly. If you are writing a paper on disciplinary problems of school children for a psychology course, your professor may not allow you to use magazine articles from *McCalls, Reader's Digest,* or even *Psychology Today.* If he or she specifies that you are to use journal articles, then your research job will be easier if you consult *The Social Science Index* or *Psychological Abstracts.* These journals contain more scholarly articles than the magazine articles featured in the the *Readers' Guide to Periodical Literature.*

*Use Abstracts and Summaries*

Indexes like *Psychological Abstracts, Historical Abstracts,* or *Chemical Abstracts* have an added benefit. In addition to giving you the bibliographical information for an article, they also present abstracts or summaries of the articles. Each index of these volumes is numbered. The number assigned to the citation in the index volume under author or subject heading corresponds to numbers printed on the spine of the abstracts volume. If you look up that abstract number, you will find a paragraph that summarizes the article. This summary gives you a better idea than the article's title as to whether that article would really be useful for the paper you are writing.

*Check the Periodical Holdings List*

*Ask About Interlibrary Loan*

Once you are using the more specialized indexes, you will undoubtedly find that your library does not subscribe to all the journals listed in the index. You will need to check the list of periodical holdings located at the reference desk or in the periodicals area to see which periodicals your library does own. If the library does not subscribe to a particular journal that you need, ask whether they will order the article for you through an interlibrary loan system. This service is usually free, but you will probably have to wait two to three weeks before you receive the article.

*Use Computer Search for Your Bibliography*

Another bibliographical service that may interest you is the computerized literature search. You can have the library's computer search through various indexes and generate a bibliographical list for you. Some colleges make this service available only to faculty and advanced students. At other institutions, the service is available to everyone; the user, however, must pay for the computer search. These searches vary in price, depending on the breadth of the topic and the particular data bases consulted. If you have the computer complete a search for you, you will have to define your topic very carefully, and you may have to consult a specialized manual or thesaurus for descriptors or subject headings.

Research skills, like writing skills, improve with practice. The more you work in the library, the easier you will find it to locate information. As the quality of your information improves, so does the quality of your papers and your education. Give yourself the time and practice to develop solid research skills.

**EXERCISE: USING THE CARD CATALOG**

Go to your library and fill in the following requested information.

1. Look in the title section of the card catalog, and locate a book entitled *The Myth of Mental Illness.*

   Author (last name, first name, and middle initial): _____

   _____

   Year and city of publication: _____

Name of publisher: _____

Number of pages: _____

Does the book have a bibliography or illustrations? _____

Under what subject headings is this book listed? _____

_____

_____

2. In the author's section of the card catalog, look up two books by Ernest Hemingway. Write down the bibliographical information required for a book.

|  *Book 1*  |  *Book 2*  |
|---|---|
| Author: | Author: |
| _____ | _____ |
| Year of publication: | Year of publication: |
| _____ | _____ |
| Title of book: | Title of book: |
| _____ | _____ |
| _____ | _____ |
| City of publication: | City of publication: |
| _____ | _____ |
| Name of publisher: | Name of publisher: |
| _____ | _____ |
| _____ | _____ |

**EXERCISE: RESEARCHING A TOPIC WITH THE CARD CATALOG**

Choose a topic. If you have a paper due this semester, use the topic for that paper. Otherwise, choose one of the following topics: the Olympics, women's fashions, alcohol, disarmament, or the social security system.

1. Check the *Library of Congress Subject Headings* for three approved headings that will give you information about your subject. Write them down.

Library of Congress Headings

_____

_____

_____

2. Look at the subject section of the card catalog, and write down the following bibliographical information for two books about your subject.

Author: (last name, first initial, and middle initial)

Book 1                           Book 2

_____        _____
_____        _____
_____        _____

Year of publication

Book 1                           Book 2

_____        _____
_____        _____

Title of book

Book 1                           Book 2

_____        _____
_____        _____
_____        _____
_____        _____

City of publication

Book 1                           Book 2

_____        _____
_____        _____

Name of publisher

Book 1                           Book 2

_____        _____
_____        _____

Call number

Book 1                           Book 2

_____        _____
_____        _____

On what floor of the library would you find these books?

Book 1                           Book 2

_____        _____
_____        _____

**EXERCISE: RESEARCHING A TOPIC WITH THE *READERS' GUIDE TO PERIODICAL LITERATURE***

Use the *Readers' Guide to Periodical Literature* to find an article on your topic. Write down the following information.

Subject heading: _____

Author if it is listed (last name, first name, and middle initial): _____
_____

Date of magazine (month, day, year, if listed): _____

Title of article: _____

_____

Name of magazine: _____

_____

Volume number of magazine: _____

Page numbers of the article: _____

Does your library own the magazine? (Check the periodical holdings listing at the reference desk or periodical section.)

Yes _____        No _____

If your library has open stacks, write down the call number of the journal and find the journal. If your library does not have open stacks, fill out a call slip and get the journal.

Call number: _____

Is the journal bound together with other issues of the journal, or is it available as a single copy? Is it printed on paper or microfilm?

| | | |
|---|---|---|
| Bound | Yes _____ | No _____ |
| Single copy | Yes _____ | No _____ |
| Microfilm | Yes _____ | No _____ |

Find the article and copy down the first sentence.

_____

_____

**EXERCISE: RESEARCHING A TOPIC WITH ANOTHER INDEX TO PERIODICALS**

Use a periodical index other than the *Readers' Guide to Periodical Literature* (e.g., *Business Periodicals Index, Psychological Abstracts, Art Index, Historical Abstracts*) to find an article on your topic; write down the following information.

Title of index you used: _____

Author (last name, first initial, and middle initial): _____

_____

Year of publication: _____

Title of article: _____

_____

Name of journal: _____

_____

Volume number (and issue number if listed): _____

Page numbers of article: _____

Does your library own the journal? (Check the periodical holdings list at the reference desk or in the periodicals section.) If your library does not own the journal, fill out an interlibrary loan request and staple it to this page.

Yes _____      No _____

If your library has open stacks, write down the call number and get the journal. If your library does not have open stacks, fill out a call slip and get the journal.

Call number: _____

Is the journal bound together with other issues of the journal, or is it available as a single copy? Is it printed on paper or microfilm?

| | | |
|---|---|---|
| Bound | Yes _____ | No _____ |
| Single Copy | Yes _____ | No _____ |
| Microfilm | Yes _____ | No _____ |

Find the article, and copy down the first sentence.

_____

_____

_____

_____

**EXERCISE: RESEARCHING A TOPIC WITH AN INDEX TO NEWSPAPERS**

Use *The New York Times Index, The Wall Street Journal Index,* or another newspaper index to find an article on your topic. Write down the following information.

Name and year of index used: _____ _____

_____

Subject heading used: _____

Author (if listed): _____

Date of article: _____

Name of newspaper: _____

Title of article (if listed) _____

_____

_____

Section, page, and column of article: _____

Where would you find the article? Is it on paper or microfilm? _____

Location _____

| | | |
|---|---|---|
| Paper | Yes _____ | No _____ |
| Microfilm | Yes _____ | No _____ |

# Chapter 9

## Papers

### *Thinking and Writing Logically*

**THE WRITING PROCESS**

Do you have difficulty translating your thoughts into words? Do you try to avoid courses that require term papers? Do you encounter a "mental block" when you sit down to write a paper? Many students dread writing papers more than they dread taking exams. This is understandable. The writing process often results in feelings of frustration, and it does require a lot of time and planning. Even professional writers often find it hard to get started, and once they are writing, they spend hours revising their work before it's ready for public view.

### The Purpose of Writing Assignments

This chapter presents hints and techniques that will make the writing process less painful, but first a few words about the purpose of writing assignments that may help you to approach these tasks more enthusiastically. It is true that papers, like exams, give your professor a means for evaluating how much you have learned. The primary purpose of writing assignments, however, is to help you learn about a topic and to teach you how to think, organize, and communicate your thoughts.

When you put ideas into your own words, when you summarize, compare, and criticize them, you become actively involved with them. You remember your ideas and are able to use them long after the course is over. That is the real reason that instructors assign papers. They want you to make the assigned material a part of yourself. They want you to learn how to research a topic and how to communicate about it.

## Research and Communication

The ability to carry out research is one of the most useful skills you will learn in college. You will find that it helps you later in life, for instance, when you are aiming for a competitive job and need to find out more about the company that is about to interview you. You will use it as you advance in your career to keep up with the latest developments in your field. You will need it when you have to decide what type of car to buy, how to go about buying a house, or where to send your child to college.

The ability to communicate clearly is also one of the most important skills you can learn in college. You will find that you are called upon to communicate more often and at more advanced levels as you progress from your freshman year to your senior year at college. You will also find that virtually any career you might choose will require this skill. This becomes particularly true if you want to rise into the managerial or executive ranks.

Once you have learned some basic rules about writing, the key to improving your writing skills is practice. Take the time to review your instructor's comments and suggestions when he or she returns your papers. Try to apply the instructor's suggestions to the next paper you write. Writing is a cumulative skill; each paper you write should help you improve your skill for the next round.

## SELECTING A TOPIC

The first step in writing a paper usually involves choosing a topic. Before you even tackle the topic, be sure that you understand the assignment. A lab report has different goals than a literary critique. A case study in social work uses a different format from a case study in political science. Professors in history expect different elements in a research paper than do professors in communications.

*Review the Assignment*

If your instructor has given you written guidelines, read them carefully. If the instructions for the assignment are verbal, take down your professor's words carefully. Ask questions about anything that is not clear, and then review those notes before you choose your topic. If you are absent when an assignment is given, make an appointment with your professor to find out firsthand about the assignment.

*Choose an Interesting Topic*

When you choose a topic, choose one that interests you and one that you know something about. It is easier to motivate yourself to write if you are interested in your subject. You will also have a head start if you have some idea of where or how to approach your topic.

## Topic Definition

*Narrow Topic Down*

Once you have chosen a topic, you have to define it. This usually means narrowing it down. Most students make the mistake of choosing topics that are too broad. This then results in a paper that is superficial. You never get a chance to really discuss or evaluate the topic because you are covering too many bases. You do not have the opportunity to deal with your topic in depth because you are too busy describing all its parameters at a very general level.

Let us say, for example, that you have chosen to do a two-page paper on cars. The subject of cars is much too broad a topic for a two-page paper. Will you discuss types of cars? Production techniques for cars? Advertising for car sales? Environmental impact of cars? To produce an effective paper, you will have to narrow your topic down to one of these, but even they are likely to be too broad. Let us say you are interested in the environmental impact of cars. You will need to narrow your topic down even further. Will you examine fuel economy? Air pollution? Road construction? Encroachment on wilderness preserves? The outline in figure 12 will give you examples of how you might narrow down your subject until you have a topic you can handle competently within the scope of your assignment.

Once you have defined your topic, check it with your professor. He or she will be able to tell you whether the topic is too broad or too narrow. If it is too narrow, you will not be able to find enough information to write a paper of the required length. If it is too broad, you will end up with a superficial paper in which you cannot demonstrate your analytical or critical skills and for which you will receive a poor grade. Your professor will also be able to tell you whether the topic you have chosen is too advanced for you to handle and whether you will be able to find information on it at your level of expertise. It is wise to have more than one idea about possible topics when you go to see your instructor. He or she may guide you as to which one will be easier to research or will result in a better paper.

**EXERCISE: NARROWING DOWN A TOPIC**

Choose one of the following topics and list five major subtopics that narrow it down. Then choose one of the subtopics you have identified and narrow it down again into four narrower topics that might be used for a shorter paper. If you have difficulty thinking of subcategories, try the brainstorming technique. Give yourself five minutes to list all words or phrases that come into your mind when you think about that topic. Do not evaluate the phrases, and do not worry about spelling or handwriting. Just write as much and as quickly as you can in the five minutes. When the time limit

I. Cars
  A. Types
    1. Family
    2. Sports
    3. Four-wheel drive
    4. Van
  B. Effect on Lifestyle
    1. Method of commuting to work
    2. Types of vacations taken
    3. Number of cars owned
    4. Level of debt sustained
  C. Production Techniques
    1. Assembly line production
    2. Multinational company structure
    3. Union participation
    4. Management restructuring
  D. Environmental Impact
    1. Improved fuel economy
    2. Reduced air pollution
    3. Necessity for road construction
    4. Destruction of wilderness preserves

**FIGURE 12. SAMPLE OUTLINE FOR NARROWING DOWN A TOPIC**

is up, go back and review your list. Cross off the words that are not appropriate. Recopy the ones that might be appropriate subtopics for a short paper.

1. Choose one of the following listed topics, cross out the other two, and list five major subtopics under your choice.

*Sports*             *Occupational Choices*             *Changing Sex Roles*

_____

_____

_____

_____

_____

_____

_____

_____

_____

_____

_____

_____

_____

_____

_____

_____

_____

2. Choose one of the five subtopics you identified, and narrow it down into four smaller subtopics suitable for a short paper. Use the brainstorming technique.

_____

_____

_____

_____

_____

_____

_____

_____

_____

_____

_____

_____

_____

_____

_____

_____

_____

_____

_____

## COLLECTING INFORMATION

*Determine the Purpose of your Paper*

Once you have defined your topic, check with your instructor about the purpose of the paper. Usually he or she will tell you whether to describe something, to explain it, to prove something, to convince your audience of a certain point of view, or to inform your reader about a topic. Each of these assignments has a different purpose and will require different research and writing strategies.

*Use Index Cards for Notes*

The type of assignment will determine what type of information you will need. You may be using your own thoughts and experiences, others' experiences or opinions, assigned readings, or reference materials from the library. If you are doing a paper that requires sources other than your own experience, you will have to take notes from those sources and organize your material. Use three-by-five-inch index cards to take notes. Put one idea on each card. Number the cards so that related or supporting material for ideas follows the original ideas. You will later be able to shuffle these cards and rearrange them to help you organize your material. Look over your cards while you are doing the research so that you can think about the best ways to organize the information.

*Use Index Cards for Sources*

Keep a separate set of three-by-five-inch cards to use as bibliography cards. Each time you use a new source, write down the complete citation. You will have to prepare a bibliography or a list of references for any research paper you write. Keeping track of the bibliographical information as you go along will save you a great deal of time in having to go back and track down a missing date of publication or the page numbers of an article. For each journal article, write down last name and first initial of the author, year of publication, title of the article, title of the journal, volume number of the journal, and page numbers.

*Record Author Name, Year of Publication, Title, Journal, Volume Number, Page Numbers, City and State of Publication, Publisher, and Edition*

If you are using a book, you will need author's name, year of publication, title, city and state of publication, name of publisher, edition (if it has been reprinted more than once), and pages used. When it is time to type up your list of references, you will be able to arrange your bibliography cards in alphabetical order and type directly without having to recopy all that information or run to the library to track down missing information.

*Give Each Source Card a Number*

As you write your paper, you will probably wish to quote or give credit to the authors whose works you are using. In order to cite these sources appropriately, you will need to know the source of the information on your note cards. Give each of your bibliography cards a code number. When you take notes from a book or article, on three-by-five-inch cards, you can put that code number on top of the corresponding information cards. Then as you write your paper from your note cards, you will automatically have the source of each idea, quotation, or statistic available without the bother of writing down the bibliographical information on each note card.

*Find Research Library*

Where should you look for information about your topic? In order to research most of your college papers, you will need a research library. These may be found in colleges, universities, medical schools, or specialized libraries in large cities. Very few local libraries will have the reference materials or sources necessary for college-level research papers.

*Check Subject Headings of Card Catalog*

*Find the Guide to Subject Headings*

The best advice is to go from the more general sources to the more specialized ones. Start out with an encyclopedia and get an overview of your topic. This will give you an idea of subtopics that you might look for in more specialized works. Check the card catalog under your subject heading for books on your topic. The appropriate subject headings are not necessarily obvious, and you may have to check several headings before you find books that zero in on your topic. Ask a reference librarian to help you locate the appropriate headings in the Library of Congress guide to subject headings. This is a thesaurus to the subject section of the card catalog. When you find a book that looks promising, write down the author's name, the title, and the call number. The card catalogs of many research libraries are computerized so that you may actually be carrying out this part of your research on a computer screen rather than on a small wooden box.

*Check Journal Indexes*

Magazine, journal, and newspaper articles give you more specific, and often, more up-to-date information on a topic. If you will be including these sources for your paper, check indexes such as the *Readers' Guide to Periodical Literature, The Humanities Index, The New York Times Index.* More specialized indexes also exist for fields like psychology, biology, and so on. Ask a reference librarian to show you how to find, through these indexes, articles that relate to your topic. Your reference librarian may also be able to make a computer literature search for your paper. This service is available in some schools for advanced undergraduate papers. You must define your topic carefully, and the computer will then check a variety of appropriate indexes to locate books, articles, and dissertations about your topic.

*Use Current Sources*

Try to use sources that are current. Books or articles more than fifteen years old may no longer be accurate. This is particularly true in fast-changing fields like science or medicine; statements made about acquired immunodeficiency disease syndrome (AIDS) six months ago may no longer be accurate. It is also true in areas like history and literature where new theories or discoveries change current views. There may be older classic material that you will wish to consult, for instance, Freud's original case description of Little Hans. Secondary evaluative literature, however, should be of a more contemporary nature.

*Begin Research Early*

Begin your research as early as you can. This will give you the opportunity to order materials that your library doesn't own. Many college libraries are able to get you any book or article published free of charge through an interlibrary loan system, but the process can take up to three weeks. Give yourself time to gather the best possible materials. Beginning your research early will also allow you to use the materials your library has on hand before they have been checked out by everyone else in the class. If you have to change your topic or gather additional research to complete the paper, you will have time for it. The final advantage of an early start is that it allows you to think about your paper before you have to write it; this will result in a better paper. Your instructor might even be willing to look over the first version of the paper and return it with suggestions so that you can rewrite it for a better grade.

# PREPARING TO WRITE

*Schedule Prime Time*

*Choose Good Writing Area*

Give some thought to the time and place in which you will write. You should set aside time for writing when you are most alert and your concentration is at its best. Like your study area, your writing area should be organized with all the materials you need; it should be free of distractions; and it should allow you to work comfortably (e.g., good lighting, proper support for your back, etc.).

*Brainstorm for Ideas*

If you are writing a paper from your own experience and need ideas to flesh out your topic, use the brainstorming technique. Sit down for five minutes and write, as quickly as you can, everything that comes to mind. Don't censor or evaluate this material; just write. When the five minutes are up, go back over your writing and see what you can use in your paper. Eliminate some ideas. Add others that occur to you while you are reviewing your notes.

*Pose Questions for Ideas*

An alternative technique to brainstorming that generates ideas to get you started is the question technique. Set aside five minutes and, in that time, write as many questions as you can think of that relate to your topic. Again, don't criticize or censor the questions. Write all questions as quickly as you can and as soon as they occur to you. After five minutes, review the questions you have written and make additions or deletions as appropriate.

**EXERCISE: GENERATING AND ORGANIZING IDEAS**

1. Take a topic on which you have been assigned a one- to two-page paper, or choose one of the following listed topics. Set aside five minutes and use the brainstorming technique to generate as many ideas as possible for your paper. Edit your ideas to see which ones are usable. Add additional ideas that occur to you while you are editing. Then set aside an additional five minutes and try out the question technique. Which technique works better for you?

*Use the brainstorming technique with one of the following topics:*

The corruption of politicians

A national health insurance program

The high salaries of celebrities

_____

_____

_____

_____

_____

_____

_____

_____

_____

_____
_____
_____
_____
_____
_____
_____
_____
_____
_____
_____
_____
_____
_____
_____
_____
_____
_____
_____

*Use the questions technique with one of the following topics:*

The corruption of politicians

A national health insurance program

The high salaries of celebrities

_____
_____
_____
_____
_____
_____
_____
_____
_____
_____

_____

_____

_____

_____

_____

_____

_____

_____

_____

_____

_____

_____

_____

_____

_____

_____

_____

2. After generating ideas for your paper, organize those ideas into an outline so that related ideas follow each other. Use patterns such as cause and effect, classification, chronological order, and compare and contrast to help you organize your thoughts in a logical manner. If you are doing a lengthy research paper, go through your note cards and look for patterns. Arrange cards into piles that reflect the major categories of your paper. Then go through and arrange each pile into smaller subcategories. Place the categories and subcategories into order so that they follow a logical train of thought.

Take the ideas you generated for one of the three topics in the preceding section of this exercise, and organize those ideas into an outline in which related ideas follow each other logically.

_____

_____

_____

_____

_____

_____

_____

_____

_____

_____

_____

_____

_____

_____

_____

_____

_____

_____

_____

_____

_____

_____

_____

_____

_____

_____

_____

_____

_____

## FORMULATING A THESIS STATEMENT

*Write Thesis Statement*

You are now ready to formulate a thesis statement. Look over your outline and check for patterns, trends, or relationships. Summarize your ideas into one clear, detailed sentence that defines the purpose of your paper. This is the sentence that will organize and control your paper. The rest of your paper will be dedicated to explaining, supporting, and defending this thesis statement. The following examples of thesis statements might be used for a short paper called The Changing Trends in Exercise Today.

- An appropriate program of exercise can lead to a more satisfying lifestyle and to a healthy old age.
- Exercise can lead to health problems if it is pursued to extremes.
- The growing popularity of exercise reflects our culture's obsession with the "thin is beautiful" doctrine.

A thesis statement is not always easy to write. If one does not come forth after a review of your outline, try the brainstorming technique. Write all possible thesis statements that occur to you in a five-minute period. Then examine each statement to see how much of your outline it would include or exclude. Try to combine several of the thesis statements if you do not wish to eliminate any of your material. If you are still not sure about a statement, let it sit over night. Your brain will continue to work on the problem, and you may have some new insights on the next day.

*Revise Outline*

Once you have chosen a thesis statement, you may have to revise your outline to support it. You may wish to discard some of your research or to complete additional research to answer new questions. The complexity and specificity of your thesis statement will depend on the length of your paper and the type of paper you have been assigned. You may wish to check with your instructor as to whether your thesis statement is appropriate to the assignment.

**EXERCISE: WRITING A THESIS STATEMENT**

Look over the outline you generated in the preceding exercise, and write a thesis statement that might be appropriate for a two-page paper.

_____

_____

_____

_____

_____

_____

_____

_____

_____

_____

_____

## THE FIRST DRAFT

*Read Assignment Again*

*Do Not Edit, Just Write*

Now that you have your thesis statement and outline, you are ready to write your first draft. Check your professor's instructions for the assignment once again. Make sure that you have followed these instructions, and then begin with an introduction. Your introduction should include your thesis statement. Do not worry about being witty at this point. Do not worry about grammar, spelling, punctuation, or choice of words. Just get your ideas down on paper. Write as though you were telling a story to a friend. Follow your outline and put the ideas down in order. Explain each idea thoroughly, supporting it with examples, reasoning, quotations, or any other supportive material you may have. If new ideas occur to you as you are writing, jot them in the margin and return to them later. Take breaks while you are writing. Never try to finish a major paper in one day.

## USING CRITICAL ANALYSIS AND LOGICAL THINKING

*Revise Draft Next Day*

Let your draft sit overnight or for several days. Your mind will continue to work on it even if you are not consciously aware of it. You will return to the paper

*Supply Transitions*

*Be Brief*

*Check Vocabulary*

*Write, Rewrite, and Rewrite Again*

the next day with new perspectives and better judgment. A paper involves communicating information in a logical, effective manner. You may see patterns in the material; comment on them. Make comparisons and discriminations. You may see holes in your presentation that you did not notice the day before. Fill them in with additional information or transition sentences. You may notice repetitions or inappropriate phrases. Rewrite your material. Be as brief and concise as possible. Do not try to impress your instructor with the length of the paper by adding filler material. Your instructor will just write "redundant" or "repetitious" in the margin. Most professors do not judge quality by the pound. They will get bored, and they will downgrade a repetitious, lengthy paper for poor organization.

Do not use fancy words unless you know what they mean and know how to use them. Misusing complicated words is much worse than using monosyllables correctly. Misused words obscure your meaning and make you seem pompous. Check your words in the dictionary if you have any doubts about their meaning.

## REVISIONS AND FINISHING TOUCHES

*Check Style, Organization, Content, Clarity, and Support*

*Check Order and Transition Statements*

The best papers have gone through several drafts. Write, rewrite, and rewrite again. Give yourself two to three revisions and three to five days before completing the final copy of a major paper. Now is the time to check your content, organization, and style. Be aware that your writing style should be different from your speaking style. Slang expressions and contractions do not belong in formal written work. Be sure that you have an introduction and a conclusion or summary. Be sure that your ideas are clearly expressed. Explain, justify, and support your ideas even if you are not writing a research paper. Your instructor is interested in teaching you how to think. He or she does not want just your opinions, so include the foundation on which those opinions are based.

Check to see whether your ideas are presented in the order you announced in your introduction. Be sure that you have included transition sentences that lead the reader from one idea and paragraph to the next. Be careful in citing the ideas or work of others. Be sure that you include the complete source in the proper format for each quotation or citation. Check to see that the ideas you have presented support your entire thesis statement. Arrange a mutual support system with a friend so that you read each other's papers and give each other feedback on items such as clarity and organization of ideas.

### Quotations

*Provide Citations*

Take care with the citation of material from your research. If you quote an author's work word for word, use quotation marks before and after the excerpted material, and then give the author credit, either in parentheses following the quote, in a footnote at the bottom of the page, or in an endnote at the end of the paper. It is generally better to paraphrase an author's ideas rather than to string together long quotations with your brief transition sentences. Use quotations only when you feel that you cannot present the material in words that are different from the author's or when the exact words are important to the point you are making. If you are paraphrasing an author's ideas in your own words, you need not use quotation marks, but you should still give that author the proper credit for his or her ideas. If you present statistics, these should also be footnoted or cited appropriately.

# Proofreading

*Proofread with Care*

Now it is time to proofread. Check your punctuation, your grammar, and your spelling. These will influence your grade even if your instructor is trying to ignore them. Most instructors, however, do not ignore them. They assign part of the grade for the mechanics of writing. After all, a college graduate is supposed to write like a college graduate. Your supervisors at work will expect this as well.

*Proofread with a Friend*

*Proofread Out Loud*

The best way to proofread is to arrange with a friend to proofread each other's papers. Our eyes tend to skim over the mistakes we have made when we are rereading a paper. Choose a friend who spells and writes reasonably well. If you cannot find someone to read your paper for you, read it to yourself out loud. You are more likely to hear missing words and awkward grammatical constructions. Keep a dictionary by your side and check your spelling. The list shown in figure 13 includes errors that are constantly found even in seniors' papers. These errors should not occur in college-level writing.

*Type Your Paper*

Almost all college instructors require that papers be typed. You will find that the same standard applies in the business world, and you may not have your own secretary when you are first starting out. Even if your professor does not require a typed manuscript, you are likely to find that your grade is better when your paper presents a neat, professional appearance. It is a good idea to number your pages and type your last name at the top of each page in case your pages should become separated.

*Include a Title Page*

*Keep a Copy*

Give your paper a title page that includes your name, the course title, your instructor's name, the date, and the title of your paper. Put your paper in a cover, or at least staple the pages together so that your instructor has all the pages in the proper order when he or she is ready to read your paper. Make a copy of your paper, and keep it in case your instructor loses it.

## CITATIONS AND REFERENCES

A few words about honesty and plagiarism are in order at this point. It is dishonest to hand in a paper that you have not written. If you are caught, and it is likely that you will be caught, you may fail the course in question, and a letter describing this instance of cheating may be placed in your permanent file at the college. In certain institutions, you may also be expelled from the school. Review your college's policies regarding academic misconduct.

*Do Not Plagiarize*

It is also illegal to use another author's ideas, opinions, words, or statistics without giving credit to that author. This practice is called plagiarism, and it can result in sanctions as serious as a failing grade in the course, dismissal from the college, loss of one's job, and imposition of substantial fines by a court of law. A review of your school's policies on plagiarism will convince you that this is a serious offense.

*Choose a Citation Format*

Ask your professor about his or her preferred style for citations. There are several accepted formats for doing this. If your professor has no preference, use the simplest format, as shown in figure 14. This format, endorsed by the *Publication Manual of the American Psychological Association,* includes the author's last name, the year of publication, and the page number of the citation. This information is presented in parentheses in the text of your paper immediately following the citation. You need not include any footnotes nor endnotes, but be sure that the complete bibliographical information appears in your list of references at the end of the paper.

*It's* means "it is."
*Its* is the possessive pronoun for an object.
*Its'* does not exist in the English language.

*There* refers to a location.
*Their* is the plural form of the possessive pronoun.
*They're* means "they are."

*Your* is a possessive pronoun.
*You're* is a contraction for "you are."

*To* is used in two ways.
　　It directs you to a location. ("I am going *to* school.")
　　It precedes a verb. ("I want *to* play.")
*Too* is used in two ways.
　　It means "also." ("I am coming, *too*.")
　　It is an adverb. ("I have *too* much money.")
*Two* is the number that comes after one.

*Effect* (as a verb) means to bring about. ("His greed *effected* the murder.")
*Affect* (as a verb) means to have an influence on something. ("The murder *affected* his future tremendously.")

*Effect* (as a noun) means that something has been influenced. ("The murder had a tremendous *effect* on him.")
*Affect* (as a noun) is used by psychologists to mean an emotion. ("He showed no *affect* even at his mother's funeral.")

*Everyone, anyone,* and *no one* are indefinite pronouns that call for a singular verb. ("*Everyone* has HIS or HER own opinion." However, "Everyone has *their* own opinion" is *incorrect*.)

*Receive* is spelled with the *e* first: *i* before *e* except after *c* and in *neighbor, weird,* and *weigh.*

*Develop* has no *e* on the end.

*Environment* and *government* each have an *n* in the middle.

Certain words form the plural by dropping *on* and adding *a.*
*Criterion* and *phenomenon* become *criteria* and *phenomena* when they are plural.

**FIGURE 13. COMMON ERRORS IN GRAMMAR**

*Choose a Bibliography Format*

If you have used sources other than your own inspiration in researching or writing your paper, these must be listed on a separate page of references at the end of your paper. As there are several acceptable formats for bibliographical listing, ask your instructor which format he or she prefers. In the event that your professor has no preference, use the format presented in figure 14. This format is endorsed by the *Publication Manual of the American Psychological Association.* The third edition of this volume was published in 1983, in Wash-

1. A direct quote requires quotation marks.

   "College students today are more optimistic about career opportunities after graduation" (Smith & Jones, 1990, p. 15).

2. A paraphrase does not require quotation marks, but you must still cite the author and the source.

   Research shows that today's college students believe they will easily find jobs after they graduate from college (Smith & Jones, 1990, p. 15).

3. The following example is a bibliographical reference for a journal article.

   Smith, R. M. & Jones, A. M. (1990). Attitudinal trends in the college class of 1956. *Journal of Higher Education. 14,* 177–181.

4. The following example is a bibliographical reference for a book.

   Smith, R. J. & Jones, A. M. (1990). *Current trends in higher education.* (pp. 177–181). New Jersey: Prentice Hall.

FIGURE 14. EXAMPLES OF CITATIONS AND REFERENCES

ington, D.C., by the American Psychological Association. Another popular format is presented in the *MLA Handbook for Writers of Research Papers, Theses, and Dissertations,* published in 1984, in New York, by the Modern Language Association. Finally, K. L. Turabian's *A Manual for Writers,* published by the University of Chicago Press in 1983, is an old classic in the field of writing manuals. Figure 14 gives several examples of references and citations.

# Chapter 10

## The Computer
### *A Student's Best Friend*

### COMPUTERS AND LEARNING

Welcome to the age of the computer! Some people hate computers, and other people love them. Nearly everyone finds them useful, and many people cannot live without them. Regardless of your feelings for computers, there will be few places to hide from these machines when you go out into the work world. For this reason many colleges now insist that each student own or have access to a computer. If you are new to the world of computing, prepare yourself for some wonderful discoveries and a few frustrations.

Many college courses today use computers as an integral part of the learning process. In some courses, computers help students work their way through practice exercises in accounting, engineering, or statistics. In other courses, computers simulate laboratory experiments in psychology, biology, or physics. Social work students might use computers to practice the interviewing skills they will need with clients; premed students may try their hand at solving challenging diagnostic cases. One of the most widespread uses for computers in the classroom is in the area of writing.

### COMPUTERS AND THE WRITING PROCESS

Many writing instructors are now holding their classes in computer laboratories rather than in conventional classrooms. Students report that computers make writing more fun. Those who used to dread writing find that word processing takes the drudgery out of composition.[1] They no longer have to retype whole pages in order to correct a typographical error or to make changes in organizational structure.

Students who once hated writing say that computers make writing enjoyable and exciting.[2] Because corrections and changes are so easy to make, they feel free to try out new ideas. There is no longer such a thing as a mistake; students can keep making changes until their texts are perfect. They can add sentences, delete words, move paragraphs around, and check spelling, executing each action with a single command. Students may rely on the computer's memory so that they are free to move back and forth in their work, focusing on ideas, organization, spelling, or revisions of different sections at various times. Because computers save so much time, students are willing to experiment with new techniques. They can try free-writing, brainstorming, or heuristic aids to composition.[3] They can compare several drafts to see which organizational structure works best. Writing skills improve because students are more willing to "play" with their work and develop it.

Students who have experienced difficulty sitting still and concentrating on a piece of paper find that the lighted screen captures their attention. Students who have lost their train of thought, during the laborious process of writing out ideas by hand, report that the keyboard makes communication a snap. Students who were not willing to edit because it was too difficult to read their handwriting are eager to read over their printed pages. Students who were not willing to reorganize their papers because retyping was so boring and time-consuming find the computer's "cut-and-paste" options to be fun and efficient. Reluctant writers become enthusiastic writers. They write more; they are more willing to revise their work; and they take greater pride in their writing.[4]

Computers offer special advantages for students who have physical challenges. Students with visual impairments find that special software with large-print letters makes reading easier. Many students who cannot write because of motor disabilities are able to use the keyboard. For students with motor impairments, the new voice-activated computers nearing the production stage will provide a way to express their thoughts in writing.

Some reasons students give for using computers are the following:

- Computers make writing fun.
- Corrections and changes are easy to make.
- Fewer errors appear in the finished work.
- The final product looks neat and professional.
- Writer's cramp is eliminated.
- New techniques can be explored.
- Minor errors do not create the need to retype whole pages.
- Several drafts can be prepared and the best one chosen.
- Papers can be prepared over several work sessions; the computer can keep track of notes and outlines.

One word of caution before you go on to the magic keyboard. Although you are about to discover the many advantages of working with a computer, you are also about to discover some of the limitations. The computer can make writing easier and more enjoyable. It can also produce a more professional-looking product that has fewer spelling and grammatical errors, but it cannot write for you. *You* must produce the ideas, *you* must develop them, and *you* must organize them. This still takes time and work.

If you have not worked with a computer before, you will have to learn the system and practice with it. It is likely to take you a few hours of study and practice before you are feeling comfortable with the word processor. The more you use it, the more competent you will become.

Following are some typical frustrations overcome by beginning students:

- It takes time to learn the command keys. If you hit the wrong key, you may erase a word or a sentence unintentionally. On the other hand, the computer makes it very easy to correct such errors.

- If you have never typed before, you will have to learn. With a little practice, you will find that keying on a computer keyboard is much faster and easier than using a typewriter.

- You may lose your work if you are not careful about storing it in the appropriate places.

- You will have to learn to control the appearance of your work on paper. It will take some time to learn how to produce double-spaced printing, to position the printer in the right place, and to produce a title page.

All of these problems can be avoided or overcome through practice sessions on the computer. Most students report that the pains of this learning process are well worth the final rewards.

## BASIC WORD-PROCESSING SKILLS

The word processor is a set of instructions, or a program, that tells your computer what to do. It allows you to create, edit, and print a document. Some of the most-popular word-processing programs are WordPerfect, WordStar, Word, AppleWorks, and MacWrite. There are too many of these programs on the market to go through the specific steps of using each one. The programs do share many common features, however, and a review of the basic features will help you use the computer to improve your writing.

If your word-processing program comes with a tutorial, work your way through it. The step-by-step directions will give you the basic procedures necessary to begin writing. If you do not have a tutorial, read the manual that comes with the word-processing program and practice the basic procedures. It is best to do this when you have a friend or a tutor close by who is familiar with the program you are using.

The first thing you must learn is how to start up your word-processing program. Most college computer laboratories provide students with access to microcomputers that use diskettes to store information. Your computer may use either $5\frac{1}{4}$-inch floppy diskettes or $3\frac{1}{2}$-inch hard shell diskettes. Ask the laboratory assistant about the type of diskette your computer uses; you will probably have to buy one so that you have a place to store your work.

*Format a Blank Diskette Only Once*

Before you use a new diskette, you must first format, or initialize, it. This process sets up the storage space on the diskette so that your computer and word-processing program can work with it. Initializing a diskette is a very quick, easy process. Read about it in your manual, or ask the laboratory tutor to show you the procedure. Do not use a diskette that has not been properly formatted; you will lose your work! Be careful to format a diskette only once. Formatting a diskette wipes out all the information you have stored on it. If you have stored a draft of your paper on the diskette, you probably do not wish to lose it by formatting the diskette again!

*Load the Word-Processing Program*

Many microcomputers require that you place a diskette containing the word-processing program in one drive of the computer and that you place another personal, or data, diskette, on which you store your work, into a second drive. Be sure that you place the diskettes in the correct drives. Find out if the diskettes should be placed in the disk drives before or after you turn on the computer. If your computer has only one drive, you will have to load the word-processing program first, remove that diskette, and then place your personal, or data, diskette into the slot.

*Insert Your Personal or Data Diskette*

If your computer uses an internal hard drive, you may not need to insert a program diskette. Select the word-processing option when it appears on the screen, and then insert your data diskette so that you will be able to save your work.

## Storing Your Work

Before you type any work onto a computer, learn how to store your work. Most word-processing programs call this "saving." While you are working on the computer, your work will be held in a temporary memory system. This memory is temporary in the sense that your work can be lost if you exit from the word-processing program or turn off the computer.

*Store Your Work Frequently*

My most frustrating computer lesson occurred one morning, when, after I had been working on the computer for three hours, the electric power to my home was momentarily interrupted. I had not saved my work during this time, so that momentary blip in electric power cost me three hours of work! I had to reconstruct my work as best I could and key it in from the beginning. I have never made that mistake again. I now save my work every few minutes.

Once you store your work on a hard disk or on a diskette, a permanent record is made. You can retrieve that piece of work at any time in the future. It is wise to get into the habit of saving your work every fifteen minutes or so. Saving your work is a quick and easy process. Consult your manual or laboratory tutor for the proper procedure. You will have to tell the computer the name of the piece on which you are working; you must also tell the computer where to store your work.

*Name Your File*

*Check Manual for Appropriate File Names*

Each time you begin a new document, the computer will ask you what you wish to name it. Naming a document sets up a text file for it in the computer so that you can store it and return to work on it at another time. Choose a name that will help you remember which work you stored in that particular file. A laboratory report on DNA might be called DNALAB. Check your manual to find out the maximum number of letters you may use in the file's name and whether your computer allows spaces or numbers in the name.

*Store Later Drafts Under Different Names*

When you write several drafts of a document, you might wish to store each of them under a separate name: DNALAB1, DNALAB2, and so on. This will allow you to compare drafts and to incorporate material from earlier drafts. It will also serve as evidence that the work is yours, should a question of plagiarism ever arise, and it will give you a backup in the event that your most recent draft is accidently erased.

In addition to telling the computer the name of your document, you must also tell it where you want the work stored. If your machine has a hard drive, you may want to store your document there. In that case, you might specify "C:DNALAB" to indicate that your laboratory report should be stored on Drive C. If you share the computer with other students or if your computer does not have a hard drive, you will want to store the document on your personal diskette. If you placed that diskette in Drive A, then you will key in "A:DNALAB" after giving the command to store your work.

*Back Up Your Work*

It is always a good idea to back up your work. Make two copies so that, if one is lost or damaged, you still have the second disk. You may store one copy on the computer's hard disk and one copy on a data disk, or you may choose to make a duplicate copy of your data disk.

*Save Before Printing*

*Store Before Exiting*

Remember to save your work every fifteen minutes or so. Saving your work frequently and regularly may save you hours of frustration. Also remember to save your work before you print it. Your work can get lost between the computer and the printer, but as long as you have saved the work, you can quickly retrieve it and reissue the print command. Always store your work before you walk away from the computer and before you exit from the word-processing program.

## Handling Disks

*Label Disks*

Label your disk so that you know what work it contains and under what name you have stored a particular document. Write on the label before you put it on the diskette. If you wish to write on it later, use a felt-tip pen. A labeled disk gives you some insurance against accidently reformatting a disk that contains documents you wish to save.

*Handle Disks Carefully*

*Retrieve Your Work*

Handle your disks carefully. Keep them in their protective covers when they are not in the computer. Avoid bending or exposing them to high temperatures. Damaged disks result in lost work that you cannot retrieve. When you wish to work on a document or print it out again in the future, you need only give the computer the file name after entering the retrieve command. If you do not remember the file name or if you enter it incorrectly, issue a display or directory command, and the computer will list the names of all files contained on that disk.

## Keying in Work

Keying work on a computer keyboard is much easier and faster than typing on a typewriter because it is so easy to correct errors. Since you will not be worrying about accuracy, you will find yourself keying much more quickly.

*Find the Function Keys*

The computer keyboard has more keys than a regular typewriter. You will find a whole set of function keys (usually labeled F1, F2, F3, etc.) that allow you to give the computer various commands such as "move a paragraph" or "underline a sentence." You will find yourself pressing many of these function keys, in conjunction with the Ctrl key, the Alt key, or the shift key (↑), to issue a variety of commands.

*Find the Keys that Move the Cursor*

You will also find a number of keys that allow you to move the cursor. The cursor (the blinking bar on your screen) tells you where on the screen your next keystroke will take effect. Some keys move the cursor one letter at a time; other keys move it to the end of the next word, to the end of a line, to the end of the page, or to the end of the paper. You will find yourself moving the cursor in order to add words, delete sentences, or rearrange the order of paragraphs.

*Note the Wrap-Around Feature*

*Note the Hard Carriage Return*

As you are keying, you will notice that the computer automatically takes you to the next line when you come to the edge of the right-hand margin setting. You do not have to keep track of margin settings in order to move to the next line. If you wish to move to the next line before you come to the edge of the margin, just press the enter key (↵) and the computer will move the cursor to the next line.

*Note Insert, Delete, and Escape Keys*

You will also notice keys that allow you to insert (Ins) and delete (Del) characters, backspace (←) to delete characters, escape (Esc) from various options, and move to various tab settings (⇄). Practice using these keys with your tutorial or manual until you feel comfortable with them. Many word-processing programs come with templates that you can mount on the keyboard to help you remember which keys control which functions. Most of these programs also use a help key with which you can call up a display of the key functions. This display will tell you which keys control which functions. As long as you memorize which key calls up the help menu, you will not need to memorize all of the key functions. As you work with the word-processing program, you will find yourself automatically remembering the keys that you use most often.

*Memorize Help Key*

## Printing Work

You must learn how to send your work from the computer to the printer in order to hand your instructor a "hard copy" of your paper. Each word-processing program uses a slightly different method for accomplishing this. Ordinarily, you select the print option from the menu, tell the computer which text you wish to print, and press the enter or return key.

*Save Before Printing*

Again, be sure that you have saved your work before you issue the print command. Work is often lost on the way to the printer, and is sometimes lost when several computer terminals in a laboratory are connected to the same printer. Before you issue the print command, check that the printer is turned on, that it is connected to the computer, and that it has enough paper. You are less likely to lose your work. If you have saved your work and it is lost on the way to the printer, you can easily retrieve it and issue the print command again.

*Check Printer and Paper*

**EXERCISE: PRACTICING THE BASICS OF WORD PROCESSING**

It is time to sit down and begin work with your computer! Ideally, you will be able to schedule a class session at the computer laboratory when an instructor or a laboratory assistant will be available to assist you. If this is not possible, choose a time when you have at least an hour to work with the computer. It might be helpful to work with a friend; two heads are often better than one in finding solutions to problems that arise.

*Bring this book and two blank diskettes with you* when you begin work with your computer. This exercise will take you through the steps to begin using your word-processing program. Write down the answers to the questions in your text so that they are available for reference should you forget any procedures during future writing sessions.

If your instructor or the computer laboratory tutor is available, he or she can help you with the answers to these questions. The answers can also be found in the tutorial or the manual that accompanies your word-processing program.

1. Turn on the computer. If the monitor (screen) does not light up, find its switch and turn on that, too.

2. If you are using a new data disk that has not been formatted, insert the disk in the appropriate drive and format it before you begin to work. What steps are involved in formatting a disk?

_____

_____

_____

_____

_____

3. Insert the program disk into the appropriate drive, and load the word-processing program, if necessary. Which is the proper drive for the program disk?

_____

4. Insert your data disk into the appropriate drive, if you have not already done so. (If your computer has only one drive, you will have to remove the program disk before you insert your data disk.) Which is the proper drive for your data disk?

_____

5. Which option must you select from the menu to begin writing or editing? Select that option now, and press enter (↵) if necessary.

_____

6. If you are creating a new file, must you name it before you begin writing or may you name it when you are ready to save? Let LESSON.TXT be the name of your file.

_____

7. List any restrictions that govern your choice of file names. (E.g., What is the maximum number of letters in a name? Are spaces or numbers permitted? Must the file have a name "tag" or extension like the one in FILE.TXT?)

_____

_____

_____

_____

_____

_____

8. What command must you issue to create or open a new file? Issue that command and name your file LESSON.TXT if you have not yet done so.

_____

9. What command must you issue if you wish to work on a file that already exists?

_____

10. Type in the following text. (Do not worry about any typographical errors you make at this point.)

> I pledge allegiance to the flag of the United States of America and to the republic for which it stands, one nation, under God, indivisible, with liberty and justice for all.

> My country 'tis of thee
> Sweet land of liberty
> To thee I sing.
> Land where my fathers died
> Land of the pilgrims' pride
> From ev'ry mountainside
> Let freedom ring.

11.a. In each of the following situations, write, on the answer line, which key(s) you would press to move the cursor (the blinking, lighted bar).

_____ move(s) the cursor one character to the left without erasing text

_____ move(s) the cursor one character to the right without erasing text

_____ move(s) the cursor one word to the left

_____ move(s) the cursor one word to the right

_____ move(s) the cursor to the right-hand margin

_____ move(s) the cursor to the left-hand margin

_____ move(s) the cursor to the bottom of the screen

_____ move(s) the cursor to the top of the screen

_____ move(s) the cursor to the end of the text

_____ move(s) the cursor to the beginning of the text

_____ move(s) the cursor to indent a paragraph

(On many computers you cannot use the space bar to move the cursor to a new position in your text without erasing text as you move. It can be frustrating to break this habit if you are accustomed to a typewriter where the space bar is used to move from one point to another.)

b. Position the cursor at the beginning of the Pledge of Allegiance, and try out each of the cursor movements listed above.

12.a. Must you press a particular key to insert text? Or does your word-processing program automatically move existing text to the right to make room for additional material as you key it? Many word-processing programs have a toggle switch (a key on the keyboard) that controls this function. (That key is often labeled *Ins.*) Once you have pressed the key that activates insert mode, you will remain in that mode until you press the key again.

How do you activate insert mode?

_____

_____

b. Insert the following text after the word *flag* in the first line of the Pledge of Allegiance material that you typed: *which is red, white, and blue.*

13.a. Must you press a particular key to type over text that you wish to delete? Or, does your processor automatically erase existing text as you type on top of it? In many word-processing programs, pressing the insert (INS) key will activate type-over mode so that existing text is erased as you type over it.

How do you activate type-over mode?

_____

_____

b. In place of "and to the republic for which it stands," type the following text: *and to the nation it represents*

14.a. Does your word-processing program automatically reform your paragraph to eliminate blank spaces and line up your margins as you insert or delete material? If it does not do this automatically, which key must you press to reform your paragraph so that the blank spaces are eliminated?

_____

b. Before you press that key, be sure to place a hard carriage return, by pressing the enter key, or the end-of-paragraph symbol that your program uses at the end of the paragraph. (Press the enter key after "and justice for all.") If you do not perform this operation, the Pledge of Allegiance will be merged into one paragraph with "My Country 'Tis of Thee."

c. Press the correct key and reform your paragraph.

15. Which key(s) would you press to delete—

_____ a single character?

_____ a single word?

_____ a whole line?

_____ a whole section of text?

a. Delete the *g* in *flag.*

b. Delete the word *pledge.*

c. Delete the second line of "My Country 'Tis of Thee."

d. Delete the last three lines of "My Country 'Tis of Thee."

e. Recover sentences or paragraphs you have previously erased. (Many programs allow you to change your mind about material you have deleted.)

16.a. How do you save your file?

_____

_____

_____

b. Save your text on your personal disk.

17.a. How do you back up your file (make a second copy in a different location)?

_____

_____

_____

b. If your computer has a hard drive that you can use, save your text onto the hard drive.

c. If the hard drive is not available to you, copy the contents of your diskette onto a second diskette. Write down the steps involved.

_____

_____

_____

18.a. After you have saved your file and wish to end your computer session, how do you exit from the program?

_____

_____

   b. Exit from the program now.

19. Call up the program again.

   a. How do you retrieve your text (LESSON.TXT)?

_____

_____

_____

   b. Retrieve your text and add the following to the end of your text: *Congratulations to me!*

   c. Save your text.

20. Check that the printer is turned on and connected to your computer and that it has an adequate supply of paper.

   a. How do you tell the computer to print your text?

_____

_____

_____

   b. Print your text.

   c. Collect your printout.

   d. Exit from the program.

   e. Collect your data disk.

   f. Turn off the computer if this is appropriate.

Congratulations! You have made it through the first session on your word-processing program. Best wishes for a long and productive relationship with computers.

## WORD-PROCESSING ALL STAGES OF WRITING

Instructors generally identify four processes that are necessary to produce a finished piece of writing:

   **1.** Prewriting, or planning

   **2.** Writing, or drafting

   **3.** Rewriting, or revising

   **4.** Editing, or proofreading

## Stage One: Prewriting

Prewriting is the planning process where you define a topic, explore what you know about it, find out what you need to know, generate ideas, do research,

```
Mary Jane Doe                    Assignment 1
Freshman Seminar                 Due: September 30
Professor Starke                 Suggested Length: Five pages
```

Description of Assignment

The scandals surrounding college athletes have tarnished the image of team sports. I will discuss the factors responsible for these problems and suggest solutions that might help the institutions and teams regain their integrity and original focus. I will use my own experiences along with newspaper or magazine articles to write a five-page paper that describes the problem, analyzes the causes and effects, and makes recommendations for change.

Audience

The audience will be college freshmen who are familiar with the problem through their readings and experiences as athletes or as spectators at sports events. I hope to show that competition should be reduced and that limits should be placed on the amount of money distributed to college teams.

Organization Strategies

I will begin with a description of the issues, by giving examples of abuse and by describing the magnitude of the problem. I will describe the effects of the abuses on athletes and on colleges. I will compare high school sports with college sports to show how levels of competition increase as fund-raising pressures become more important. I will then recommend guidelines for academic standards and fund-raising that should bring college athletics back as a respected part of the undergraduate experience.

Thesis Statement

I will try to convince my readers that current economic and psychological climates encourage colleges and universities to exploit athletes and to subvert academic standards in an attempt to produce winning teams. As long as college sports remain a key factor in fund-raising and publicity, team managers will knuckle under to strong pressures to win at any cost.

Sources of Information

My own knowledge and experience. Newspaper and magazine articles (with bibliographical references).

FIGURE 15. EXAMPLE OF ASSIGNMENT PAGE

read, take notes, and produce an outline. Professional writers usually spend more time on this planning phase than they do in the writing stage.

## The Assignment Page

Sitting down and planning a paper is often the most difficult part of writing. The computer can be very helpful at this stage. Some instructors recommend that you begin by generating a one-page assignment sheet that will guide your writing.[5] Figure 15 provides a sample assignment page that considers the following items.

- Key in a heading that gives your name, the course title, the instructor's name, the due date, and the suggested length for the paper. Then key in a description of the assignment.

- Consider your audience. Are you writing for the general public or for a specific group with special knowledge, background, and attitudes? What is your goal in addressing this audience? Will you inform them of a certain position? Will you try to influence their beliefs or attitudes? Will you try to change their behavior?

- What type of organizational strategy will you use? Will you compare and contrast? Will you use cause and effect? Will you present advantages and disadvantages?

- You might next consider the content of the assignment and the sources of information you will use. You may have to collect information through library research or personal interviews. You may be able to rely on your own experiences or on the information in your text.

- Finally, formulate a thesis statement that describes your goals and tells your reader the direction you will follow.

The example of an assignment page in figure 15 incorporates the elements listed above.

**EXERCISE: CREATING AN ASSIGNMENT PAGE TO ORGANIZE YOUR PAPER**

Create an assignment page for a paper that has been assigned in one of your courses. Save the document and print it. Show the page to your instructor and ask whether it fulfills the requirements for the assignment. Many students receive poor grades on their papers because they have misunderstood the assignment.

This exercise instructs you to put an assignment into your own words and to seek feedback from your instructor. You will then find out whether you have interpreted the assignment correctly. As you begin to write, refer back to the assignment page in figure 15. Use it as a guide for your paper's organizational structure. You should also use it as a checklist to be certain that you have covered all aspects of the assignment.

### Generating Ideas Through Free-Writing

Instructors often recommend "free-writing" as a way to cope with the sudden blanks or the panic that attacks many writers when they are confronted by an empty page and the pressure to produce a paper.

The goal of free-writing is to stimulate the flow of thoughts into words. Choose a topic and write about that topic for ten minutes without stopping. Write whatever comes into your mind. Do not stop to correct, criticize, or edit anything. If you draw a blank, just repeat the last word until a new idea comes along. Before you begin, turn down the brightness knob on your monitor. When you cannot see the words on the screen, you are less likely to be distracted from your train of thought. Here is an example of a free-writing exercise complete with all the typographical errors.

### An Example of Free-writing

The beginning of a paper is always the hardest point for me. I don't know what I want to say or where to start.I It is so tempting to just put off the whole thing, but I know that I have a deadline, and so I have to get this wtritten. I would like to write about vacation time when the stressis off and I don't have to be on a rigid timeschedule all of the time. I can read for pleasure or just lie on a beacch and soak yp the sun. I can stay up all night and not have to worry that I will be exhausted the next morning because I won't have to get up the next morning if I don't feel like it! I only have to make "difficult" decisions like whether to go sailing or windsurfing or snorkeling or just putter around the house enjoyuing the quiet and the freedom to b unproductive. This might be a good place to start pa paper on the benefits of escaping from stress. It certainly does wonders for the mind. I wonder what it does for the body? I am certainly in a better mood for a few weeks after I return from vacation. Daily irritations just seem to roll of my back. My body gets a break and I return ready to face work with new reservews of energy.

A list of ideas elicited by this free-writing episode might include the following:

**I.** Work Pressures
   A. Difficulties of writing
      1. Finding a starting point
      2. Procrastination
      3. Stress and pressure
         a. Deadlines

**II.** Vacations: Relief from Pressure
   A. No rigid time schedule
   B. No stress
   C. Preferred activities
      1. Basking on the beach
      2. Reading for pleasure
      3. Sailing
      4. Wind surfing
      5. Snorkeling
   D. Effects on—
      1. Body
      2. Mind
      3. Mood

**EXERCISE: GENERATING IDEAS THROUGH FREE-WRITING**

Choose a topic for a paper assigned in one of your courses and take ten minutes to free-write on the computer. Save your text and print out a hard copy. Read over your text and write a brief sentence that summarizes your main ideas. List those main ideas and use them as a basis for an outline of your paper. Save and then print your outline of ideas.

You may wish to engage in several free-writing sessions to generate more ideas, or you may wish to try brainstorming and list all ideas that come to mind within a ten-minute time span. Once you have listed your ideas, go back and look for similarities, patterns, and connections among your ideas. Group the ideas based on those connections. Give each group a heading. Arrange these groups in a logical order. This outline can then form the basis of an organizational structure for your draft.

### Heuristic Questions

Aside from its utility in generating ideas, the computer can also be helpful, during prewriting, in gathering information and organizing it. Some writers use a "shell," or template, as a frame on which to construct a paper.

*The Journalist's Shell*   One example of this kind of strategy involves the six heuristic questions traditionally asked by journalists:

- What?
- Why?
- Who?
- Where?
- When?
- How?

**EXERCISE: GATHERING INFORMATION THROUGH A JOURNALIST'S SHELL**

If you were going to do a paper on watermelons, for example, you might start out with the word *what* on your screen. You would then insert, under that heuristic word *what,* several paragraphs on what watermelons are like. Define watermelons and describe them. Discuss different types of watermelons; how do they look, taste, feel, and smell?

When you have finished writing all that comes to mind under the *what* of watermelons, go to the word *why* and insert as many paragraphs as you can on why people grow watermelons, why they eat watermelons, and why they enjoy watermelons.

Continue inserting paragraphs under each of the heuristic words that answer the questions prompted by that particular key word. You will find that the ideas for your first draft practically write and organize themselves.

*The Classical Shell*   A more sophisticated form of the shell technique uses a framework proposed by classical Greek writers. Like the journalist's questions, this framework can help you discover or remember important information about your topic. Aristotle proposed twenty-eight items, but the five that follow should give you a good idea about how to proceed:

- Definition
- Comparison and contrast
- Connections
- Testimony
- Circumstance

If you were writing a paper on sin, you might begin with

- A definition of sin—
  How is sin defined?
  Is there more than one definition?
  Does sin really exist?
  What are the different kinds of sin?
  Are there various components to sin?

- A comparison and contrast of sin—
  What does sin resemble?
  How does sinful behavior differ from other behaviors?
  What is sin most like? Why?
  How do sins differ from each other?
  How do various sins resemble each other?

- Connections of sin—
  What are sin's origins?
  What are the consequences of sin?
  Does sin serve any purpose?
  Is sin related to any other traits?

- Testimony—
  What do the experts say about sin?
  What is your own experience with sin?
  How do most people feel about sin?

- Circumstance—
  How do we gather information about sin?
  Is there such a thing as sin?
  What circumstances make sin possible or impossible?

**EXERCISE: GATHERING INFORMATION THROUGH A CLASSICAL SHELL**

1. Key in the framework and questions described above, but substitute an *X* for the word *sin.* Save that text under the file name SHELL. Doing this will preserve your blank shell so that you can call it up for a future paper.

2. Now go back and systematically answer the questions in relation to a topic on which you have to write a paper. This exercise will give you some idea about what you know and what you still have to research for your paper. It will also help you to organize your information.

When you are ready to store your work, save your text under a name that will remind you of the file's content. If you were writing a paper on sin, you might name the file SHELLSIN. When you have completed your research and filled in as much information as you can under each question, you may erase the questions and begin organizing your paragraphs into a draft of your paper.

### Using an Outline Program

Some word-processing systems include an outline program. When you activate this program, the computer will display an outline structure beginning with the Roman numeral I. After you have keyed in your heading and pressed the appropriate key, the heading will automatically be indented and you will be presented with an *A* for a subheading. When you give the appropriate command, the outline will then indent further and print a 1 so that you may enter the next level of subheadings. This type of outline program allows you to insert, delete, and move headings and sections so that you can change the organization of your outline quickly and easily. The computer keeps track of your categories so that you do not have to remember whether the next subheading should be a *b* or *c;* the word-processing program will automatically print the correct prompt for you.

Such outlines are a lot of fun, and they can help you to organize the topics for your paper. If your word-processing program does not contain an outline program, you may purchase a separate program. PC-Outline is one example of an outline program designed for personal computers. You may use the outline headings as a shell while you type in appropriate sentences or paragraphs under each heading. When you are ready to write your first draft, it is easy to erase the titles of the outline's categories. You will then be left with a neatly organized set of paragraphs.

If you have access to an outline program, check the manual or documentation for it and try it out. Many of these programs come with on-screen directions and help options available at a keystroke. These may be so simple and helpful that you do not need the manual.

## Stage Two: Writing, or Drafting

Once you have defined your topic, generated some ideas, and thought about the overall organization of your paper, you are ready to write your first draft. Word-processing programs have a number of options that can be very helpful at this point.

### *Working with Several Files Simultaneously*

Many word-processing programs allow you to work with several files at the same time. You may have your notes or an outline in one file and your draft in another. If your processor has a split screen option, you will be able to see the outline on half of the screen and to incorporate parts of it into the draft you are writing on the other half of the screen. You can also use the split screen to view two drafts of your paper at the same time. In this way, you can choose the best features of each and integrate them into one paper.

Instead of using a split screen, some word-processing programs allow you to work with two or more files simultaneously by placing material from several files in "windows." You are able to view material from various files by opening and closing windows that are located in different segments of the screen.

If your word-processing program offers options that move material back and forth among files and that merge files, learn to use them. They will save you much time in scrolling back and forth through lengthy documents to find the sections you want. They will also eliminate the need to copy lengthy sections of text from one file into another.

## Stage Three: Rewriting or Revising

Professional writers rarely present their first drafts to the public. In fact, the difference between a poor writer and a competent writer usually lies in the revision stage. Many writers require three and even four drafts before their work is refined enough for publication. The word-processing program takes the drudgery out of revisions. Making corrections and changes is quicker, easier, and more fun.

### *The Block Move*

Once you learn to move the cursor efficiently, you will find that it is very easy to make changes in your work. One or two keystrokes will take you to a place in your document where you can insert or delete material. You may add or subtract letters, words, sentences, paragraphs, or even whole pages with a single keystroke.

If you have written material in one part of your paper that you would like to move or copy to another place, you can do this easily by marking the boundaries of the material that is to be moved and then indicating the new location with the cursor. This operation is often called block moving or cut and paste. It allows small or large sections of text to be erased, moved, or duplicated without the need to retype the material. Learning this procedure will make your editing much easier.

### *Paragraph "Busting"*

Paragraph "busting" can be a useful technique for checking on cohesiveness, organization, and transitions in your paper. One option is to use the search and replace command described below to search out each instance of a period and to replace it with a hard return. Each sentence of a paragraph will then be displayed on a separate line. You will be able to examine sentences more easily to be sure that they are related and that they flow logically into each other.

Another option involves the display of the first and last sentences of each paragraph. When you see these two sentences without the distraction of intermediate material, you can readily judge whether you have consistently followed through with the thought you introduced. You can also check whether you have provided a smooth transition between the last sentence of one paragraph and the first sentence of the one that follows.

You may use a similar strategy to check the cohesiveness of the paper by isolating the thesis statement and comparing it with the conclusions in your final paragraph.

## Stage Four: Editing, or Proofreading

The word-processing program is a very handy aid when you reach the last phase of writing: proofreading. A number of options make this task more accurate and less boring.

### *The Search-and-Replace Command*

One useful procedure is the search-and-replace command that is available on many word-processing programs. This feature allows you to specify a group of letters, a word, or a punctuation mark for which your computer will mount a search. When it comes to the designated symbol, it will pause and automatically replace that word or punctuation mark with another one that you have specified. If you do not want automatic replacement, the computer will pause and allow you to decide whether you wish to make a change in that location. It will then go on to find the next instance of the designated word so that you may examine that piece of text. It will continue to search and pause until it ferrets out each instance of the designated characters in the entire document.

If you know, for example, that you tend to confuse *their* with *there,* you may instruct the computer to stop each time it finds the word *their.* You can then examine each instance and decide whether you wish to replace it with *there.* On the other hand, if you find that you have consistently misspelled Sigmund Freud's name in a twenty-page psychology paper, you may instruct the computer to search for each instance of *Frued* and automatically replace it with the correct *Freud.*

If you know that you tend to get caught up in run-on sentences, you may instruct the computer to pause at each period. Isolating each sentence in this way will make it easier to judge whether or not you are dealing with a run-on sentence.

A final example of the usefulness of search-and-replace commands involves the elimination of sexist language from a paper. If your instructor criticizes your prose on this basis, instruct the computer to replace each instance of the word *he* with *he or she.* You might also have the computer search for all instances of the word *man* so that you can replace *chairman* with *department chair, post-man* with *mail carrier,* and *policeman* with *police officer.*

### *The Spell Checker*

The "spell checker," available as part of many word-processing systems, is one of the most-popular editing options. You may instruct the computer to search through your text and to pause each time it comes to a word it does not recognize. You then have the option of activating a display of words that resemble the one you tried to spell. One of them is likely to be the correct version of the word you misspelled.

Some spell checkers work as you are typing; the computer will automatically beep when you type in a word it does not recognize. You may then correct the word or activate a list of words that resemble the one you were trying to spell. In addition to helping you with spelling, this type of checking will alert you to many typographical errors. It cannot, unfortunately, serve as a substitute for careful proofreading. The computer will not beep if you mistakenly keyed in *heroin* for *heroine,* because *heroin* is a properly spelled word that also appears in its dictionary.

## SPREADSHEETS

Spreadsheets like Lotus 1-2-3 and EXCEL have opened up exciting possibilities for students in areas as varied as engineering, mathematics, manufacturing, management, economics, and statistics. These programs allow students to build and play with models in their fields much the way a word-processing program allows writers to play with the component parts of the writing process.

A student in manufacturing might build a model of an assembly line and try out different ways of breaking down the task to see which would be most efficient. A spreadsheet can give a mathematician access to Monte Carlo programming, the analysis of complex statistical probabilities through the use of multiple random events. Models for complex economic phenomena can be readily constructed and examined by students in economics and political science.

I was converted to spreadsheets when I had to perform the statistical analysis on data from a large research project. After some preliminary preparation, I found that a single keystroke was able to complete in one second calculations that had taken me six hours on a hand calculator. I had to perform more than ten of these analyses, so I was very impressed! Since most of the work took place in creating the spreadsheet, I just typed in the ten different sets of data and each calculation was done in a second. The total saving in time was sixty hours!

Spreadsheets can also be helpful outside of the classroom. You can create a spreadsheet to keep track of your personal investments, noting dividend and interest payments, sales, purchases, profits, losses, and maturity dates. As each payment comes in, you just log it in the appropriate slot. As April 15th rolls around, the press of a single button can tally your reckonings for the Internal Revenue Service.

A spreadsheet can also help you keep track of the courses you must complete to graduate from your college. Create a spreadsheet that lists the categories of courses you must complete for your degree. As you complete each course, key it in under the appropriate category: basic skills requirements, general education requirements, requirements in your major, requirements in your minor, or requirements for certification in a specialty area. Whenever it is time to register for the upcoming semester's courses, you will know exactly what you have to take.

## WIDENING YOUR COMPUTER HORIZONS
## TO OTHER FIELDS

Mathematics students rejoice in programs like TK Solver or MathCAD that allow them to watch as the computer actually goes through the steps of solving complex mathematical formulas on the screen. These students can now understand and play with various aspects of complex mathematics formulations in a way that was previously impossible.

Music majors may enjoy working with a program that helps them compose, orchestrate, transcribe, and play their original compositions. The computer also helps poetry students with their creative process. Students may specify a given structure, and the computer will help them write poetry by keeping track of meter and phrase length, by suggesting words and rhymes.

Students who request counseling (personal or vocational) can find answers to their needs from a computerized "counselor" like Sigi or the Discover program. Chess, backgammon, bridge, and Go enthusiasts can refine their skills by practicing against computerized "opponents."

Indeed, there seem to be almost no limitations to the variety of ways that computers are helping students in the learning process. It is well worth the investment of your time to become familiar with this fascinating technology.

## NOTES

1. J. Strickland, "The Reluctant Writer and Word Processing," *Conference for Secondary School English Department Chairpersons (CSSEDC) Quarterly* (1988), pp. 4–5.

2. T. Hughes, "Word Processing: Changes in the Classroom, Changes in the Writer," *CSSEDC Quarterly* 10 (1988), 3:2–3.

3. W. W. Wresch, "Computers and Composition Instruction: An Update," *College English* 45 (1988), 8:794–799.

4. W. V. Costanza, *The Electronic Text: Learning to Write, Read, and Reason with Computers* (Englewood Cliffs, N.J.: Englewood Cliffs Publications, N.J. Educational Technology, forthcoming).

5. H. M. Smith and M. L. Kennedy, *Word Processing for College Writers* (Englewood Cliffs, N.J.: Prentice-Hall, 1989).

# Chapter 11

## Relationships

### PERSONAL CHANGE

As you enter college, you will find that your relationships with others change. You may not see as much of your old friends as they go off to different schools or begin careers instead of continuing with their educations. You now may be living in a dormitory or in an apartment with roommates rather than with your family. If you continue to live at home, you may find that your relationships with family members change as you mature and take on new responsibilities. If you are returning to college after some years in the work force or as a home-maker, you may find that your new perspectives and the demands of course work lead to changes in your relationships with family and friends.

### COMMUNICATION

These changes in relationships are important and exciting, but all changes require some adjustment. Now that you are taking on new roles and responsibilities, you will have to cope with more varied interpersonal situations on your own. If you are going to get what you need from your college years, you will have to learn to communicate effectively with professors, administrators, classmates, roommates, and friends.

### Listening

One of the basic components of communication involves listening. In order to communicate effectively, you must first understand what the other person is saying. Many people fail to really hear what others say because they are too concerned with making or defending their own points. If you are silently rehearsing what you will say while another person is talking, you will miss large portions of the communication.

- Face each other.
- Make eye contact.
- Listen while the other person is speaking.
- Do not prepare your response while the other person is speaking.
- Take a moment to consider what was said and your reaction to it before you respond.
- Restate the speaker's ideas and feelings in your own words.
- Ask the speaker whether your restatement is complete and accurate.

FIGURE 16. STRATEGIES FOR EFFECTIVE LISTENING

If you are guilty of "selective listening," you will hear only those parts of the message that confirm your own views. If you are afraid to change, you will block out those aspects of the communication that do not agree with your position. If your main goal is defending yourself, you will not be able to consider the other person's points. If your major objective in listening is to evaluate others, you will make judgments before you have time to really understand their point of view.

One way to be sure that you are listening accurately is to restate what the other person has said and to confirm your interpretation with him or her. It is often helpful to do this when you are bogged down in an argument with another person. If you each restate the other's view before responding, you will be more likely to promote accurate communication. This is also a way to reassure each other that you are genuinely trying to understand both points of view. The exercise that follows will allow you to practice effective listening skills. When you are communicating, try to follow the guidelines shown in figure 16.

**EXERCISE: LISTENING AND PARAPHRASING**

Break into pairs and choose one of the following topics. Decide which of you will be the listener first. The speaker will express his or her thoughts on the subject in four or five sentences. The listener will restate the speaker's ideas and feelings and will then ask the speaker if he or she is satisfied with the paraphrasing. Is it accurate and complete? If it is not, the speaker will correct the restatement. Then switch roles so that the speaker becomes the listener, choose another topic, and repeat the exercise.

Some suggested topics are—

Abortion

Death penalty

Minimum age for alcohol consumption

Military draft

Euthanasia

## EXPRESSING YOUR IDEAS

Listening constitutes one-half of the communication process. Expressing your ideas and feelings makes up the other half. If you are going to get what you need from your college experience, you will have to learn to communicate your thoughts. Assertion involves the appropriate sharing of thoughts and feelings with others. If you communicate your needs and emotions to other people without putting those people down, then you will feel good and your relationships will flourish.

If you nonassertively keep your needs and feelings to yourself, then you may become hurt or angry, and others may lose respect for you. On the other hand, if you become aggressive and abuse others or force your ideas on them, you may find yourself facing interpersonal problems. People will become angry and avoid you. The goal is to communicate your needs and feelings appropriately without abusing others or depriving them of their rights.

## Aggressive, Nonassertive, and Assertive Behavior

As an example of the different ways you can react to any set of circumstances, consider the following situation. A customer in a restaurant orders a steak and requests that it be prepared rare. When the steak arrives well done, the customer may make one of the following responses.

1. *Aggressive:* The customer rants and raves at the waiter, accuses him of negligence, refuses to leave a tip, and threatens to never patronize the restaurant again.

   *Result:* The customer's needs are met, but the waiter feels abused, and the other members of the customer's party may feel embarrassed.

2. *Nonassertive:* The customer eats the steak and says nothing about the poor service. She then feels angry about paying for a meal that she did not enjoy. She becomes angry at herself for being a "wimp," and other members of her party may also lose respect for her.

   *Result:* The customer feels frustrated and loses respect.

3. *Appropriately assertive:* The customer politely explains to the waiter that the steak was not prepared according to her instructions, and she requests a substitution. She then enjoys her meal and leaves the waiter an appropriate tip for good service.

   *Result:* Both the customer's rights and the waiter's dignity and tip are preserved.

In general, nonassertive behavior (example 2) is emotionally dishonest. The person denies her true needs and feelings. She does not stand up for her rights and allows people to take advantage of her. Other people may feel sorry for her, they may get angry at her, and they may even become disgusted with her spineless behavior. Her resentment may result in emotional outbursts if she has been pushed over the brink by a relatively minor incident. This outburst does not make sense to the other people involved because the issue that triggers it might seem so trivial. This resentment and these temper outbursts may eventually jeopardize relationships with others.

Aggressive behavior (example 1) is inappropriately honest and direct. The aggressive customer may be rude and hurt others by blatantly criticizing and intimidating them. She gets her way by trampling over others' rights and feelings. In other areas of life, the aggressive person may often engage in verbally or physically abusive behavior by yelling at them, belittling them through the use of sarcasm, or even using physical force against them. The aggressive person may often feel superior or righteous while in the midst of a temper outburst, but then feels guilty or regretful about her behavior afterwards. She may jeopardize relationships with others by hurting and humiliating them. People will often be angry at her; they will avoid her or seek revenge for their humiliation.

Assertive behavior (example 3) is emotionally honest. The assertive person expresses her true feelings. She respects herself and demonstrates that respect by standing up for her rights. She also respects others involved and does not put them down in order to make herself look better. The assertive person gets what she wants more often than the nonassertive person, yet she is not as likely to anger people as the aggressive person. Other people involved in relationships with her usually value her and respect her opinions.

Assertive behavior does involve risks, and you may not wish to be assertive in all situations. For example, it may not be in your interest to tell your boss that he is running the company the wrong way, especially if he is someone who does not take kindly to criticism. If you criticize him, you may risk losing your job. On the other hand, if the situation at work really bothers you and you bottle up your emotions, you will end up feeling angry and resentful. You may eventually blow up at your boss unintentionally and really give him a piece of your mind. In that case you will definitely lose your job. If you can afford the possibility of a job change, it may be worthwhile to make some tactful suggestions for change before events reach the boiling point. If you make constructive suggestions while you are in control of your emotions, you might find yourself with improved working conditions and a raise in pay!

The same situation holds true in personal relationships. You may not wish to refuse your roommate when she asks to borrow your new sweater. On the other hand, if she continually borrows your clothes and returns them in poor condition or fails to return them at all, you will eventually resent her behavior. You will become angry at yourself and at her, and your relationship will suffer even though you give in to her requests. If you assertively tell her how much it disturbs you when your things are not returned and mention that you will only allow her to borrow them if they are returned in good condition, she may change her behavior. In that case, your friendship can continue on a basis of mutual respect.

## EXERCISE: DIFFERENTIATING AMONG ASSERTIVE, AGGRESSIVE, AND NONASSERTIVE BEHAVIORS

This exercise will help you to differentiate among appropriately assertive, aggressive, and nonassertive behaviors. Read each situation and classify the response as *assertive* (+), *aggressive* (−), or *nonassertive* (N). Compare your responses with the answers printed at the end of the chapter.

| Situation | Response | +, −, or N |
|---|---|---|
| 1. A friend has asked you for the second time in a week to babysit for her child while she runs errands. You have no children of your own and respond, | You're taking advantage of me and I won't stand for it! It's your responsibility to look after your own child. | _____ |

"Discrimination Test on Assertive, Aggressive and Nonassertive Behavior," is reprinted from a test by Patricia Jakubowski-Spector. It is excerpted from A. J. Lange and P. Jakubowski, *Responsible Assertive Behavior: Cognitive Behavioral Procedures for Trainers* (Champaign, IL: Research Press, 1980), fifth printing. Copyright 1976 by Research Press. Excerpted with permission.

2. An attendant at a gas station you frequently stop at for gas neglected to replace your gas cap. You notice this and return to inquire about it and you say,

One of you guys here forgot to put my gas cap back on! I want it found now or you'll buy me a new one.

———

3. You'd like a raise and say,

Do you think that, ah, you could see your way clear to giving me a raise?

———

4. Someone asks for a ride home and it is inconvenient because you're late, and have a few errands, and the drive will take you out of your way. You say,

I am pressed for time today and can take you to a convenient bus stop, but I won't be able to take you home.

———

5. A student enjoyed the teacher's class and says,

You make the material interesting. I like the way you teach the class.

———

6. A committee meeting is being established. The time is convenient for other people but not for you. The times are set when it will be next to impossible for you to attend regularly. When asked about the time, you say,

Well, I guess it's OK. I'm not going to be able to attend very much but it fits everyone else's schedule.

———

7. In a conversation, a man suddenly says, "What do you women libbers want anyway?" The woman responds,

Fairness and equality.

———

8. You've been talking for a while with a friend on the telephone. You would like to end the conversation and you say,

I'm terribly sorry but my supper's burning, and I have to get off the phone. I hope you don't mind.

———

9. At a meeting one person often interrupts you when you're speaking. You say,

Excuse me. I would like to finish my statement.

———

10. You are in a hard-sell camera store, and you have been pressured to purchase an item. You say,

Well, OK, I guess that's pretty much what I was looking for. Yes, I suppose I'll get it.

———

11. A good friend calls and tells you she desperately needs you to canvass the street for a charity. You don't want to do it and say,

Oh gee, Fran, I just know that Jerry will be mad at me if I say "yes." He says I'm always getting involved in too many things. You know how Jerry is about things like this.

———

12. You are at a meeting of seven men and one woman. At the beginning of the meeting, the chairman asks you to be the secretary. You respond,

No, I'm sick and tired of being the secretary just because I'm the only woman in the group.

———

13. A man asks you for a date. You've dated him once before and you're not interested in dating him again. You respond,

Oh, I'm really so busy this week that I don't think I will have time to see you this Saturday night.

———

14. The local library calls and asks you to return a book which you never checked out. You respond,

What are you talking about? You people better get your records straight—I never had that book and don't you try to make me pay for it. _____

15. You are in a line at the store. Someone behind you has one item, and asks to get in front of you. You say,

I realize that you don't want to wait in line, but I was here first and I really would like to get out of here. _____

16. A parent is talking with a married child on the telephone and would like the child to come for a visit. When the child politely refuses, the parent says,

You're never available when I need you. All you ever think about is yourself. _____

17. Plans to vacation together are abruptly changed by a friend and reported to you on the phone. You respond,

Wow, this has really taken me by surprise. I'd like to call you back after I've had some time to digest what's happened. _____

18. Your roommate habitually leaves the room a mess. You say,

You're a mess and our room is a mess. _____

19. Your husband wants to watch a football game on TV. There is something else that you'd like to watch. You say,

Well, ah honey, go ahead and watch the game. I guess I could do some ironing. _____

20. It is your turn to clean the apartment, which you have neglected to do several times in the last month. In a very calm tone of voice your roommate asks you to clean up the apartment. You say,

Would you get off my back! _____

21. An acquaintance has asked to borrow your car for the evening. You say,

Are you crazy! I don't lend my car to anyone. _____

22. A loud stereo upstairs is disturbing you. You telephone and say,

Hello, I live downstairs. Your stereo is loud and is bothering me. Would you please turn it down. _____

23. A friend often borrows small amounts of money and does not return it unless asked. She again asks for a small loan which you'd rather not give her. You say,

I only have enough money to pay for my own lunch today. _____

24. A neighbor has been constantly borrowing your vacuum cleaner. The last time, she broke it. When she asked for it again, you reply,

I'm sorry, but I don't want to loan my sweeper anymore. The last time I loaned it to you it was returned broken. _____

25. Your mate wants to go out for a late night snack. You're too tired to go out and say,

I really don't feel like going out tonight. I'm too tired. But I'll go with you and watch you eat. _____

# EFFECTIVE COMMUNICATION

Issues involving assertiveness come up frequently. These issues may arise when friends pressure you to have another drink or to take a drug when you do not wish to. They may arise when you are urged to party but feel you should be studying for an important exam the next day. They may come up when your spouse or partner wants to have sex, but you do not wish to. These issues may arise when your mother insists that you eat another piece of the cake that she baked even though she knows you have been dieting strenuously for the past three weeks. They may come up when your spouse buys a new set of golf clubs with the money you have been saving for the children's orthodontist. They may arise when your roommates continuously "borrow" all the food that you buy or when your children blast the stereo while you are trying to study.

## "I" Statements versus "You" Statements

The preceding statements describe situations in which emotions run high and in which it is easy for people to lose their tempers. One strategy for keeping things under control while at the same time working toward a constructive solution is to use "I" language rather than "you" language. If you say to someone, "You are inconsiderate," that person is likely to respond, "No, I'm not. You're the inconsiderate one!" The two of you may then get into an argument in which voices keep rising, tempers are lost, and nothing useful is accomplished. If, on the other hand, you say, "I am hurt," and you explain exactly what it is that the other person does that hurts you, that person is more likely to listen to you without becoming defensive.

"You" statements make the other person feel defensive because they criticize, judge, and label. They force the person to come back with a rebuttal to your accusation, and they usually lead to an argument. "I" statements, on the other hand, tell the other person how his or her behavior makes you feel. "I" statements express your feelings, opinions, observations, and goals or desires without putting the other person down. Observe how the following "you" statements can be turned into "I" statements. Imagine someone saying first one and then the other to you. Do you feel less defensive and angry in response to the "I" statement?

| *"You" statement* | *"I" statement* |
|---|---|
| You are crazy. | I don't understand. |
| You make me furious. | I feel angry. |
| You don't listen to me. | I feel so frustrated. |
| You don't help me. | I feel overwhelmed. |

When you use "I" statements, the other person is more likely to listen to you and to understand your position. The other person is also more likely to sympathize with you, because he or she is not using so much energy in self-defense. Try to use "I" language wherever possible in the exercise that follows and in any confrontations that you face.

EXERCISE: USING
EFFECTIVE
COMMUNICATION
TO SOLVE
DISPUTES

This exercise will give you practice in finding solutions to problems and in expressing yourself assertively. Take an index card and write down at least three situations that raise issues of assertiveness for you. Pass those cards to your instructor. (Do not put your name on the card. This part of the exercise is *anonymous.*) Three volunteers will list all of these areas on the board for the class.

Break down into small discussion groups of four students. Your instructor will then assign two problem areas from the list to each of the small groups. Discuss the situations and brainstorm possible solutions to the problem. Then have two of the group members role-play the situation; each of you will take a part and act out the situation and the solution. Each skit should last no more than one or two minutes. Coach each other about the script, the body language, the tone of voice, the eye contact, and so on, so that your skit is as effective as possible. When you have finished with the first problem situation, act out the second one, giving the other two members of the group a chance to star in this skit. Then regroup as a class, and each of the pairs will present its skit. After each skit, have your fellow class members offer suggested improvements or alternate solutions to the problem. Here is a sample script from a sexual situation where the woman wishes to use a condom and the man does not. She is responding assertively in a sexual situation.

**He:** I know I don't have any diseases; I haven't had sex with anyone in six months.

**She:** Thanks for telling me. As far as I know I am disease-free, too. But I would still like to use a condom since either of us could have an infection and not know it.

**He:** I don't have any condoms and we don't want to go out and get any.

**She:** Well, I just happen to have some condoms with me. What color do you like best?

**He:** It will interrupt sex.

**She:** Let me put it on for you. You'll love it.[1]

## UNDERSTANDING AND AVOIDING DATE RAPE

You may wonder why a section on rape is included in a chapter on relating to others. There is a disturbing increase in a phenomenon on college campuses today that professionals call "acquaintance rape" or "date rape." In this situation, women are forced to have sex with men whom they know when they go out on a date. Ninety-thousand rapes are reported in the United States each year, and 60 to 70 percent of these are acquaintance rapes.[2] This section is presented so that you will recognize the tragic consequences that such an incident can have. It will also suggest ways that you can avoid becoming a rape victim or perpetrator.

In the years I have practiced as a therapist and a college professor, I have seen and heard of unfortunate cases where women have been forced to drop out of college because they could not deal with the emotional trauma caused by a rape. There have also been cases where young men have been suspended from college and faced criminal proceedings because of a rape incident. A rape can have unfortunate effects on the college careers of both the man and the woman involved.

Even in those cases where the students involved were not forced to withdraw from college, they still spent so much time and energy agonizing over the incident that they neglected their studies and found themselves failing courses.

Rape incidents can also have negative effects on students' social relationships. Some young women have come to fear all men and could not enter into a close relationship with any male for many years after a rape experience. Other women have lost the ability to participate in any sexual relationship because of the painful memories this type of relationship elicits. Some young women have lost all sense of security and could not remain in their rooms alone without experiencing tremendous anxiety and panic attacks. Some men have suffered from tremendous feelings of guilt after performing an act that they thought was alright at the time. The consequences of a rape can be tragic for both people who are involved.

If you believe that you need not be concerned about this subject because it could not happen to you, you are wrong! Acquaintance rape occurs more frequently among college students, and it is more common among freshman than any other group.

A survey of college women conducted by Carol Pritchard revealed that one-fourth of these women had been raped or were victims of an attempted rape; almost one-half of the women in the survey personally knew someone who had been raped. One-fourth of the men surveyed admitted that they had used aggression in sexual situations with women. In this college survey, 84 percent of the rapists were dating partners or acquaintances! The number of incidents is probably greater than figures suggest because many women feel too embarrassed to report rape, especially rape by someone they know.[3]

**EXERCISE: CHECKING STEREOTYPICAL VIEWS OF MALE AND FEMALE BEHAVIOR**

1. Many tragic incidents of date rape are the result of misunderstandings or misreadings of the other person's behavior. Our culture offers certain stereotypes, or false models, of male and female behavior that result in misleading beliefs about both sexes. The following questions are meant to help you explore your views about male and female behavior and to help you share those views with your classmates. Write *A* for "agree," next to the following statements with which you agree, and write *D* for "disagree" next to the statements with which you disagree.

_____ a. The man should be the aggressor in a sexual situation. He should take control and initiate sexual activity.

_____ b. The woman should be passive. She should wait for the man to make the moves.

_____ c. If a man does not make a pass, the woman will feel hurt or rejected.

_____ d. If a man does not make a pass, the woman will think that he is not a man.

_____ e. If a woman protests against sex, she is just acting because she does not want the man to think that she is too easy. She really wants sex, even if she says "No."

_____ f. If a woman says "No," she does not want to have sex with the man at that time.

_____ g. If a woman does not flirt or dress in a sexy way, she will not be able to attract any men.

_____ h. If a woman flirts or dresses in a sexy way, it is because she wants to have sex.

_____ i. If a woman stops a man before the kissing gets too hot and heavy, he will think she is a prude and will lose interest in her.

_____ j. If a woman allows the kissing to get serious, it is because she wants to have sex.

_____ k. If a woman shows warmth and caring, it is because she wants to go to bed with the man.

_____ l. If a woman shows warmth and caring, it is because she likes a man and wants to get to know him better.

_____ m. If a woman goes to a man's room with him, it is because she wants to go to bed with him.

_____ n. If a woman goes to a man's room with him, it is because she wants to be with him somewhere private where they can talk and get to know each other better. She does not necessarily want to sleep with him.

2. When you are finished with part 1 of this exercise, write the numbers 1 through 14 on a slip of paper and copy your answers from part 1, next to the appropriate numbers. Do not write your name on the paper, but do write "male" or "female" to indicate whether you are a man or a woman. Hand the papers in to your instructor. Have your instructor tally, on the chalkboard, the number of agree and disagree answers for each question, in male and female response categories.

**Improving Communication Between Men and Women**

3. When you have completed part 2 of this exercise, consider the following questions in a class discussion. Use the discussion as a learning experience to show you how to improve communication between men and women.

• Is there much disagreement among class members about the answers? Why?

• Do the males in the class tend to see the situations differently from the females? Why?

• How do your answers compare with your classmates'? Is there a majority view? Why do you agree or disagree with it?

• Do the men think it is fair that they are pressured into the aggressor role? How might you change this?

• Do the women think it is fair that they are expected to be passive and play hard to get? How might you change this?

• How can a man or a woman say "No," so that the other person knows it is a real "No"? Is there more involved in saying "No" than just the actual words used?

• How do you think men and women might work toward a more equal and honest relationship between the sexes so that embarrassing or even tragic errors in communication can be avoided?

- Know your sexual intentions. Be aware of what you want to do and what you don't want to do.

- Decide, before you go out on a date, how far you want to go with your partner. Stop things (tactfully, but assertively) when you have reached those limits. Do not allow yourself to be coerced or bullied into going beyond your limits.

- Communicate your intentions clearly. If you wish to say "No," say it firmly and clearly so that your partner knows you really mean it.

- Respect your partner's right to say "No." If your request for sex is turned down, it does not mean that you are not a "real man" or a "real woman." It does not mean that you are not a worthwhile human being. It does not even mean that your partner does not like you.

- You may *want* to have sex, but *you do not have to have sex.* You can control your actions.

- You do not have the right to demand sex from another person if he or she does not wish to have sex, even if you have spent money on that person.

- You are not obligated to have sex because someone has "wasted" time or money on you. A date is a situation where two people go out to enjoy each other's company and get to know each other better. Sex is not part of the contract.

- Be aware that flirting, dressing in a sexy way, or going to a man's room may be interpreted by some men as an agreement to intercourse. It is not necessarily wrong to do these things, but try to communicate your true intentions clearly so that you can avoid unpleasant misunderstandings.

- Using drugs or alcohol may cloud your ability to read another person's messages accurately or it may hamper your ability to communicate your own intentions clearly. Know your limits and act responsibly. Getting drunk or high is no excuse for seriously hurting another person.

- If you are raped, seek help at the college counseling center. The counselor will not blame you, embarrass you, or force you to report the incident if you do not wish to do so. He or she will help you come to terms with your own feelings so that the experience does not continue to haunt you.

FIGURE 17. GUIDELINES FOR ASSERTIVE COMMUNICATION IN SEXUAL SITUATIONS

People often have very different views or interpretations of the same situation. The subtle communications of tone and body language involved in an intimate encounter can easily be misread, and the result may be tragic for both parties. Life is much simpler if we are honest about our feelings and desires and if we state those feelings assertively and clearly. In the sexual arena, clear communication is particularly important because it is so easy to misread another's signals. Do not expect your partner to read your mind unless you tell him or her what it is you want. Do not assume that your partner wants one thing when your partner is telling you he or she wants another.

All individuals have the right to make their own decisions about what to do with their bodies. Respect your partner's right to make those decisions; assume that what your partner says is what he or she means. Figure 17 presents some guidelines that may help you avoid an unpleasant or even traumatic situation.

## Answer Key for Differentiation Test

| | | |
|---|---|---|
| 1. − | 10. N | 19. N |
| 2. − | 11. N | 20. − |
| 3. N | 12. − | 21. − |
| 4. + | 13. N | 22. + |
| 5. + | 14. − | 23. N |
| 6. N | 15. + | 24. + |
| 7. + | 16. − | 25. N |
| 8. N | 17. + | |
| 9. + | 18. − | |

## NOTES

1. R. A. Hatcher et al., *Contraceptive Technology 1988–1989,* 14th ed. (Atlanta: Printed Matter, Inc.; New York: Irvington Publishers, 1988).

2. Ibid.

3. C. Pritchard, *Avoiding Rape On and Off Campus* (Wenonah, N.J.: State College Publishing Co., 1985).

# Chapter 12

---

# Responsible Intimacy

## VALUES AND DECISIONS

You will find that the area of interpersonal relations requires a number of important value decisions. This process of learning about yourself, becoming close to others, and making decisions about values is often a difficult one. It may become even more difficult during college, since you will be experimenting with greater freedom from your parents and you may be experiencing considerable pressure from your friends about adopting the value systems they share.

Remember that only you can judge which values work for you. People who respect and value you as a friend will ultimately accept the standards that you set for yourself. Try to resist the pressure to do what everyone else is doing if it does not feel right for you. Often, the "everyone else is doing it" view is misleading. For example, although it may seem that everyone in college is sexually experienced, national surveys of eighteen-year-olds reveal that *only 50 percent have actually engaged in sexual intercourse.*[1] Apparently *not* everyone is doing it! It is possible to have a close and meaningful relationship that does not involve sex.

## INTIMATE RELATIONSHIPS

Intimate relationships involve give and take and sharing. Partners must be willing to disclose themselves to each other. This does not necessarily involve sharing every secret, but it does mean sharing what is important to the relationship and allowing your partner to know about your joys, expectations, frustrations, dreams, fears, excitement, and other important feelings. Each person must have a desire to give to the other, help the other, and support the other, so that both partners are fulfilled. Each makes a commitment to stay with the other through times of crisis and conflict, to give support, and to work things out. The partners agree to accept each other and to tolerate and respect the differences between them.[2]

## Sexual Relationships

An intimate relationship *may* involve a sexual relationship although many intimate friendships do not include sex. Nor must a sexual relationship necessarily involve sexual intercourse. There are ways to share warm, affectionate, physical feelings without engaging in intercourse.

All human beings need touching—for affection, for comfort, for communication. Most people enjoy erotic touching as well. For many, this involves sexual intercourse: sexual contact that results with the penis in the vagina. But most people enjoy as well a wide range of sexual expressions that gives them pleasure: holding hands, kissing, massaging, mutual masturbation, dancing, oral-genital sex, fantasy, and sharing erotic movies can all be expressions of sexual feelings. Taste, smell, vision, hearing, and imagination matter just as much as touch in erotic situations.[3] Sexual expression and affection can be communicated without intercourse. Only you can judge what you should be doing and under what conditions you might be willing to experiment with various types of sexual behavior.

### *Precautions*

If you make a commitment to abstinence, family planners recommend that you stay sober, stay out of the empty house, and stay out of the back seat. Otherwise, abstinence may be just too difficult to accomplish.[4] On the other hand, if you decide to have a sexually intimate relationship, there is certain information about birth control and sexually transmitted diseases with which you should become very familiar. When these subjects come up, many students say, "Yuck!" These subjects are often considered unromantic, awkward, embarrassing, or even disgusting.

Such hang-ups in communicating openly about sexual matters seem to be particularly American. As a result, the rate of unwanted pregnancies in the United States is *higher than in any other industrialized nation.* Couples in other countries do not seem to have the same unrealistic ideas about what is romantic. That is probably because we get our notions of romance from the media, and the media does not portray relationships between people who live in the real world.

Sharing and caring enough to help each other avoid disease, death, and the emotional trauma of unwanted pregnancy are warm, loving things to do with a partner. There is nothing romantic about getting AIDS or going through an abortion.

There is also nothing romantic about the number of students who are forced to drop out of college each year because they or their partners become pregnant. Nor is there anything romantic about the students who spend so much time worrying whether they have contracted a disease that they neglect their studies and flunk out of college. Do not allow these types of mistakes to ruin your college career.

Even if you think you know everything there is to know on these subjects, please read the following information carefully. It has been estimated that *over one-third* of all females between the ages of fifteen and twenty years in the United States have *at least one unwanted pregnancy.*[5] In 1981, four of five pregnancies, among women under twenty years of age, were conceived out of wedlock. Of these, more than one-half were terminated by abortion.[6] Of the 50 million women who have abortions throughout the world each year, approximately 150,000 die from botched abortions![7] Apparently, many young men and women do not know as much about birth control as they should.

What is even more disturbing than the number of unwanted pregnancies are the consequences of those pregnancies. The pregnancies in this young age group result in an astoundingly high percentage of abnormal, physically damaged babies due to birth complications and inadequate prenatal medical care. They also result in a very high number of medical problems for the mothers. Both the mothers and the babies usually experience severe psychological problems and lives of poverty due to interrupted educations, stressful parental responsibilities, and restricted social opportunities.

Researchers are constantly developing new information and techniques in the area of birth control, and surveys show that many adults are misinformed on these vital subjects. Familiarity with this information could lead to the difference between a satisfying sexual experience and a nightmare involving abortion, unwanted pregnancy, serious illness, or even death. It is not in your interest to become one of these unfortunate, but all too common, statistics.

## METHODS OF BIRTH CONTROL

If you decide that you are ready to enter into a sexually intimate relationship with a partner, you should be mature and caring enough about your welfare and the welfare of your partner to take responsible action about birth control. The following information will help you to decide what type of birth control to use if you make the decision to become sexually active. The Planned Parenthood Federation of America, with branches listed in the telephone directories of most cities and towns, offers excellent literature and individual counseling should you have additional questions about contraception.

### Abstinence

The only method of birth control that is 100 percent effective is *abstinence*. If you do not have sexual intercourse, you cannot become pregnant. If you wish to have intercourse, however, there are a number of methods that can greatly reduce the chance of pregnancy. They vary in effectiveness and ease of use, but they only work if they are used according to directions every single time you engage in intercourse. If you have sex just one time (even if it is your very first time) without birth control protection, you risk the chance of pregnancy. If you find a particular contraceptive method uncomfortable or inconvenient, try another one until you find one that suits you and your partner. An uncomfortable method will not work because you will be tempted to "skip it just this once." That one time will open you to the risk of pregnancy.

Certain methods of birth control are more popular among different age groups because of their convenience or effectiveness. The Alan Guttmacher Institute reports in the National Survey of Family Growth that in the group of 15- to 19-year-old women, more than 15 percent use the pill, 5 percent rely on condoms, one-and-one-half percent use the diaphragm, but more than 9 percent expose themselves to the risk of pregnancy by not using any birth control. It is interesting that 55 percent of the respondents in this age group reported that they had not been sexually active in the past three months. This last method, abstinence, is the most-effective form of birth control.

In the group of 20- to 24-year-old women, more than 30 percent use the pill; the condom and the diaphragm are about equally popular, each claiming almost 6 percent of the contraceptive users. In the next age group of 25- to 29-year-old women, the pattern looks about the same, although the pill drops in popularity (down to 23 percent) as the diaphragm, condom, and intrauterine device (IUD) each pick up approximately 7 percent of the contraceptive market.

## The Pill

There are three effective birth control methods that require a medical prescription: the pill, the IUD, and the diaphragm. All three methods are used by the woman. The pill seems to be the most-common contraceptive used by women, probably because of its convenience and effectiveness. The pill is a contraceptive device containing hormone-like substances; it is taken orally. Some pills work by preventing a woman's ovaries from releasing eggs; others work by changing the environment in her uterus and cervix so that it is difficult for an egg to be fertilized. When a woman wishes to become pregnant, she will stop taking the pill. Her regular menstrual cycles should return within one to three months.

Taking the pill must be coordinated with your menstrual cycle, and you must follow your doctor's directions carefully if you expect the pill to work. Some pills must be taken every day; others are taken during just twenty-one days of your cycle. The pill can be dangerous for women who have had blood clots, liver disease, unexplained bleeding from the vagina, or cancer. It is also more dangerous to women who smoke because of increased risk of blood clots and phlebitis. A medical examination is necessary in order to prescribe the right pill for you and to be certain that the pill is safe for you.

The pill is the most-effective temporary birth control technique available. Of 100 women who use the pill, approximately 3 will become pregnant during the first year they use the pill.[8] If these women always take the pill when they should, they have less chance of becoming pregnant. The pill has other advantages as well: many women find that their menstrual cycles become more regular, and they experience less severe cramps when they are on the pill. There is also evidence that the pill may protect some women from developing certain serious illnesses.

Some women find that the pill results in problems like nausea or weight gain. It may also increase the likelihood of more serious disorders like stroke, heart attack, blood clots, or liver cancer. There are certain signs that can warn you of developing problems. If you are taking the pill and experience any of the following symptoms, consult your doctor as soon as possible: pain, redness, or swelling in your leg; pain in your stomach, chest, or arm; shortness of breath, blurry vision, or painful headaches. Do not take the pill if you have a history of serious headaches.

Pills can be purchased in a drugstore or in family planning clinics if you have a doctor's prescription for them. The medical examination, in which the physician determines whether the pill is safe for you and which pill you should take, can be given in a physician's office. Both the examination and the pills may cost less in a family planning clinic that operates on a sliding scale fee than in a private doctor's office or drugstore.

## The Intrauterine Device (IUD)

The IUD is the next-most-effective prescription birth control technique. Of 100 women who use the IUD, only 6 will become pregnant during the first year.[9] The IUD is a device made of plastic or copper that is inserted into a woman's uterus by a gynecologist or obstetrician. The IUD prevents pregnancy by changing the lining of the uterus so that it is more difficult for pregnancy to take place. Menstruation will continue while the IUD is in place. When a woman wishes to become pregnant, she asks her doctor to remove the IUD.

The IUD is not suitable for women who have heavy menstrual bleeding, anemia, or certain abnormalities of the uterus, ovaries, or cervix. It may also be dangerous for women who have had recent infections in their tubes or ovaries or a history of tubal pregnancy. The IUD may also cause some discomfort (cramps, bleeding, backaches) during the first few months after it is inserted. When an IUD has been inserted, you should return for a checkup soon after your first period, to be sure that the device is still in place. Most pregnancies that occur in IUD users happen because the device falls out and the woman is not aware of it. If you have had an IUD inserted and you think you may be pregnant, notify your physician as soon as possible. A pregnancy that proceeds while an IUD is in place can be very dangerous.

Although IUDs are one of the most convenient and effective contraceptive devices, they can result in some problems. Consult your doctor if you experience severe cramps or pain in your lower abdomen. You should also report any pain that is experienced during sex or unexplained fever, chills, or discharge from your vagina. There is a greater risk for pelvic infection in IUD users, and some of these can be quite serious if they are not promptly treated by a physician.

## The Diaphragm and Cervical Cap

The diaphragm is a small rubber disk that the woman coats with a spermicidal cream such as nonoxynol-9 and inserts into her vagina each time she has intercourse. It prevents pregnancy by blocking the passage through which sperm swim to unite with the egg. The cream serves as a backup contraceptive by stopping the sperm if the diaphragm becomes dislodged during sex or if it was not properly inserted in the first place. A medical examination is necessary so that the woman can be fitted with the correct size and model of diaphragm.

Studies regarding the effectiveness of the diaphragm report various figures; failure rates vary from 2 to 19 pregnancies for every 100 women who use the diaphragm during their first year.[10] This risk of pregnancy is lowered if you use the diaphragm conscientiously and properly each time you have sex. If the diaphragm does not fit correctly or if it is not inserted properly, the sperm will be able to swim through and pregnancy may result. For this reason, the fit should be checked by a physician every two years or sooner if your weight has changed markedly (up or down) or if you have experienced pregnancy.

Diaphragms are not as effective as the pill or the IUD, and they must be inserted each time you have sex. The diaphragms should be left in place for six to eight hours after intercourse. On the other hand, they do not result in any medical complications of the type mentioned above in connection with the pill or the IUD. They can be used safely by most women, especially those who are not eligible for one of the other methods because of their medical histories or other problems. The medical exam and fitting for a diaphragm is done by a gynecologist in his or her office. It can also be performed in a family planning clinic. Diaphragms are sold in both drugstores and clinics. Given proper care, a diaphragm should last up to two years.

The cervical cap is now available in the United States. It looks something like a miniature diaphragm and fits over the cervix to prevent the sperm from uniting with the egg. Like the diaphragm, it should be used in conjunction with a spermicidal cream such as nonoxynol-9. First year failure rates vary from 8 to 27 pregnancies per 100 women, depending on the study consulted.[11]

The cervical cap should not be used if you have a history of toxic shock syndrome or an allergy to rubber (latex) or spermicide. It is also contraindicated for women who are prone to urinary tract infections.

## The Condom

The condom (also known as prophylactic, rubber, or safe) is a contraceptive device that is used by the male during intercourse; it requires no prescription.

It is placed over the erect penis before the man enters the woman so that the condom catches the sperm and prevents them from entering the woman to join with an egg. The condom offers protection from sexually transmitted diseases in addition to protection against pregnancy.

Like the diaphragm, condoms result in no medical complications. They are disposable and inexpensive, and they can be purchased in drug stores, clinics, and through many mail order catalogs. They are not always prominently displayed in drug stores, so you may have to ask for them. Be prepared to tell the druggist whether you prefer lubricated or unlubricated condoms. He may also ask you for a brand preference. Plain rubber condoms are the least expensive, and just as effective as animal tissue, lubricated, textured, or colored condoms. In addition, rubber condoms are more effective than those made of animal tissue in preventing the spread of AIDS. They can be purchased by men or women, and there is no restriction on the sale of condoms based on age.

Condoms are effective if they are conscientiously used during each act of intercourse. Of 100 couples who use condoms, only 12 pregnancies may occur during the first year of use.[12] Condoms can be even more effective if they are used with an additional backup contraceptive such as a spermicidal cream or foam. Should the condom break during intercourse, the cream or foam would stop the sperm from swimming to join with the egg.

Condoms may break if they are handled roughly, although lubricated condoms are less likely to tear. They also tend to weaken with exposure to light or heat. Do not store condoms in your wallet next to your body or in other warm places like your glove compartment for long periods of time. Use or dispose of condoms by the expiration date printed on the package. They weaken with age and should be disposed of within two years of purchase.

## Vaginal Sponge

The sponge is a soft, round, two-inch device that is saturated with a spermicidal solution such as nonoxynol-9. The woman inserts it into her vagina where it blocks the passage to the uterus. In addition to blocking the sperms' path, the spermicide reduces the sperms' movement so they cannot swim to join with an egg. Of 100 women who use the sponge, between 17 and 25 become pregnant during the first year.[13]

There is no special fitting required for the sponge as it comes in only one size. The woman moistens it with approximately two tablespoons of water, which lubricates it and activates the spermicide. It should not be removed from the vagina for six hours after the last act of intercourse so that the sperm are effectively neutralized by the spermicide. The sponge may be left in the vagina for twenty-four hours. Do not use it when you are menstruating because it may expose you to the risk of toxic shock syndrome. The sponge is disposable and should never be used a second time.

The sponge requires no prescription. It can be used by any woman who can insert a tampon, and it is available in drugstores and clinics. Researchers report that, out of 100 women who use the sponge, 9 to 11 may become pregnant. You can make the sponge even more effective if you back it up with an additional device such as the condom.

The sponge is a fairly new birth control device. It is, therefore, too early to be certain about medical complications. Accumulating evidence is beginning to show, however, that use of the sponge exposes women to increased risk of toxic shock syndrome. If you have difficulty locating or removing a sponge, call your doctor. You should not forget about it or leave one in place longer than twenty-four hours, as you may develop toxic shock syndrome, which can be fatal. For the same reason, you should not use the sponge during menstruation, after an abortion, or after having a baby. Consult your doctor if you develop irritation, discharge, or an unpleasant odor from your vagina.

## Vaginal Foams, Jellies, Creams, Suppositories, and Tablets

All of these contraceptives are inserted into the vagina where they may offer some protection against pregnancy. They should be used in conjunction with a spermicidal cream such as nonoxynol-9 if this spermicide is not one of the ingredients in the product. They do not require medical examinations or prescriptions and cause few medical problems. Instructions on how to use each product come with the package. You should read these instructions carefully, and perhaps even practice with the product once or twice before you use it in a sexual situation.

Of 100 women who use one of these vaginal contraceptives, 21 may become pregnant during the first year's use. (More recent studies report failure rates of 36 pregnancies per 100 women.[14]) Conscientious and proper application will reduce the risks of pregnancy. These products are very useful for boosting the effectiveness of other contraceptives when used in combination with condoms or IUDs. The suppositories are less effective than the foams, and the timing involved in the use of suppositories is a little tricky. They require approximately fifteen minutes inside the vagina before intercourse in order to be fully effective. They also cannot be relied upon for more than an hour after insertion. A fresh suppository should be inserted for each instance of intercourse.

## Fertility Awareness Methods

Fertility awareness (natural birth control) methods of contraception attempt to prevent pregnancy by avoiding intercourse during the periods of the month when the woman is most fertile. You may recognize these methods by other names such as natural family planning, the rhythm method, the mucus charting method, the basal body temperature charting method, or the ovulation method. Couples use fertility awareness methods to figure out when the woman has released an egg from her ovaries. She is most likely to become pregnant just before, during, and after the time the egg is released. The couple then abstains from sex during those times.

Fertility awareness methods offer no medical complications, and they are acceptable to couples who have religious reservations about the use of other forms of birth control. Thermometers and charts for keeping records of basal body temperature may be purchased in drug stores or at family planning clinics. Among typical users of this contraceptive method, approximately 20 percent fail during the first year.[15] A couple should take a course or talk with a counselor at a family planning clinic in order to be able to practice these methods most effectively.

Fertility awareness methods are not easy to use. They take time to learn, and after they are learned, the couple must keep very careful daily records in order to ensure accuracy. If a woman does not have regular menstrual cycles, these methods will not work no matter how conscientious the record keeping. Both partners must also be willing to show considerable self-control, because there will be certain days when having sex will expose them to the risk of pregnancy. Some of the spontaneity of lovemaking is lost because of the scheduling and planning that are crucial to the success of these methods.

A woman generally ovulates, or releases an egg, from her ovaries once a month, approximately 14 days before her menstruation begins. She is fertile for 5 days before she ovulates and for 3 days after she ovulates. This results in 5 to 8 fertile days during each month. If the woman's menstrual cycle is regular and the couple has kept careful records, she should not be at risk for pregnancy if the couple has sex during the other days of the month.

The two most-accurate records to keep are mucus consistency and basal body temperature. Birth control will be much more effective if both of these signs are checked. In using these methods, the couple must refrain from having sex from the end of menstruation until three days after the woman has ovulated. The woman must take her temperature every morning, even before getting out of bed, smoking, or having anything to eat or drink. She must keep a record of her basal body temperature that is accurate to within several tenths of a degree.

The record keeping for fertility awareness methods is complicated. A couple should take a course or consult a counselor at a family planning clinic to learn which signs and times indicate fertile periods. Trying to guess when ovulation has occurred by counting forwards from the last menstruation (calendar method) is very risky. This is not an accurate method, and it should not be used unless you are also recording body temperature or checking the vaginal mucus.

## Withdrawal

Withdrawal is a method of contraception in which the male attempts to pull his penis out of the woman's vagina before he ejaculates, or "comes." If he is successful in doing this, the sperm will not have the opportunity to enter the woman's body and fertilize an egg.

This is not a reliable method of birth control for two reasons. First, a man often releases some sperm in the lubricating fluid that he secretes during sexual stimulation before he reaches his climax. The method also requires a great deal of self-control and timing because there is a reflexive reaction to thrust deeper into the woman during intercourse rather than to pull out. This method should only be used as a last resort if no other methods of contraception are available, since it poses the greatest risk of pregnancy.

## The Douche

Douching is a technique in which the woman sprays fluid up into her vagina after having intercourse. The douche is used to wash the sperm out of the woman's body before the sperm can unite with an egg. It is the most unreliable of all the techniques discussed so far. The sperm begin swimming up to meet an egg before the woman can insert the douching fluid, so many of the sperm are out of the fluid's reach by the time the woman douches. There is even the chance that the pressure of the fluid may give the slower sperm a boost up through the vagina to meet an egg!

## Voluntary Sterilization

Sterilization (vasectomy or tubal ligation) is a surgical procedure that prevents the egg from joining with the sperm in the uterus. If the egg and the sperm cannot join together, there is no risk of pregnancy. Women who have been surgically sterilized through a tubal ligation (cutting and tying of fallopian tubes) continue to menstruate, but their eggs do not enter the uterus. Men who have undergone a vasectomy (cutting and tying of the vas deferens) continue to ejaculate during sex, but their ejaculate does not contain sperm.

Neither operation should have any effect on a person's sexual behavior. There is no tampering with the hormones so there should also be no change in the person's feelings of femininity or masculinity. The total number of sterilized adults in the American population is estimated at more than 16.5 million. A failure rate of 4 pregnancies per 100 individuals is reported.[16]

This procedure is generally permanent, and it is not reversible. For this reason, a couple must be certain, when they make this decision, that they do not wish to have any more children.

Women's sterilization method, tubal ligation, is more complicated than men's, and it is performed in a hospital. It involves more risk for medical complications than does the vasectomy, which is usually performed in a doctor's office or a clinic and does not require hospitalization.

As you can see, there are many birth control methods available, and researchers continue to develop new contraceptives; studies are currently underway on a pill taken by men, a condom used by women, and a "morning after" pill. Therefore, it pays to update your knowledge about birth control from time to time, through your physician or your family planning clinic. Choose an effective method that is most comfortable for you and your partner. If the method you choose does not work out for any reason, discuss it and try another method. The Planned Parenthood Federation of America, a neighborhood family planning clinic, or your college's health services division can be very helpful in offering you additional information or individual counseling. Keep trying out different methods until you find one that suits you, but *do not have sex without using some form of birth control.* You owe that to yourself and to your partner.

**EXERCISE: MAKING DECISIONS ABOUT BIRTH CONTROL**

The major goal of this exercise is that you practice talking with others about this important subject so that you will be comfortable communicating about birth control in the event that you decide to enter into a sexually intimate relationship. Break up into groups of four and discuss each situation; decide on the general advice you would give to each couple, the method of contraception you would recommend, and the reasons for your recommendations. Record your answers so that you may share them with the class as a whole.

**Directions:**

In each of the following cases a couple is making decisions about intercourse and birth control. Discuss the situation with your group and together decide: (1) What general advice would you give the couple? and (2) What birth control method do you recommend for them? Why?

*Choices may include:*

abstinence—no sex
outercourse—sex without intercourse
condom                foam          diaphragm
condom and foam       sponge        pill

"Choice and Consequences: Making Decisions About Birth Control" is reprinted, by permission, from Peggy Brick and Carolyn Cooperman, *Positive Images: A New Approach to Contraceptive Education* (2d ed.) (Planned Parenthood of Bergen County, 1987), 45–46.

1. Jane and Jim have been going together for over a year. When they began to have intercourse, Jane got the pill—she took it for about six months. Then a month ago they had a fight and decided not to see each other for awhile. Jane stopped taking the pill. Last night they got together, talked things over, and decided to continue with their relationship. Tonight, they're alone at Jim's and really want to resume their sexual relationship . . .

Advice: _____

_____

Birth Control: _____

Why: _____

_____

2. Jeff and Susan are crazy about each other. For the last three months they've done a lot of heavy petting, but never had intercourse. Tonight is very special because tomorrow Susan leaves the city for a summer job at the shore. They know they won't see each other for at least a month and both want to show their love for each other by having intercourse. They've been to a late movie, parked the car, but they don't have any birth control.

Advice: _____

_____

Birth Control: _____

Why:_____

_____

3. Dave and Janet have been having intercourse once or twice a week for six months. They've been using "withdrawal" and it seemed to work OK—until two weeks ago when Janet's period was late. For ten days they worried that she was pregnant and they both vowed that they'd never have unprotected intercourse again. Finally, Janet's period came—but now she's embarrassed to go to a family planning center. Dave doesn't want to use a condom.

Advice: _____

_____

Birth Control: _____

Why: _____

_____

4. Ken's family has strong religious values including the belief that intercourse should be saved for marriage. Ken respects both his parents and his religion. Ken is dating Cindy and he cares for her a great deal. Cindy has already had intercourse in a previous relationship (she took the pill then, but stopped it when the relationship broke up three months ago). Cindy thinks it's natural and right that she and Ken should express their love for each other by having intercourse.

Advice: _____

_____

Birth Control: _____

Why: _____

_____

**EXERCISE: "PUTTING BIRTH CONTROL INTO ROMANCE"**

Break into groups of two (male and female in each pair, if possible) and work with someone of the opposite sex who was not in your group for the previous exercise. Complete this exercise, and record your answers so that you may share them with the whole class. Once again, the goal of the exercise is to reinforce your knowledge about birth control and to help you become more comfortable in discussing birth control with another person.

**Directions:**

You are to describe a romantic scene in which the couple is discussing the possibility of using birth control. Your description should include the following parts.

**The Setting:**

Describe the place where the couple is having their conversation. Try to make it as vivid as possible so the reader can "see" the spot.

_____

_____

_____

**Characters:**

Describe, briefly, each of the partners. Include their names, ages, personal characteristics and interests.

Female: _____

_____

_____

Male: _____

_____

_____

**The Relationship:**

Tell how the couple met, how long they have known each other, and the present status of their relationship.

_____

_____

_____

_____

"Putting Birth Control into Romance" is reprinted, by permission, from Peggy Brick and Carolyn Cooperman, *Positive Images: A New Approach to Contraceptive Education* (2d ed.) (Planned Parenthood of Bergen County, 1987), 30–31.

**The Feelings:**

Tell how each partner feels about the possibility of getting and using birth control.

Female: _____

_____

_____

Male: _____

_____

_____

**The Dialogue:**

Write the verbal exchange between the partners in which they are discussing the possible use of birth control. There should be at least three quotations from each partner.

Here are some examples:

| | |
|---|---|
| **First Partner:** | I won't feel as much if I have a condom on. |
| **Second Partner:** | Well, you won't feel anything if you don't have a condom on. |
| **First Partner:** | It will interrupt sex. |
| **Second Partner:** | Let me put it on for you. You'll love it. |
| **First Partner:** | Condoms are a total turnoff. |
| **Second Partner:** | There's nothing great about getting pregnant either. Please give the condom a try or let's look for alternatives. |
| **First Partner:** | What alternatives do you suggest? |
| **Second Partner:** | Just petting and kissing. We could postpone sex, even though we both want it. |

Now make up your dialogue for the partners who are discussing the use of birth control.

**First Partner:** _____

_____

_____

**Second Partner:** _____

_____

_____

**First Partner:** _____

_____

_____

**Second Partner:** _____

_____

_____

**First Partner:** _____

_____

_____

**Second Partner:** _____

_____

_____

## SEXUALLY TRANSMITTED DISEASES (STDs)

Aside from birth control, the other important topic that belongs in a discussion of intimate relationships is sexually transmitted diseases (STDs). If you are involved in a relationship that includes sex, information on this subject is literally a matter of life and death. Of course AIDS is the disease on everyone's mind today, but other STDs can also result in severe illness, sterility, and even death if they are not treated.

### Acquired Immunodeficiency Disease Syndrome (AIDS)

AIDS involves a set of symptoms caused by the body's inability to fight infection. When your body's natural immune system is destroyed, you become susceptible to a host of diseases that are not troublesome to people with normally functioning immune systems. AIDS was first described in 1981, but the disease is contagious, and cases have now been reported in all 50 states of this country and in 125 countries around the world. The number of people affected continues to increase as the number of new cases doubles every six to twelve months. The Centers for Disease Control predict that 270,000 people in this country will have AIDS by the end of 1991.

There is no medical treatment available at this time that will cure the disease nor is there any vaccine that can protect you against contracting it. Although recent research indicates that the drug zidovudine (formerly known as AZT) may be effective in slowing the progress of the disease, AIDS is almost always fatal. Half of the 48,000 people who have been diagnosed as suffering from AIDS have died already, and the other half are expected to die within the next few years. Aside from those people who have actually been diagnosed as having AIDS, the Public Health Service estimates that 1.5 million people have been infected with the AIDS virus and are, therefore, capable of spreading the disease to others.[17]

Diagnosis of AIDS is made when a person contracts a disease that indicates that his or her body's natural defense system is not working. The two most-common diseases that are used in the diagnosis of AIDS are Kaposi's sarcoma, a rare form of cancer that results in purplish blotches and bumps on the skin, and *Pneumocystis carinii* pneumonia, a lung infection characterized by a persistent cough and fever with difficulties in breathing. Since these diseases are not usually found in people whose natural immune systems are working properly, they are indicative of the damaged defense systems found in AIDS patients.

AIDS seems to be caused by the T-lymphotropic human immunodeficiency virus: (HTLV). We now have accurate tests available, such as the enzyme linked immunosorbent assay (ELISA), which can detect antibodies to AIDS virus in the blood. These antibodies are almost always present when an individual has AIDS or one of the AIDS-related conditions. Current research indicates that 20 to 30 percent of the individuals who have been infected by the HTLV virus will develop AIDS and die. Among the other 70 to 80 percent are those who will develop AIDS-related complex (ARC) with symptoms ranging from mild to severe illness.

A certain percentage of the people who have the HTLV virus do not seem to develop any symptoms, but they are contagious and can transmit the disease to others. Even in those who do eventually develop symptoms of AIDS, nine years may pass between the time they are infected with the virus and the time the symptoms first appear. A person may, therefore, be contagious to others without even knowing that he or she has the disease. The Public Health Service estimates that the number of people in this country who are infected with the AIDS virus ranges between one and two million.[18]

Research shows that less than 1 percent of the general population is infected with the HTLV virus. AIDS does occur, however, in much higher percentages among certain groups of people. These high-risk groups include gay or bisexual men (25 percent), illegal drug users who inject their drugs intravenously (25 percent), individuals who require frequent blood donations (35 percent), partners (male and female) of people who are infected with AIDS, and babies born to women who have AIDS. The disease is much more widespread among men than women, among blacks and hispanics than other races, among people from ages twenty to forty-nine than other ages, and among city dwellers than rural residents.

### Transmission of AIDS

Researchers have determined how the virus is transmitted, and their findings explain why the groups listed in the paragraph above are at much higher risk of contracting the disease. The virus is spread through contact with bodily fluids such as blood, semen, fluids from the vagina or penis, urine, and feces. If such infected fluids come in contact with another person's body, the AIDS virus may gain entrance through a cut or a place where the skin is very thin and porous. The skin is thin around the mucus linings of the sex organs, the anus, the mouth, and the eyes. Contact between these parts of the body and the infected fluids from another person's body is likely to result in transmission of the virus.

AIDS is spread through sexual contact, but certain sexual practices, such as anal sex, are more likely to result in transmission since the virus can cross the thin mucus linings that are often damaged during this type of sex. The virus in the semen then has the opportunity to enter into the partner's blood system through the torn or damaged area. Oral sex is also risky because of the increased likelihood of contact between the damaged mucus linings in the mouth and throat and the infected body fluids.

These high risk behaviors are common among homosexual and bisexual men, and they explain why the incidence of AIDS is higher among these groups. Heterosexuals who participate in these types of sex, however, are also more likely to get AIDS if they have sex with a contagious partner. If you must engage in these high-risk sexual practices, use a condom to minimize the likelihood of contact between infected body fluids from your partner and your mucus membranes. Studies have shown that condoms, especially those treated with nonoxynol-9, are effective in decreasing the probability that you will contract the disease. Use synthetic (latex) condoms rather than natural (animal membrane) condoms.

The second-most-common way that AIDS is spread is through the sharing of infected needles between illegal drug users. The virus, present in the blood and on the needle of the infected user, is directly injected and transmitted into the blood of the partner. The common practice of sharing needles among intravenous drug users explains why AIDS occurs more frequently among this group of people. If you must use illegal drugs, do not share needles with other people.

If you travel in other countries, be alert to medical facilities that do not use disposable needles. Sharing needles with other patients is a high-risk practice because you cannot be sure that the other patient does not have AIDS or some other contagious disease. Medical facilities in this country use disposable needles so you need not fear infection if you donate blood or require injections for other medical reasons. If you come into contact with needles that have not been properly disposed of or blood vials that may be infected, handle them carefully. If you puncture your skin with the needle or broken glass, you may become infected with the AIDS virus.

The third way that AIDS is contracted is through infected blood products. This explains the higher incidence of AIDS among hemophiliacs, who require frequent donations of blood products, and among babies, born to infected women, who share blood systems with their mothers. We now use tests in this country to screen all blood products for the presence of the AIDS virus. The ELISA test is reasonably accurate for this purpose, and testing has reduced the number of people who contract AIDS because they require blood transfusions or the donation of blood products. If you are injured while traveling in a foreign country, be aware that careful screening of blood products is not practiced in many places. If you have AIDS and become pregnant, consult your doctor, as your baby will most likely be born with the disease.

AIDS cannot be spread through casual contact with people who are infected. Studies show that even family members who live in close contact with AIDS victims and share food, towels, cups, and other personal possessions do not become infected. It is also a myth that AIDS can be spread through contact with infected insects, cats, dogs, toilet seats, or swimming pools. Nor can you contract AIDS from donating blood in this country. Disposable needles are used, so it is not likely that you will come in contact with a needle that had been used for another donor. AIDS can only be spread through sex or contact between infected body fluids and an opening into your blood system. If you do not expose yourself to these things, you are not likely to be infected by the virus.

The most-certain way to avoid AIDS is to totally abstain from sex and to avoid contact with infected body fluids. However, if you have decided to go ahead with a sexual relationship, there are certain precautions you can take to lower the risk of contracting the disease. Figure 18 lists a number of precautions that you can take to lower your risk of contracting AIDS.

## Other STDs

### Herpes

Herpesvirus is a virus of the same sort that causes colds, mumps, measles, chicken pox, or the flu. Type I herpes causes cold sores around the mouth, while Type

1. *Know your partner's medical and sex history.* Do not have unprotected sex with someone who has been infected with the AIDS virus. Unfortunately, it is difficult to know whether a person has AIDS; many people do not even know when they have the disease. If, in the last nine years, your partner has had sex with anyone who was infected with the disease, your partner may be infected with the virus. Although AIDS seems to spread more easily from men to women, reports from Africa indicate that female prostitutes are spreading the disease among their male clients. You do not have to be gay or bisexual to get AIDS!

2. *Use a condom whenever you are having sex.* Unless you are absolutely certain that, in the past nine years, your partner has not slept with anyone who might have been exposed to AIDS, use a condom. Unfortunately, the virus is present in the body fluids that might be touched even before intercourse actually takes place. The virus could enter through a cut on your hand or in your mouth unless a condom is worn throughout the entire sexual interaction. Using condoms, especially those treated with nonoxynol-9, lowers the probability of contracting AIDS and also protects you against other STDs.

3. *Limit the number of people with whom you have sex.* The more people with whom you sleep, the more likely it is that you will be exposed to the virus. If you have sex with partners who come from the high-risk groups, such as homosexual or bisexual men, intravenous drug users, or persons who require regular blood donations, use a condom and avoid high-risk sexual practices.

4. *Avoid high-risk sexual practices like oral and anal sex.* Avoid high-risk sexual practices with both male and female partners. If you must engage in these practices, use a condom throughout your sexual encounter.

5. *Avoid contact with body fluids of people who might be infected.* Never share needles with anyone. Handle needles or body fluids of infected people with care. Do not allow these items to touch parts of your body where the virus might be able to enter your blood system.

6. *Do not have sex with anyone who has ever used illegal intravenous drugs.* People in this high-risk group are very likely to be carriers of the AIDS virus.

**FIGURE 18. PRECAUTIONS AGAINST AIDS.**

II is usually involved in the small, painful sores that develop on the sex organs. These sores may last from two to three weeks, and they may be accompanied by fever, swollen glands, and an overall itchy feeling. If you have active herpesvirus on your skin, there is a good chance that you will spread it to your partner when you have sex.

After the sores heal, the virus is in a dormant, or inactive, phase. You won't experience any uncomfortable symptoms and you won't be contagious to other people, but the virus is still in your system. Approximately one-third of the people who become infected with herpes will never experience another infection. For the other two-thirds, however, recurrent infections are likely sometime in the future. For some people, these repeated infections do not occur frequently, perhaps as rarely as once a year. For others, recurrent infections may appear every month or two. For some people, the recurrent infections are just as painful as the first one; for others, there is less pain or even no pain at all. We do not know why people have different reactions to the herpesvirus, nor do we know what triggers the repeated infections.

Herpes is contracted by contact with active herpesviruses. Thousands of these viruses are present in the sores. A person may experience an itching or tingling feeling before a sore appears on a certain area of the skin. Contagious virus is present on that part of the skin from the time the tingling or itching occurs until the sore has healed and disappeared. If you touch a sore, or liquid from a sore, to another part of your body where the skin is thin, such as your eye, your mouth, or your genital area, the herpesvirus will enter and another sore may appear. This is also likely to happen if you touch a sore and then touch a part of your body that has a cut or other opening into your blood system. You can spread herpes by touching one of your sores and then touching another part of your body or by touching the sore of another person to your own skin.

If you avoid touching the sores and don't allow anyone else to touch the sores, you can stop the spread of herpes. Obviously, it is not wise to have sex when active herpesvirus is on your skin. This will be true from the time you experience the first tingling or itching until the time the sore has completely healed and disappeared. Occasionally, small numbers of herpesvirus may also be present even though you have not experienced any symptoms. This may happen in the case of someone who doesn't even know that he or she has herpes. In order to prevent the spread of herpes, it is wise to always use a condom and nonoxynol-9 spermicide whenever you have sex.

Outbreaks of herpes should be treated by your physician. There is no cure at the present time that will prevent future infections of the herpesvirus.

### Chlamydia

Chlamydia is caused by a parasite that resembles bacteria, and it is currently the most-common sexually transmitted bacterial infection in this country. The parasite can infect the internal sex organs or the eyes. In many men and women, the infection results in itching and burning during urination, and it also results in pelvic inflammatory disease in women. These symptoms generally appear two to seven days after infection. In some cases, however, the infection is more problematic because the person experiences only mild symptoms or no symptoms at all after contracting the infection. The infected person does not realize that he or she requires treatment, nor does the person know that he or she is contagious to others. The disease can lead to blindness and to more serious urinary problems if it is not treated.

Diagnosis is made by a doctor who will prescribe antibiotics to cure the disease. Physicians are currently seeing many cases where an individual contracts both chlamydia and gonorrhea at the same time, so the medical examination should cover both diseases. You will not contract chlamydia, syphilis, or gonorrhea from toilet seats, swimming pools, or from casual contact with infected people. These diseases are only transmitted through contact with infected sexual organs.

### Gonorrhea

Gonorrhea is caused by bacteria (gonococcus or GC), and it can result in a discharge (pus) from the urinary tract, a frequent urge to urinate, a burning sensation during urination, an inflammation of the vagina and internal sex organs, and rash, fever, and sores in the mouth. Symptoms usually appear two to eight days after you have been infected. Gonorrhea is particularly dangerous when it does not cause any symptoms because the person does not know that he or she needs treatment, nor does the person realize that he or she can spread the disease to sex partners.

If gonorrhea is not treated, it will infect the internal sexual organs and can lead to sterility. It can also infect the liver and cause serious urinary problems so that the person is unable to urinate. Arthritis, infection of the heart valves, and widespread infection all through the body may also occur. If a pregnant woman has gonorrhea, her newborn infant will also contract it; this leads to blindness in the baby. The disease can be successfully treated by a course of antibiotics.

### Syphilis

Syphilis is caused by a type of microorganism called a Treponema pallidum. It may result in a chancre, or sore, on the skin of the sex organs or mouth. The sore is usually painless and appears two to six weeks after the infection. The sore disappears after a short time, but the organism is still active in the body. If the person is not treated, the disease may spread throughout the body, infecting many organs, specifically the eyes, the kidneys, and the bones, eight to nine weeks later. When the disease spreads through the body, the person may also experience a rash all over his or her body.

If the disease is not treated at this time, all symptoms will disappear as the organism becomes inactive for anywhere from two to forty years. During this time, the treponeme spreads through the blood and lymph glands to all parts of the body. When the symptoms appear again, they are very serious, resulting in severe damage to brain, heart, liver, kidney, and other vital organs. The person may, for example, develop a mental disorder; a certain percentage of people even die from the disease when it has reached this advanced stage. Syphilis can be diagnosed and successfully treated by antibiotics.

### Pediculosis Pubis

Pediculosis pubis (''crabs,'' or pubic lice) is a condition in which lice are spread from one sexual partner to another. (Fleas can also be transmitted in the same way.) The lice generally remain in the hair surrounding the sex organs, although they may travel up to the hair on the chest, the eyelashes, and the eyebrows. The lice multiply rapidly and feed on the person's blood, causing tremendous itching. The condition can be successfully treated with a physician's prescription for a medicated shampoo.

## Your Responsibilities

If you contract an STD, it is important that you get treatment for it. It is also important that you tell your sex partner about it so that he or she can get treatment; otherwise, your partner will infect you again and may also spread the disease to other sexual partners.

A number of courts have recognized a legal and moral obligation to inform a partner about a sexually transmitted disease. A court recently awarded $14 million to the lover of a famous actor because the lover was not informed that the actor had AIDS. For these reasons, it is important that you learn to feel comfortable while talking about this subject.

**EXERCISE: COMMUNICATING ABOUT STDs**

This exercise is designed to answer any questions that you may have about sexually transmitted diseases, to make you aware of where you can go to get answers to your questions, and to help you become more comfortable in talking about this important topic.

1. Take three index cards and write a question about STD (or any question about sex, if you do not have one about STDs) on each of the three cards. If you really cannot think of three questions about sex, just write that you have no questions; you must write something on the cards. Do not put your name on the cards; this part of the exercise is *anonymous.*

2. Hand the cards to your instructor. He or she will have the questions typed or written on new cards and will distribute them to the class at the next session so that each person receives between one and three questions to research. Take the cards to the health services office at your college, or call your physician or a family planning clinic and explain that you have a class assignment to find the answers to the questions on your cards. Ask the questions and any others that you may have. Then come back to class and report on your research.

**EXERCISE: COLLECTING INFORMATION FROM A FAMILY PLANNING CENTER**

This exercise is meant to familiarize you with the location and workings of a local family planning clinic; it is also meant to give you more practice in communicating about STDs.

Choose one of the following STDs for a research project. Visit a family planning clinic. (Planned Parenthood holds clinics on many college campuses, so you may not have to leave campus to complete this assignment.) Ask for a pamphlet about the disease. If the pamphlet does not present complete information or if the center has no pamphlet on the disease you have chosen, interview a counselor at the center to find information about the disease. Write down the name of the person you interview and the location of the center.

### Sexually Transmitted Diseases*

- Acquired immunodeficiency disease syndrome (AIDS)
- Acute urethral syndrome, or cystitis
- Cervical intraepithelial neoplasia
- Chancroid
- Chlamydia
- Cytomegalovirus infections
- Enteric infections
- Genital warts
- Gonorrhea
- Granuloma inguinale
- Hepatitis B
- Herpes genitalis
- Lymphogranuloma venereum
- Molluscum contagiosum
- Mucopurulent cervicitis
- Nongonococcal urethritis
- Pediculosis pubis
- Pelvic inflammatory disease
- Scabies
- Syphilis
- Vulvovaginitis
- Trichomoniasis
- Bacterial vaginosis
- Candidiasis

---

*Reproduced, with permission, from R. A. Hatcher et al., *Contraceptive Technology 1988–1989* (Atlanta, Ga.: Printed Matter, Inc., and NY: Irvington Publishers, Inc.) Fourteenth ed., 14.

Bring the pamphlet back to class and present a report to the class. If your instructor does not have enough class time to process this exercise, he or she may prefer that you hand it in as a written assignment. In that case, attach the pamphlet to your report.

## NOTES

1. E. F. Jones et al., "Teenage Pregnancy in Industrialized Countries," in *Contraceptive Technology 1988–1989,* 14th ed., R. A. Hatcher et al. (Atlanta: Printed Matter, Inc.; New York: Irvington Publishers, 1988), p. 51, fig. 3.3.

2. G. Corey, *I Never Knew I Had a Choice,* 2nd ed. (Monterey, Ca.: Brooks/Cole Publishing Co., 1986).

3. R. A. Hatcher et al., *Contraceptive Technology 1988–1989,* 14th ed. (Atlanta: Printed Matter, Inc.; New York: Irvington Publishers, 1988).

4. Ibid.

5. M. T. Erickson, *Behavior Disorders of Children and Adolescents* (Englewood Cliffs, N.J.: Prentice-Hall, 1987), p. 70.

6. R. A. Hatcher et al., *Contraceptive Technology 1988–1989,* 14th ed.

7. S. Greenhouse, "A New Pill, a Fierce Battle," *New York Times,* 12 February 1985, p. 23.

8. R. A. Hatcher et al., *Contraceptive Technology 1988–1989,* 14th ed.

9. Ibid.

10. Ibid.

11. Ibid.

12. Ibid.

13. Ibid.

14. Ibid.

15. Ibid.

16. Ibid., p. 337.

17. "Human Immunodeficiency Virus Infection in the United States: A Review of Current Knowledge," *Morbidity and Mortality Weekly Reports* 36, Suppl. No. S–6 (Center for Disease Control, 1987): 1–48.

18. Ibid.

# Chapter 13

## A Healthy Lifestyle

### HEALTHY BODY, HEALTHY MIND

Why is a chapter on health included in a text on succeeding in college? Because you can't survive, let alone succeed, unless your body is functioning well. Your mind cannot function effectively without a body to nurture and protect it. If you abuse your body or do not get adequate rest, proper nutrition, or sufficient exercise, your body will eventually break down on you. If you deny yourself those essentials, you compromise your immune system and fall prey to whatever diseases are lurking about. The same holds true if you abuse your body with excessive doses of stress or caffeine, nicotine, alcohol, or other drugs. Alcohol, cocaine, and other drugs may kill you faster, but any of the abuses listed above will eventually lead to serious breakdown. You can't study if your physical plant has shut down!

### GUIDELINES FOR GOOD NUTRITION

*Follow Generally Accepted Health Guidelines*

Fad diets come and go, as do nutrition "experts." There are, however, certain guidelines for a healthy diet that are generally accepted by most physicians. If you follow as many of these guidelines as possible, you will be rewarded by a mind and body that feel better, function better, and resist disease better.

*Reduce Salt, Sugar, and Fat in Your Diet*

Reduce the amount of salt, fat, and sugar in your diet. The typical American diet is one of the worst in the world. Our infatuation with meat, fried foods, and highly processed foods results in serious health problems. Leading causes of death in this country, such as heart disease, cancer, stroke, and diabetes, are all associated with our poor eating patterns. Excessive salt intake is strongly linked with high blood pressure, and foods that are high in saturated fat also increase your risk of heart attacks. Reduce cholesterol (which clogs your arteries and endangers your heart) wherever possible by switching to skimmed or partially skimmed dairy products, cutting back on the amount of meat you eat, and using margarine and vegetable oils instead of butter.

*Reduce Sugar*

Excessive consumption of sugar may be related to diabetes and mood swings such as those experienced during depression; the "empty" calories in sugar also discourage you from eating nutritious foods that your body needs. Increasing the percentage of calories in your diet that comes from complex car-

*Increase Complex
Carbohydrates*

bohydrates will automatically help you reduce fat and sugar levels. Complex carbohydrates are the ones you find in foods that are high in starch and fiber (whole-grain bread, rice, pasta, cereals, etc.) as opposed to the carbohydrates present in high-sugar foods like candy and soda. Complex carbohydrates enter the bloodstream more slowly, giving you longer-lasting energy. On the other hand, sugar will give you a sudden boost in energy followed by a sharp drop. Complex carbohydrates also prevent hunger longer. Try a toasted English muffin with jam for a snack instead of a doughnut or a candy bar.

*Read Labels*

Look at the nutrition labels of the foods you eat. You can often reduce the amount of sugar, salt, fat, and calories by choosing different brands of the same product. Many baked goods contain palm oil, coconut oil, or coconut butter, which are high in saturated fats and raise cholesterol levels. Choose products made with sesame, soy, or peanut oils instead. These unsaturated fats help to lower your cholesterol level. Processing makes a difference, too. For example, canned vegetables often contain a lot of salt. Frozen vegetables usually have no added salt.

*Substitute Foods
with Lower Calories
and More Nutrition*

At other times, you may wish to substitute a lower-calorie food or a healthier food for one you have been used to eating. For example, plain yogurt has fewer calories and less fat than sour cream, but tastes almost as good on a baked potato. One tablespoon of whipped butter has 30 calories less than a tablespoon of regular butter. Using low-fat yogurt flavored with fruit juice instead of whole milk yogurt flavored with fruit and syrup can lead to savings in both fat and calorie levels. The fat in margarine is unsaturated, so it is less harmful to your cholesterol count than the fat in butter. Remove the skin from chicken to cut both calories and fat. Try tuna packed in water instead of tuna packed in oil to reduce fat and save 30 calories. A blueberry muffin has 100 fewer calories and less sugar than a glazed doughnut. A baked apple has less fat and saves you 205 calories over a slice of apple pie.

## WEIGHT LOSS

Regulate the number of calories that you consume. The average female college student requires between 1700 and 2500 calories per day to maintain her weight. The comparable figure for the average male student is 2500 to 3300 calories per day. If you are trying to lose weight, do it gradually. Experts recommend that you lose no more than 1 to 2 pounds per week. More rapid weight loss can damage both your health and appearance; you are also more likely to gain the weight back quickly if you reduce too rapidly.

*Lose Weight Slowly*

One pound is equivalent to 3500 calories. If you reduce your daily calorie consumption by 500 calories a day, you will lose 1 pound a week (52 pounds in a year!). The pounds you lose slowly are the ones that are more likely to stay off. It is also true that losing weight too rapidly results in loss of muscle tissue (including heart muscle) as well as fat. Do not try to lose more than 1 to 2 pounds a week. Any weight loss program should incorporate extra water intake and, possibly, a multivitamin.

*Combine Diet with
Exercise*

Even better, combine a reduction in calories with an increase in exercise. Reduce your food intake by only 100 calories and burn only 100 extra calories a day through a small increase in activity level, and you will lose 1 pound every 2.5 weeks. That represents a loss of 4 pounds in just 10 weeks (almost 21 pounds in a year!) with virtually no deprivation or effort. A study at the Baylor College of Medicine showed that dieters who also exercised lost an average of 20 pounds in a year. Those who only dieted gained most of their weight back. If you combine a change in diet with an exercise program, you will lose weight faster, build up muscle tone for a more attractive appearance, and live longer.

*Do Not Cut Calories Too Much*

The minimum number of calories for a female diet is 1200. Do not go below that level unless you have consulted with a physician. Studies have shown that going below 1000 calories for a few weeks will slow down your metabolism by 10 to 30 percent so that you will burn calories more slowly. You'll be depriving yourself of food, but you won't be losing weight as fast, and much of the weight you lose will come from muscle, not from fat deposits. When you go back to your old eating habits, you will gain the weight back, and you may even gain more weight since your metabolism may remain in low gear. Instead of reducing your calories below 1000, add exercise to burn those extra calories. You'll feel and look better.

## Eating Disorders

*Do Not Lose Too Much Weight*

If you find yourself losing too much weight or weighing considerably less than the ideal weight for your height and frame, see a physician. You may have an illness that requires medical treatment. Aside from various parasites, muscular diseases, and hormonal imbalances that may cause unnatural weight loss, a psychological disorder called anorexia nervosa results in dangerously high levels of weight loss. Anorexia is an eating disorder in which young women try to lose weight, but lose control over their eating. They lose too much weight, upset the chemical balance in their bodies, and become dangerously undernourished. A percentage of anorectics even die from complications caused by the disorder.

Bulimia, an eating disorder that may be related to anorexia, also seems to be spreading among young women. Women who have this disorder go on eating binges, consuming huge quantities of high-calorie foods; they then attempt to control their weight gain by abusing laxatives or inducing vomiting. It is a dangerous disorder that may lead to serious medical problems. Bulimia can result in severe damage to the digestive system over a period of several years. It can also destroy the body's delicate electrolyte balance, leading to death in the short term. One survey estimates that one in every five college women is bulimic.

Bulimia, like anorexia, seems to strike most heavily at women in their teens and twenties. It is at least partially caused by our culture's obsession with the "thin is beautiful" syndrome. As a matter of fact, thin was not always beautiful, as can be seen in the pleasingly plump models of classic painters like Rubens or da Vinci. Thin did not become popular in our country until the 1920s, and even in the 1940s and 1950s, female movie stars had voluptuous figures rather than the type of thin frame popularized by Twiggy. In many European countries, in Africa, and in the Arabic world, a woman today must be "pleasingly plump" in order to be considered attractive.

Yet American women blindly embrace the "thinner is better" doctrine. Most dieters in this country are women, and most women are on perpetual diets. The preoccupation with thinness is beginning at earlier and earlier ages. One survey even found that one-half of a group of fourth graders were dieting! It seems that many women are trying to lose more weight than is medically recommended. The truth is that women's bodies are biologically meant to have some fat on them. This fat is necessary in order to insure regular menstrual cycles, normal pregnancy, and the ability to breast-feed. The following charts present ideal weights according to the statistics gathered by life insurance companies. The ideal weight is the one that will allow you to live the longest time. Calculate your ideal weight. Do not attempt to go below it, or you will face a frustrating, never-ending battle that you cannot win. In addition, you may damage your health.

| | Men | | Women | |
|---|---|---|---|---|
| Height in 1-inch Heels | Elbow Breadth | | Height in 1-inch Heels | Elbow Breadth |
| 5'2"–5'3" | 2 1/2"–2 7/8" | | 4'10"–4'11" | 2 1/4"–2 1/2" |
| 5'4"–5'7" | 2 5/8"–2 7/8" | | 5'0"–5'3" | 2 1/4"–2 1/2" |
| 5'8"–5'11" | 2 3/4"–3" | | 5'4"–5'7" | 2 3/8"–2 5/8" |
| 6'0"–6'3" | 2 3/4"–3 1/8" | | 5'8"–5'11" | 2 3/8"–2 5/8" |
| 6'4" | 2 7/8"–3 1/4" | | 6'0" | 2 1/2"–2 3/4" |

This table is reprinted from "How You Can Control Your Weight," 1983, courtesy of Metropolitan Life Insurance Company.

**FIGURE 19. STATISTICS FOR MEDIUM FRAMES**

**EXERCISE: DETERMINING YOUR IDEAL WEIGHT**

1. First determine whether you have a large, medium, or small frame. To approximate your frame size, extend your arm and bend the forearm upward at a 90-degree angle. Keep your fingers straight, and turn the inside of your wrist toward your body. If you have a caliper, use it to measure sideways the space between the two prominent bones on either side of your elbow. Without a caliper, place the thumb and index finger of your other hand on these two bones.

Measure the space between your fingers against a ruler or a tape measure. Compare it with the tables (shown in figure 19) that list elbow measurements for medium-framed men and women. If your measurements are lower than the ones listed, you have a small frame. If your measurements are higher, you have a large frame.

2. Now, to find your ideal weight, look up your height and your frame size in the chart that appears in figure 20. Ideal weights are presented for men

| | Men | | | | | Women | | | |
|---|---|---|---|---|---|---|---|---|---|
| Height Feet | Inches | Small Frame | Medium Frame | Large Frame | Height Feet | Inches | Small Frame | Medium Frame | Large Frame |
| 5 | 2 | 128–134 | 131–141 | 138–150 | 4 | 10 | 102–111 | 109–121 | 118–131 |
| 5 | 3 | 130–136 | 133–143 | 140–153 | 4 | 11 | 103–113 | 111–123 | 120–134 |
| 5 | 4 | 132–138 | 135–145 | 142–156 | 5 | 0 | 104–115 | 113–126 | 122–137 |
| 5 | 5 | 134–140 | 137–148 | 144–160 | 5 | 1 | 106–118 | 115–129 | 125–140 |
| 5 | 6 | 136–142 | 139–151 | 146–164 | 5 | 2 | 106–118 | 115–129 | 128–143 |
| 5 | 7 | 138–145 | 142–154 | 149–168 | 5 | 3 | 111–124 | 121–135 | 131–147 |
| 5 | 8 | 140–148 | 147–157 | 152–172 | 5 | 4 | 114–127 | 124–138 | 134–151 |
| 5 | 9 | 142–151 | 148–160 | 155–176 | 5 | 5 | 117–130 | 127–141 | 137–155 |
| 5 | 10 | 144–154 | 151–163 | 158–180 | 5 | 6 | 117–130 | 127–141 | 137–155 |
| 5 | 11 | 146–157 | 154–166 | 161–184 | 5 | 7 | 123–136 | 133–147 | 143–163 |
| 6 | 0 | 149–160 | 157–170 | 164–188 | 5 | 8 | 126–139 | 136–150 | 146–167 |
| 6 | 1 | 152–164 | 160–174 | 168–192 | 5 | 9 | 129–142 | 139–153 | 140–170 |
| 6 | 2 | 155–168 | 164–178 | 172–197 | 5 | 10 | 132–145 | 142–156 | 152–173 |
| 6 | 3 | 158–172 | 167–182 | 176–202 | 5 | 11 | 135–148 | 145–159 | 155–176 |
| 6 | 4 | 162–176 | 171–187 | 181–207 | 6 | 0 | 138–151 | 148–162 | 158–179 |

This table is reprinted from "How You Can Control Your Weight," 1983, courtesy of Metropolitan Life Insurance Company.

**FIGURE 20. CHART OF IDEAL WEIGHTS**

and women ages 25 through 59. The weights are given in pounds, assuming indoor clothing weighing 5 pounds for men and 3 pounds for women. Height measurement includes 1-inch heels.

*Beware of Malnutrition*
    Studies show that female adolescents are likely to be the most undernourished members of the American family, and many of them are actually suffering from malnutrition. Malnutrition seems impossible in a wealthy country where food is plentiful. It is due, however, to improper dieting and to the American love affair with easily available junk foods that contain few nutrients. If you do not get the vitamins, minerals, and protein that your body needs, you are endangering your health. You may also be endangering the health of your child. One-third of the women in this country between the ages of fifteen and twenty years experience at least one unwanted pregnancy.[1] This is the most undernourished group in our country, and we know that malnutrition in the mother before and during pregnancy is likely to result in birth defects in her baby.

*Eat Frequently*

*Eat Early in the Day*
    Regulate the number of meals you eat. Smaller, more-frequent meals work better. Your body is less likely to store calories as fat if you eat more frequently and engage in some activity before going to bed. Eat at least three meals a day, and don't skip breakfast! Breakfast should make up approximately 25 percent of your daily calories. People who skip breakfast actually end up eating more calories during the day than if they had eaten a meal in the morning. Try to eat your largest meals early in the day so that you have a chance to burn the calories. Avoid large dinners and late-night snacking.

## THE BALANCED DIET

*Eat a Balanced Diet*
Eat a balanced diet. The four basic food groups, summarized in figure 21, are still the best guide. If you cannot eat enough servings from the vegetable and fruit group, take a vitamin and mineral supplement. Try to obtain at least 60 percent of your calories from complex carbohydrates (starches, rather than sugars). Limit your fat intake to no more than 25 percent of your calories; no more than half of those fat calories should come from animal sources (eggs, meat, dairy products). Keep your consumption from the protein group to no more than 15 percent of your calories: dried beans, low-fat dairy products, and fish and chicken contain less fat than red meat, frankfurters, pork, or sausage. Lean meats, light meats (chicken breast instead of chicken legs), and meat without skin contain less fat and fewer calories.

    Make sure that you get enough calcium. If your body doesn't take in enough calcium from the foods you eat, it will draw the calcium out of your bones. This can result in a crippling disease called osteoporosis (weak and brittle bones) that afflicts many women as they grow older. Teenagers need 1200 milligrams of calcium a day; adults require 1000 milligrams. It is better to get your calcium naturally from milk and cheese products, but if this is not possible, take a calcium supplement.

*Eat Less Fat*
    The average American eats the equivalent of almost a whole stick of butter a day. That's almost 800 calories worth of fat, or 40 percent of the total day's calories, rather than the recommended 25 percent. When you eat fats, try to use unsaturated fats that come from vegetable products like oil or margarine rather than saturated fats that come from meat or meat products like butter or

*Use Unsaturated Fats*
cream. Use monosaturated oils like olive, soy, peanut, or sesame instead of coconut or palm oils that are saturated and raise cholesterol. Include skimmed dairy products that will give you the calcium you need without adding too much fat. It is the saturated fat in the American diet that is mainly responsible for the heart attacks that kill such a large number of people in this country each year.

---

**I. Meat (Up to six ounces a day)**

Meat, poultry, fish, shellfish, eggs

A serving consists of three-and-a-half ounces of cooked meat or fish. In order to lower cholesterol, choose fish, shellfish, and poultry over red meat. Trim fat and skin, and limit eggs to no more than two yolks a week.

**II. Dairy products (Two servings per day)**

Milk, cheese, ice cream, yogurt, sour cream

A serving consists of 8 ounces of milk, 4 ounces of cottage cheese, 1 ounce of other cheeses, one cup of ice cream, or 4 ounces of yogurt. Pregnant women and nursing mothers need three servings a day.

In order to lower cholesterol, choose skimmed or partially skimmed versions of the product. Whipped butter and cheeses contain fewer calories than the regular versions. Ice milk contains almost half the calories of rich ice cream.

**III. Breads and cereals (Six or more servings per day)**

Bread, cereal, pasta, rice, dried beans, and peas

A serving consists of one slice of bread, 6 ounces of ready-to-eat cereal, or one-half to three-quarters of a cup of pasta, rice, or cooked cereal.

This group contains the complex carbohydrates that you should favor over high-sugar foods for energy. Dried beans and peas contain a great deal of protein and no fat. They may be substituted for meats, particularly when combined with milk at the same meal.

**IV. Fruits and vegetables (Five to nine servings per day)**

Fruits, vegetables, fruit juices

A serving consists of a piece of fruit, one-half of a grapefruit, one-half cup of cooked vegetable, or 6 ounces of orange juice.

Choose at least one serving every day from the group that is high in Vitamin C (citrus fruits or berries), and one serving at least every other day from the group of deep green or yellow vegetables high in Vitamin A.

FIGURE 21. THE FOUR BASIC FOOD GROUPS

## Fast Food

*Cut Down on Fast Food Consumption*

Fast food chains can present a problem to a healthy diet in terms of adding too much salt, too much sugar, too much fat, and too many calories. Catsup, pickles, sauces, and other condiments are usually very high in salt content. Buns and catsup are often loaded with sugar. Fried foods and meats contain a great deal of fat, and it is easy to consume more than one-third of the daily calories you should be having at any one meal. If you know that you will be eating a fast food meal during the day, try to make your other meals that day lower in fat and salt.

Although it will be high in salt, calories, and saturated fats, a meal at McDonald's consisting of a Big Mac, fries, and shake is reasonably well balanced. It breaks down to 41 grams of fat, 40 grams of protein, and 143 grams of carbohydrates. That comes out to a distribution of 18 percent fat, 18 percent protein, and 62 percent carbohydrates, which is within the guidelines of the Public Health Service. A Whopper, fries, and shake at Burger King has a similar distribution, although it totals 1200 calories instead of the 1100 for the McDonald's meal. At 1200 calories, this meal is higher than the 625 to 950 calories that the average female college student should have at lunch or dinner, and a bit high even for the 950 to 1250 calories suggested for the average male.

Meals at many of the other fast food restaurants vary in calories and fat content. With 48 grams of fat, an extra-crispy dinner (two pieces of chicken, mashed potatoes, gravy, cole slaw, and roll) at Kentucky Fried Chicken will set you back a total 902 calories. Add 145 calories to that total if you are drinking a 12-ounce soda. The Fish & More platter (two pieces of battered fish, "fryes," cole slaw, and two hush puppies) at Long John Silver's is higher in calories and fat content at 976 calories with 58 grams of fat.

At Pizza Hut you can indulge in a 10-inch Supreme Thin 'N Crispy pizza, with sausage, pepperoni, mushrooms, and so on, for 1200 calories and 35 grams of fat. Or, you can share a 13-inch pie with a friend for only 800 calories. That pizza is reasonably well-balanced at 13 percent fat, 28 percent protein, and 59 percent carbohydrate. If you are willing to leave off the toppings except for cheese and tomato sauce, you can save 12 grams of fat, 600 milligrams of salt, and 120 calories on half of a 13-inch pie. Mexican fast food can be low in both calories and fat if you go easy on the sour cream, guacamole, and meat fillings.

## CUTTING BACK ON CAFFEINE

*Decrease Caffeine Consumption*

Improving your diet will help you lead a healthier life. There are, however, other substances you may consume that affect your health. Caffeine is one substance that is abused by many. Caffeine is found in coffee, cocoa, chocolate, tea, cola, and other soft drinks. There is evidence that people who drink more than five cups of coffee a day are at greater risk for heart attacks.[2] Caffeine has also been implicated in research on depression, peptic ulcers, ovarian cancer, insomnia, irritability, cardiac irregularities, migraine headaches, and persistent low-grade fevers. If you are experiencing anxious or depressed feelings, caffeine may make them worse. Avoid consuming it when you are feeling "down" or depressed.

## THE IMPORTANCE OF EXERCISE

Improvements in your exercise patterns can be as important as changes in your diet when it comes to leading a healthier lifestyle. Exercise can help you to lose weight and to maintain an ideal weight. It can energize you, and it can also curb your appetite. Exercise relieves stress; it can help you to relax and get a better night's sleep. There is also some evidence that it can help to control and counteract feelings of depression.

*Increase Activity*

Exercise improves your blood circulation and helps your heart, lungs, and other vital organs to work more efficiently. A strong heart does not have to beat as often, and it pumps more blood with each stroke. Exercise also seems to counteract some of the unhealthy effects of high cholesterol levels in your diet.

Studies show that people who exercise regularly live longer, and they are able to work and play more efficiently for longer periods of time. Finally, exercise tones your muscles and gives you a more attractive appearance regardless of your weight level.

*Perform Aerobic Activity*

Increase your activity level. Aerobic activity, which stimulates the heart and lungs, is most beneficial in reducing the risk of heart disease. Examples of aerobic activity include brisk walking, cycling, rope jumping, swimming, rowing, and jogging. Obviously increased activity also burns calories and tones muscles for a more attractive appearance.

Experts used to recommend that you engage in aerobic activity for at least a twenty-minute session, three times a week, in order to receive the above health benefits. More recent research indicates that twenty minutes of exercise three times a week is not enough to prolong your life. Many researchers now agree that a minimum of 2000 calories burned in exercise during the week is required to keep the heart in prime working order over the long term. The chart in figure 22 gives you some examples of the type and amount of exercise you need per week to become and to remain physically fit.[3]

It is not only the amount of time you spend exercising that counts, it is also the intensity or rate at which you exercise. For example, if you are going to walk, you must walk at a rate of at least 4.4 miles per hour in order to get cardiovascular benefits, and you must do that for 5 hours and 30 minutes each week. If you wish to walk 5 days a week, you can fulfill your duty to your heart by covering about 4.5 miles in an hour on each of those five days.

## EXERCISE: BURNING CALORIES THROUGH EXERCISE

To calculate the number of calories that will maintain your weight, multiply your weight by 15. If you want to lose weight, you will either have to eat less or burn more calories through exercise. It is better to lose weight by doing both: reduce calories and increase activity level. Remember that 3500 calories a week equals 1 pound. Figure 23 will give you an idea of how many calories are burned in various activities by a 150-pound person. If you weigh less than 150 pounds, you will burn fewer calories; if you weigh more than 150 pounds, you will burn more calories. For example, a person between the ages of 17 and 21 who weighs 125 pounds will use approximately 219 calories per hour while watching television. A person who weighs 180 pounds will use 249 calories.

| Activity | Amount of Time per Week | Number of Sessions per Week |
|---|---|---|
| Aerobic dancing | 3 hours, 20 minutes | 40 minutes/day × 5 days |
| Swimming | 3 hours | 30 minutes/day × 6 days |
| Tennis | 4 hours, 45 minutes | 57 minutes/day × 5 days |
| Walking | 5 hours, 30 minutes | 4.4 miles in 66 minutes × 5 days |
| Running | 3 hours | 3 miles in 30 minutes × 6 days |
| Cross-country Skiing | 3 hours | 30 minutes/day × 6 days |

FIGURE 22. AEROBIC EXERCISE THAT WILL BURN 2000 CALORIES PER WEEK

| Activity | Number of Calories Consumed per Minute |
|---|---|
| Skiing (cross-country, uphill) | 18.6 |
| Running (at 7.5 miles per hour) | 13.2 |
| Squash | 14.4 |
| Basketball | 9.4 |
| Skiing (cross-country) | 9.7 |
| Football | 8.67 |
| Swimming (at 2 miles per hour) | 8.1 |
| Tennis | 7.4 |
| Skiing (downhill) | 7.1 |
| Dancing ("twist") | 7.0 |
| Aerobic dancing | 6.6 |
| Bicycling (at 9.4 miles per hour) | 6.35 |
| Golf | 5.8 |
| Walking (at 3 miles per hour) | 3.8 |
| Volleyball | 3.4 |

FIGURE 23. CALORIES BURNED PER MINUTE BY A 150-POUND PERSON

If you know that a brownie is equal to 95 calories and you want to eat that brownie, you now know that you will have to burn 95 calories by running for seven minutes, swimming for 12 minutes, bicycling for 15 minutes, or walking for 25 minutes in order to keep your weight at the same level. Using the same calculations, you will realize that a can of beer will cost you 11 minutes of running, 19 minutes of swimming, 24 minutes of bicycling, or 39 minutes of walking. In addition to burning calories, *regular,* periodic exercise increases the metabolic rate, which helps the body burn fat faster. You can lose, gain, or maintain weight by adjusting your diet and your activity level.

The following exercise will help you to become more aware of your patterns of food, alcohol, caffeine, nicotine, and other drug consumption. It will also bring your exercise habits into sharper focus.

**EXERCISE: PROMOTING HEALTHY ACTIVITIES**

### Using the Health Activities Form

For at least three days, use the form given on pages 173 through 177 to record the type and amount of food you eat and the amount of alcohol, caffeine, tobacco, and drugs you consume. You might wish to make one of those days a Saturday or Sunday. In addition, record each instance of exercise in which you engage. Record these data on a continuous basis. If you wait to record until the end of the day, you will forget many of the items that you have consumed. When you have completed three days of recording, you should be able to tell where you need to make changes in order to live a healthier lifestyle. You may wish, for example, to cut down on the amount of junk food you eat or to increase the number of fruits and vegetables you eat. Most of us are not aware of what and how much we really eat until we keep a daily record. Compare your eating habits with the balanced diet recommended by the National Institute of Health on page 168.

Health Activities Form

Name _____

Day/Date _____

| Time | Food Type & Amount | Exercise Type & Amount | Alcohol Type & Amount | Caffeine Amount | Tobacco Amount | Drugs Type & Amount | Reasons, Circumstances & Feelings at that Time |
|------|--------------------|------------------------|-----------------------|-----------------|----------------|---------------------|-----------------------------------------------|
|      |                    |                        |                       |                 |                |                     |                                               |
|      |                    |                        |                       |                 |                |                     |                                               |
|      |                    |                        |                       |                 |                |                     |                                               |
|      |                    |                        |                       |                 |                |                     |                                               |
|      |                    |                        |                       |                 |                |                     |                                               |
|      |                    |                        |                       |                 |                |                     |                                               |
|      |                    |                        |                       |                 |                |                     |                                               |
|      |                    |                        |                       |                 |                |                     |                                               |
|      |                    |                        |                       |                 |                |                     |                                               |
|      |                    |                        |                       |                 |                |                     |                                               |
|      |                    |                        |                       |                 |                |                     |                                               |
|      |                    |                        |                       |                 |                |                     |                                               |
|      |                    |                        |                       |                 |                |                     |                                               |
|      |                    |                        |                       |                 |                |                     |                                               |
|      |                    |                        |                       |                 |                |                     |                                               |
|      |                    |                        |                       |                 |                |                     |                                               |
|      |                    |                        |                       |                 |                |                     |                                               |
|      |                    |                        |                       |                 |                |                     |                                               |

Health Activities Form

Name _____

Day/Date _____

| Time | Food Type & Amount | Exercise Type & Amount | Alcohol Type & Amount | Caffeine Amount | Tobacco Amount | Drugs Type & Amount | Reasons, Circumstances & Feelings at that Time |
|---|---|---|---|---|---|---|---|
| | | | | | | | |
| | | | | | | | |
| | | | | | | | |
| | | | | | | | |
| | | | | | | | |
| | | | | | | | |
| | | | | | | | |
| | | | | | | | |
| | | | | | | | |
| | | | | | | | |
| | | | | | | | |
| | | | | | | | |
| | | | | | | | |
| | | | | | | | |
| | | | | | | | |
| | | | | | | | |
| | | | | | | | |
| | | | | | | | |
| | | | | | | | |
| | | | | | | | |
| | | | | | | | |

Health Activities Form

Name _____

Day/Date _____

| Time | Food Type & Amount | Exercise Type & Amount | Alcohol Type & Amount | Caffeine Amount | Tobacco Amount | Drugs Type & Amount | Reasons, Circumstances & Feelings at that Time |
|------|------|------|------|------|------|------|------|
|  |  |  |  |  |  |  |  |
|  |  |  |  |  |  |  |  |
|  |  |  |  |  |  |  |  |
|  |  |  |  |  |  |  |  |
|  |  |  |  |  |  |  |  |
|  |  |  |  |  |  |  |  |
|  |  |  |  |  |  |  |  |
|  |  |  |  |  |  |  |  |
|  |  |  |  |  |  |  |  |
|  |  |  |  |  |  |  |  |
|  |  |  |  |  |  |  |  |
|  |  |  |  |  |  |  |  |
|  |  |  |  |  |  |  |  |
|  |  |  |  |  |  |  |  |
|  |  |  |  |  |  |  |  |
|  |  |  |  |  |  |  |  |
|  |  |  |  |  |  |  |  |
|  |  |  |  |  |  |  |  |
|  |  |  |  |  |  |  |  |

How do your exercise patterns compare with the recommendation of burning 2000 calories through aerobic exercise each week? You may feel that you should increase the amount of exercise in your life. Should you decrease the number of cups of coffee you drink each day? Take a particularly hard look at how you use cigarettes, alcohol, or other drugs. (Yes, alcohol is a drug, too). We will talk about these in more detail in the chapter on substance abuse, but you may want to make some changes at this time. The less you use these drugs, the healthier you will be.

The last column asks you to record the circumstances and feelings you experience during consumption. An analysis of this column should give you insight into the reasons that you consume certain foods or drugs. You may then be able to find more healthy ways of dealing with tension, boredom, anger, or other emotions than having a drink or eating a pizza.

## SIGNS OF MEDICAL EMERGENCIES

*These guidelines are offered only as general advice. You may need to see a doctor earlier or under different circumstances based on your own particular medical condition. If you are concerned about a symptom or have any questions, call your doctor or the health services nurse on campus.*

Colds and influenza ("flu") are the most-common health complaints on college campuses. Unfortunately, we are all familiar with the symptoms: sneezing, sore throat, runny nose, "stuffy" head, coughing, headaches, fever, and aches and pains all through the body.

There is no cure for the virus that causes colds or flu; you just have to ride out the symptoms. You can, however, decrease the probability of contracting the virus by getting enough sleep, eating a balanced diet, and avoiding hand to nose or eye contact. (Wash your hands frequently and do not touch your nose or eyes. That's how the viruses are spread.) If your body's immune system is working well because you are rested and well fed, your natural defenses will be more likely to fight off the virus. If you do get cold or flu symptoms, you can make yourself more comfortable by using decongestants to clear your nose and throat, sucking on hard candies, and taking aspirin or aspirin substitutes. (If you have a fever [any temperature higher than 98.6 degrees], use one of the aspirin substitutes to bring it down.)

- *If your fever goes higher than 103 degrees farenheit or if a low fever persists more than three days, consult a doctor.*

- *If you get a sore throat and swollen glands and experience headaches, chills, pain when you swallow, extreme fatigue, or a rash, see your doctor. You may have either mononucleosis or strep throat. Strep throat must be treated with antibiotics in order to avoid serious medical problems.*

What if you get stomach symptoms? If you are nauseous or vomiting, suck hard candies or ice chips for a few hours. Then try water, tea, or broth. You might try dry crackers and fruit juice the next day. If you experience diarrhea, try water, tea, or broth for a day, and then try dry crackers, toast, or plain rice. Avoid fruit juices and dairy products.

- *If your symptoms do not improve within forty-eight hours or if your stomach hurts continuously, call a doctor. If you suspect that you have food poisoning (from mayonnaise salads left out too long on a warm day, canned foods or leftovers that were not reheated, meat or stuffing that was not cooked long enough), call a doctor quickly.*

- *If a pain begins near your navel and then becomes worse in the lower-right section of your abdomen, call a doctor immediately. You may have appendicitis, which can be fatal if it is not treated quickly.*

- *If you regularly experience pain in the upper part of your stomach approximately one to three hours after eating, call a doctor. You may have an ulcer. Ulcers can be dangerous if they are not treated promptly.*

- *If you have a headache or a neck ache and a fever, call your doctor immediately.*

Bring your vaccinations up to date. You should have been vaccinated against polio, mumps, measles, rubella, diphtheria, tetanus, and whooping cough as a child. Tetanus should be updated every ten years throughout your adult life. If you contract measles as an adult, you can become seriously ill. If you contract rubella when you are pregnant, you will give birth to a seriously damaged baby.

- *If you were not vaccinated during childhood, get your shots now.*

- *If you find a sore that has not healed within two weeks.*
- *If you lose more than ten pounds of weight in ten weeks or less and you see no particular reason for the weight loss.*
- *If you have severe headaches that linger, and you do not know the reason for them.*
- *If you find a mole on your skin that bleeds or changes shape or color.*
- *If you cough or vomit up blood.*
- *If you vomit although you did not feel nauseous.*
- *If you are short of breath for no reason.*
- *If you faint or experience double vision for no reason.*
- *If you find that you are bleeding from your rectum or that your bowel movements are black and tarry.*
- *If you find it difficult to urinate or if you experience pain when you urinate.*
- *If your urine is cloudy, pink, or red.*
- *If you find a lump in your breast.*
- *If you experience bleeding from your vagina in between your menstrual periods.*
- *If you find a lump or a change in a testicle.*
- *If you feel pain or pressure in your chest and you do not know any reason for it.*
- *If you have a persistent cough.*
- *If you bruise or bleed easily.*

**FIGURE 24. SIGNS OF SERIOUS ILLNESS**

If you think that you may be pregnant, consult an obstetrician (a physician who specializes in pregnancy and birth) as soon as possible. Many diseases that might not even be noticed by an adult can result in serious damage to an unborn child. These diseases are particularly dangerous during the first three months of pregnancy. You should be tested and treated for them or you may give birth to a damaged infant. You should also learn how to change your diet and take care of yourself so that you will enjoy a healthy pregnancy and give birth to a healthy baby.

- *See a doctor as soon as possible if you think that you are pregnant.*

The symptoms listed in figure 24 are reasons to see a doctor as soon as possible. They may be signs of an illness that can be treated in order to prevent more serious illness or death. Depending on your own particular medical condition, you may need to see a doctor earlier or under different circumstances. If you are concerned about a symptom or have a question, call your doctor or the health services nurse on campus.

## NOTES

1. M. T. Erickson, *Behavior Disorders of Children and Adolescents* (Englewood Cliffs, N.J.: Prentice-Hall, 1987), p. 70.

2. A. Z. LaCroix et al., "Coffee Consumption and the Incidence of Coronary Heart Disease," *New England Journal of Medicine 315* (1986): 977–982.

3. W. Stockton, "Just How Far, How Fast, for Fitness?" *New York Times,* 16 November 1987, p. C11.

# Chapter 14

## Substance Abuse

### A PRICE FOR THE INSTANT CURE

You have undoubtedly heard that we live in a "drug happy" society. Whatever your complaint, physical or psychological, someone is likely to offer you a solution that involves drugs. Are you tense, tired, depressed, or upset? There's a pill that will help you. Do you have a cold, a headache, a skin rash? Your friendly pill pusher will find a cure. Would you like to have fun, lose weight, or deliver a better speech? Modern pharmacology can fix you up with an instant "cure." Some of these drugs are legal; others are illegal. Some have short-term effects; others cause permanent damage. Some are highly addictive, others may be used with less fear of developing a dependence. Experimenting with drugs can be dangerous. You will have to pay a price in the end, no matter which ones you try.

For some students, that price is the cost of their college educations. You may be forced to withdraw from college when drugs lead you into behaviors that violate campus disciplinary codes or when drugs interfere with your ability to study and keep up your grades. Drugs can become a particular problem during the freshman year when you may be experiencing freedom from your parents' supervision for the first time. If you misuse that freedom and abuse drugs, you will find yourself expelled from college in a very short time.

### COPING WITH ALCOHOL

You may be surprised to see alcohol discussed in a section on drugs. Alcohol is classified as a drug because its main ingredient, ethanol, depresses the central nervous system just as sleeping pills do. At high enough doses it can act as an anaesthetic, numbing your sensations. Like other drugs, alcohol produces a tolerance in the user so that larger and larger doses become necessary to achieve the desired effects. It acts as a toxin, or poisonous substance, to almost all organs: brain, heart, lungs, liver, bone marrow, gut, ovaries, and testicles.

The use of alcohol in this country seems to be starting at a younger age. Studies show that many teenage boys now begin using it by the time they reach 16 years old. Earlier studies had shown that 18 was the more common age to begin drinking. A recent survey reveals that by the time boys reach the age of 18, 20 percent of them drink at least once a week and consume large quantities of alcohol on each occasion. (The comparable figure for girls is 6 percent).

**EXERCISE: TESTING YOUR ALCOHOL IQ**

Take the quiz in the following exercise and see how you score in your knowledge about drinking. You can find the answers to the questions in this chapter. Answer the ones you do not know as you read the text. You may check your responses with the answer key at the end of the chapter.

_____ 1. Which has the most alcohol?
    a. 12 ounces of beer
    b. 5½ ounces of wine
    c. 1½ ounces of liquor
    d. they all have the same amount of alcohol

_____ 2. If you want to slow down the effect that alcohol is having on you
    a. eat something before you drink.
    b. eat while you are drinking.
    c. drink more slowly.
    d. all of the above.

_____ 3. When you have had too much to drink, how do you sober up?
    a. Stop drinking and eat something.
    b. Drink a few cups of coffee.
    c. Take a cold shower.
    d. Wait 45 minutes before you have another drink.

_____ 4. If you do not want to get drunk, you should
    a. drink beer.
    b. drink wine.
    c. switch from liquor to beer.
    d. drink a nonalcoholic beverage.

_____ 5. True or False? Alcohol is an aphrodisiac. (An aphrodisiac makes sex better).

_____ 6. True or False? People can tell when they are too drunk to drive.

_____ 7. True or False? Alcohol is a depressant.

_____ 8. True or False? Alcohol is a stimulant.

_____ 9. True or False? Some people cannot metabolize alcohol. It makes them sick even if they drink only a small amount.

_____ 10. If a woman drinks while she is pregnant, her baby
    a. may be born smaller and will not grow as much or as fast.
    b. may have certain deformities of the face or limbs.
    c. may have minimal brain dysfunction.
    d. may have all of the above.

_____ 11. Most states define the level of intoxication for legal purposes at a blood alcohol concentration of
   a. .03
   b. .06
   c. .10
   d. .50
   What is the legal level of intoxication set by your state?

_____ 12. At what blood alcohol concentration level are you likely to lose consciousness?
   a. .03
   b. .06
   c. .10
   d. .50

_____ 13. How many drinks does it take for the average person to reach the level of intoxication as it is defined by the legal system?
   a. 1 to 2
   b. 2 to 3
   c. 3 to 4
   d. 4 to 5

_____ 14. If one of your parents has a drinking problem
   a. you are more likely to develop a drinking problem than the average person.
   b. you are less likely to develop a drinking problem than the average person.
   c. you have the same probability as the average person of developing a drinking problem.
   d. your parents' drinking problem has no bearing on how likely it is that you will develop a problem.

_____ 15. True or False? Alcohol is not addictive.

_____ 16. True or False? Alcohol is the leading factor in deaths of youths ages 15 through 24.

## THE CONSEQUENCES OF ABUSING ALCOHOL

Some estimates claim that one of every four teenagers is a problem drinker and uses alcohol as a means to cope with other problems.[1] Alcohol is the leading factor in deaths among young people ages 15 through 20 because it leads to fatal accidents.[2] Although alcohol is a legal drug in this country, the statistics associated with its use are harrowing. Figure 25 lists some of these statistics.

## REASONS FOR DRINKING

The reasons that many people drink are well known: to release inhibitions and feel more relaxed, to escape from problems, or to comply with peer pressures. When drinking is used to escape from problems, alcohol can set a real trap, especially for young people who still have many of life's skills to learn. Drinking does not result in a solution to a problem, just a temporary escape from it. Once the alcohol wears off, the problem is still there or it will return in the future.

- One American dies every 20 minutes from drinking too much. At least 26,000 Americans are killed every year by drunken drivers (Van Gelder, 1987).

- Of all the people killed in alcohol-related driving accidents, 60 percent are in their teens (Ellis, 1985).

- Drinking and driving continues to be the number one killer of young people ages 15 through 20. More than 40 percent of all deaths in this age group result from automobile crashes (MADD, 1988).

- A total of 2,910 young passengers ages 15 through 20 were killed in motor vehicle accidents in a recent year (MADD, 1988).

- More than 18 million Americans are "heavy drinkers"; They consume at least 14 drinks per week (National Institute on Alcohol Abuse & Alcoholism, 1987).

- Of the 18 million heavy users, more than 10 million are alcoholics. They are addicted to alcohol and experience problems in living and health associated with its use (National Institute on Alcohol Abuse & Alcoholism, 1987).

- Four-and-one-half percent of college students surveyed recently report that they have used alcohol on a *daily* basis during the past 30 days (National Institute on Drug Abuse, 1987).

- Forty-five percent of college students report that they have had *more than five drinks in a row* on at least one occasion during the past two weeks (National Institute on Drug Abuse, 1987).

- Ten percent of youths over 15 years of age drink more than 1 ounce of alcohol each day (U.S. Department of Commerce, Bureau of the Census, 1987).

- Violent crime is heavily correlated with alcohol: with 50 percent of homicides, 58 percent of suicides, 40 percent of assaults, 35 percent of rapes, 55 percent of domestic assaults, and 60 percent of assaults on children are associated with alcohol (Kinnoy & Leaton, 1982; Ellis, 1985).

- An alcoholic's life expectancy is shortened by 10 to 15 years (DeLuca, 1981; Van Gelder, 1987).

- Cirrhosis, a disease of the liver heavily associated with alcohol abuse, is the sixth leading cause of death in the United States (Gold, 1986).

- Recent studies report that even very moderate levels of alcohol consumption are associated with 50 percent to 100 percent increases in risk for breast cancer (Schatzkin et al., 1988; Willett et al., 1987).

- Close to 16 billion dollars has been spent yearly for medical treatment and support services associated with alcohol (U.S. Department of Health and Human Services, 1981).

- Approximately half of all the beds occupied in American hospitals are filled by people with problems related to alcohol consumption (U.S. Department of Health and Human Services, 1981).

**FIGURE 25. STATISTICS OF ALCOHOL ABUSE**

Since the person has not learned to cope with the problem while drinking, the only way out is to start another round of drinking when the alcohol wears off or when the problem reappears.

This can lead to a vicious cycle of addiction from which you may not be able to escape. In the meantime, you do not learn any of the social or academic skills that would allow you to solve your problem. This is, perhaps, one of the most damaging aspects of any drug addiction. The "easy way" out leads only to addiction; it does not lead to learning the skills that can help you to cope effectively with life's challenges. In particular, it is likely to ruin your college career because you will not be able to meet the academic or social challenges presented on campus.

When alcohol is used because of pressure from your friends, it can also result in problems, though they are not as severe as the ones described in the paragraph above. The danger here is that the relationships with these people may become based solely on alcohol. You may not truly become close to these people, and you may not really get to know and like them. You also may not learn any social skills about how to make friends, give support, or share feelings. In some cases, the only basis for the friendship is drinking, and that will not result in a true friendship.

The use of alcohol to release inhibitions and to help you enjoy a social event is a more adaptive reason to drink. If it is used in moderation, alcohol can help you to relax and enjoy the company of others. It can enhance the taste of food, the sound of music, and the pleasure of a social event. Just be sure that you can recognize the difference between using alcohol to make a social event more pleasant and going to a social event just so you can abuse alcohol. If you are involved in the second scenario, you are probably using alcohol to escape from some type of problem. Whatever your reasons for using alcohol, given the unsettling statistics presented above, it is in your interests either to abstain from drinking or to learn to drink responsibly.

## PROBLEM DRINKING

Drinking responsibly means making sure that alcohol does not create problems for you. If you begin partying during the week and missing classes or failing exams, then you may be sacrificing your college education and future career for a few hours worth of pleasure. If you find that you are beginning to experience hangovers, blackouts, or trembling hands, you may be giving up your health in exchange for false feelings of security and acceptance. If you are getting into trouble with the law or driving while intoxicated, you may literally be giving up your life for only a few hours of escape from feelings of anxiety or boredom.

Force yourself to think about the choices you are making each time you decide to go out and drink for an evening. Make sure that the price you pay for that outing is worth the cost. Try to limit your partying to Friday and Saturday nights. A party is not much fun, after all, if you will be constantly worrying about the exam for which you should be studying. A problem drinker is someone who continues to drink even though the drinking causes problems for him or her. Be sure that you are not creating problems for yourself when you decide to go out and drink. Do not drink and drive.

### Alcoholism in Families

Research shows that certain people are more likely to become problem drinkers than others. Swedish studies of adopted children show that, on the average, children of alcoholics are four times more likely than other people to become alcoholic. This is true even if the children are adopted by nonalcoholics at a young age. Researchers have known for years that alcoholism runs in families, but these studies lend support to the theory that a tendency towards alcoholism may be inherited.

Data from the Alcohol Research Center at Washington University[3] are typical of the strong family patterns found among alcoholics:

- 38 percent of the problem drinkers had alcoholic fathers
- 21 percent of the problem drinkers had alcoholic mothers
- 57 percent of the problem drinkers had alcoholic brothers
- 15 percent of the problem drinkers had alcoholic sisters
- 32 percent of the problem drinkers had alcoholic sons
- 19 percent of the problem drinkers had alcoholic daughters

Dr. Reich estimated that, by the age of 40, more than one-half of the men and women who have one alcoholic parent will have developed a drinking disorder. For those who have two alcoholic parents, he estimates that 60 percent will become alcoholic. By comparison, national statistics show that only 3 percent of the women and 8 to 10 percent of the men in the general population will become alcoholic. Children of alcoholic parents are at much greater risk for developing a drinking problem. Studies at the University of Kansas Medical Center showed that grandchildren of alcoholics are also at greater risk than the general population, even if their parents do not drink much.

Researchers think that the enzyme that breaks down a poisonous by-product of alcohol, acetaldehyde, may explain why some people become more easily addicted to alcohol than others. If you do not have this enzyme, the buildup of acetaldehyde after drinking even small amounts of alcohol can give you a headache and make you feel nauseous, dizzy, and uncomfortably flushed. Naturally, people who feel uncomfortable when they drink are less likely to drink much. Asian people are particularly likely to be deficient in this enzyme, and, indeed, the rates of alcoholism among Asiatics are relatively lower than for other races. Women and Jews are also more likely than Gentile men to have this deficiency. The lower rates of alcoholism among women and Jews also lends support to this theory.

A survey by the New York State Division of Alcoholism and Alcohol Abuse indicated that people who knew that they were at risk for alcoholism tried to cut down the amount they drank. Only 5 percent of the adult children of alcoholics realized that they were more likely to become alcoholic than the children of nonalcoholics, and they tried to limit their drinking. The adult children of alcoholics who did not realize that they were at greater risk drank three times as much and seven times as often as did the children who were aware of their higher risk status. Figure 26 gives a prescription for sane drinking.

- If you are male and your father was (or is) an alcoholic, don't drink at all. The risk that you will become alcoholic is very high.
- If you are male or female, and have a father, mother, or grandparent who was alcoholic, try to control your drinking.
- Do not drink when you are alone.
- Do not drink when you are upset or depressed.
- Limit your drinking to two drinks (or less) per occasion.
- If you find that your drinking is beginning to get out of control (you suffer from blackouts, you have five or more drinks on one occasion, you drink in order to get drunk), see a counselor or therapist as soon as possible. You have a problem. Do something about it!

FIGURE 26. A PRESCRIPTION FOR SANE DRINKING

**EXERCISE:**
**WARNING SIGNS**
**OF A DRINKING**
**PROBLEM**

Place a check next to any of the statements that apply to you.

_____  1. Getting into fights because of alcohol.

_____  2. Doing things when you are drunk that you regret when you become sober.

_____  3. Drinking when you have no particular reason to drink.

_____  4. Experiencing hangovers that result in missed classes, missed appointments, or missed days at work.

_____  5. Getting into accidents and hurting yourself or others while you are drinking.

_____  6. Building up a tolerance. Finding that you need more and more alcohol to get the relief or good feelings that smaller quantities used to give you.

_____  7. Experiencing blackouts. Finding that you can't remember what you did while you were drinking even though you were awake and conscious at the time.

_____  8. Finding that you are beginning to lie about your drinking or about what you are or should be doing.

_____  9. Becoming dependent on alcohol. Finding that you cannot function without it. Stockpiling and hiding alcohol so that you will never run out when you need it.

_____  10. Getting into trouble with the police or the courts because of your drinking.

_____  11. Suffering from withdrawal symptoms such as shaking hands, racing pulse, faster breathing, hallucinations, or anxiety when you have not had a drink in a while.

_____  12. Receiving warnings from your doctor about damage to your liver, heart and arteries, stomach (ulcers, gastritis), and brain (loss of memory, confusion, and permanent damage to your coordination and your vision).

_____  13. Trying to "go on the wagon."

_____  14. Taking a few drinks before you go out with friends or go to a party where alcohol will be served.

_____  15. Drinking when you are alone.

_____  16. Worrying about your drinking.

_____  17. Having your friends (or family) tell you that they are worried about your drinking.

_____  18. Drinking because you are depressed, worried, or upset.

_____  19. Going out in order to get smashed or wasted.

_____  20. Trying to control your drinking by switching brands, drinking only during certain times of the day, or sticking to only one type of drink.

If you find yourself checking off four or more of these items, talk to a counselor at your college counseling center. It is much easier to deal with a drinking problem in the early stages before it becomes serious. The counselor will be able to tell you whether or not you are developing a problem and will help you explore ways to get around your dependency. If you prefer to get help from a group rather than from an individual counselor, look up a chapter of Alcoholics Anonymous (AA), Bacchus, Al-Anon, Adult Children of Alcoholic Parents (ACOA), or any other organization on your campus that deals with alcohol problems. Most of these organizations are also listed in the local telephone directory.

## Your Body and Alcohol

The extent to which alcohol will affect you depends on many variables; the variables that make the most difference are your weight, how many drinks you have had, how fast you are drinking, and how much food is in your stomach. All of these variables affect the rate at which alcohol is absorbed into your bloodstream. The concentration of alcohol in your blood determines the extent to which alcohol impairs your ability to function.

Figure 27 outlines the effects of alcohol on your body at different blood alcohol concentration levels. At a blood alcohol concentration of .06, most people are experiencing the warm, relaxing feelings associated with alcohol. Only a small amount of alcohol is necessary to experience these feelings. If you continue drinking, you will find that your coordination and judgment become markedly impaired by the time you reach the .10 blood alcohol concentration level.

Most states define the legal level of intoxication at the .10 concentration. This is the point at which coordination is sufficiently impaired to make driving

| Effect | Blood-Alcohol Concentration | Number of Drinks |
|---|---|---|
| Warm, relaxed feelings | .06 | 2 drinks, each containing 1 1/2 ounces of alcohol<br>2 glasses wine (11 ounces)<br>2 cans beer (24 ounces) |
| Legal intoxication | greater than .09 | more than 3 mixed drinks<br>3 glasses wine (16 1/2 ounces)<br>3 cans beer (36 ounces) |
| Unconsciousness | .50 | 17 mixed drinks<br>17 glasses wine (93 1/2 ounces)<br>17 cans beer (264 ounces) |
| Death | greater than .55 | more than 18 mixed drinks<br>26 glasses wine (98 1/2 ounces)<br>24 cans beer (204 ounces) |

FIGURE 27. EFFECTS OF ALCOHOL ON YOUR BODY

dangerous. You are seven times more likely to have an accident when you have raised the alcohol concentration level in your blood to this .10 concentration level. Unconsciousness sets in somewhere between the .40 and .50 concentrations. Your body may become unconscious in order to keep you from drinking any more because drinking more is likely to result in death at higher concentrations.[4,5] These figures will vary according to the amount of food in your stomach, how much you weigh, and how fast you are drinking. It is wise to know your limitations. *It is even wiser not to drink and drive.*

Alcohol enters your blood directly through the walls of your stomach. It quickly reaches your brain, where it depresses the higher centers of your brain, resulting in a less-critical, less-inhibited attitude about your behavior. This is the reason that many people think alcohol is a stimulant. Actually, it is a depressant. You may be more talkative and outgoing because you are more relaxed and less concerned about what you are saying, not because the alcohol stimulates you to talk more.

In order to maintain this pleasant, relaxed state, you need only one drink per hour (one beer, one mixed drink, or one 5-ounce glass of wine). Your body can only metabolize one drink per hour. As long as the alcohol is active in your system, those relaxed feelings will remain with you. If you drink more than one drink per hour, you will begin raising your blood-alcohol concentration, hampering your judgment and coordination, and moving toward the levels associated with hangovers, blackouts, and unconsciousness.

### The Physiology of Alcohol

If you drink more than one drink per hour, your body cannot dispose of the poisons associated with the alcohol until you slow down your drinking rate. Some of the unpleasant side effects of alcohol are due to the effects that these poisons are having on your system. Other side effects result from your body's attempt to avoid death from an alcohol overdose. The large number of people in crisis that are brought into hospital emergency rooms because of alcohol-related problems proves that the body's defenses will not always be successful.

It is not uncommon, for example, for a person to lose consciousness from drinking too much. This frequently happens at the same time that the brain's function in regulating breathing has been depressed by the alcohol. The person may stop breathing for long periods and then be jolted into a deep breath when the lack of oxygen reaches critical levels. If the person takes this deep breath at the same time that his or her stomach is trying to get rid of the irritating effects of the alcohol by throwing up, this person may choke and die of suffocation.

Aside from helping you to feel relaxed, alcohol also increases your heart rate, changes your ability to see (blurs your vision), impairs your coordination, slows your reaction time, and reduces your judgment. It is these effects of alcohol that get you into trouble when you drive. Without your usual sense of judgment, you may take that turn too quickly to hold the car on the road. Because of slower reaction time, you may not swerve out of the way of an oncoming auto in time. Due to blurred vision and impaired depth perception, you may not turn enough to avoid that pedestrian. With poorer coordination, you may not be able to handle the turn signal and the brake at the same time, and you may end up crashing into a wall. After two to three drinks, with a blood alcohol concentration level of .10 (the legal level of intoxication in most states), you are seven times more likely to have an accident.

If you are stopped for driving while intoxicated (DWI), you may be fined or jailed. You may lose your license. Your insurance rates will go up anywhere from three to five times. You may kill or injure yourself, your friends, or other innocent drivers or pedestrians. Aside from lifelong disability, you may leave yourself with a lifetime of guilt about the other lives you have destroyed. *If you drink, don't drive.* Call a cab, call a friend, sleep over where you are, or take turns, with your friends, being the chauffeur who does not drink. If friends or family tell you that you are too intoxicated to drive, do not drive until your body has had the chance to rid itself of the alcohol. Remember that alcohol is the leading cause of death among young people ages 15 through 24.

If you abuse alcohol, you are likely to become addicted. Your body will build a tolerance for alcohol. This means that you will begin to need larger and larger quantities of alcohol to feel good after drinking. Your body will also become dependent on the drug. It will no longer be able to function normally without alcohol. When the alcohol level in your blood drops, your body will go into withdrawal, raising your blood pressure, your pulse, your temperature and your rate of breathing. You will begin to feel uncomfortable. Within the first 24 to 36 hours you will most likely experience seizures and convulsions. You may have hallucinations or memory loss, which can become permanent.

Within three to five days, major withdrawal, or delirium tremens (DTs), will set in. You will need medical help at this point. Aside from continued increases in your vital signs (blood pressure, temperature, pulse, and breathing), your brain will stop functioning properly and you will literally lose your mind. You will become confused and disoriented; you will lose your memory for past events; and you will begin ranting and raving (pink elephants, anyone?) If you do not receive medical treatment during this stage, you may die.

Some of the psychotic (ranting, raving, and hallucinating) symptoms described above are caused by a thiamine (Vitamin B-1) deficiency that is so common among alcoholics. Problem drinkers generally suffer from malnutrition. If you have a drinking problem, at least take a vitamin supplement. If liquor manufacturers were willing to add thiamine to alcohol, heavy drinkers could avoid some of those problems. These symptoms can be reversed when a physician administers thiamine, but there is nothing a doctor can do about other permanent damage to the liver, heart, brain, and stomach. This damage, along with the high incidence of accidents and suicides among alcoholics, are responsible for their steep death rates.

## COCAINE

Cocaine is known by a number of names on the street: coke, crack, snow, happy dust, toot, *C,* nose candy, and so on. Whatever the name, many health professionals are concerned that we are facing an epidemic that could destroy our society. Figure 28 presents a casual glance at some of the statistics (along with source citations) associated with cocaine.

Statistics like these illustrate the stranglehold that cocaine exerts on people who experiment with it. Students who try it for the first time often get into serious trouble because of the damage the drug can cause to their bodies or to their ability to study. Cocaine provides a very effective avenue for short-circuiting a college career.

Daily reports of murders, robberies, and assaults associated with cocaine's use have forced Americans to realize that we have a crisis on our hands. The long-term threat to our society is emphasized by events in South America where widespread corruption and terror caused by the drug's traffickers has reached into the highest levels of the government and the legal enforcement system. A

- Researchers report that more than 30 million Americans have tried cocaine, and that 5 million use it regularly (Abelson and Miller, 1985).

- Each day 5000 Americans try cocaine for the first time (Abelson and Miller, 1985).

- A household survey indicates that close to 6 million Americans have used cocaine within the past month and that almost 0.5 million of these current users are adolescents between the ages of 12 and 17 years (National Institute on Drug Abuse, 1987).

- New York State's Division of Substance Abuse reports that the largest number of new users is in the 18- to 24-year-old category.

- Cocaine-related admissions to emergency rooms all across the country have spiraled: a 121-percent increase in the New York metropolitan area, a 180-fold increase in New Orleans and a 20-fold increase in Oklahoma City, to give just a few examples (Gold, 1985).

- Rats trained to press a bar to get a drug will press it 10,000 times to obtain cocaine, compared to only 4,000 times to obtain heroin, and 250 times to obtain caffeine (Johanson et al., 1976).

- One million Americans report that they are so dependent on cocaine that they cannot stop using it even though it is destroying their lives and those of their loved ones (Gold, 1985).

**FIGURE 28. FACTS ABOUT COCAINE**

look at cocaine's history and effects may help you understand the reasons for the epidemic we face.

Cocaine is a natural stimulant that occurs in the coca plant, *erythroxylum coca,* which has existed on this planet longer than people. It grows wild in South America, but careful cultivation has resulted in successful crops in Europe, Asia, and the United States.

Native peoples in South America have chewed coca leaves for several thousand years. They believe that this practice gives them a number of benefits: increased energy, decreased appetite, greater tolerance for the effects of altitude, better digestion, and elevated mood. The Spanish Conquistadores used coca to pay their workers in the mines because they found that the drug increased the amount of work they could get out of the laborers and decreased the amount of food they needed to feed them.

Of the fourteen alkaloids present in coca leaves, it is only cocaine that became of major interest to Europeans in the nineteenth century. Europeans in the mid nineteenth century praised cocaine for its medicinal and recreational properties. It was included as an ingredient in a number of popular elixirs. Coca Cola and other colas are still made with coca leaves, although cocaine has now been removed from the product. Since the amount of cocaine contained in these drinks was small, overdoses and other medical complications did not constitute a major problem.

Cocaine became widely used as a local anaesthetic, and it was praised by medical communities on both sides of the Atlantic as a cure for everything from seasickness to head colds. We know now that cocaine is not effective as a treatment for any of these disorders, and other drugs have replaced it as an anaesthetic. By the beginning of the twentieth century, the medical community's love affair with the drug had ended, based on disastrous case reports and its highly addictive properties.

## Your Body and Cocaine

It is these negative properties of cocaine that concern professionals today. They occur because cocaine is a powerful stimulant that affects every vital system in your body. The most dramatic attention has been given to sudden, unexplained deaths in healthy individuals who have experimented with cocaine: sudden heart attacks, fatal arrythmias, strokes, seizures, and suicides. These deaths have occurred in chronic users; they have also been reported in young, healthy people when they used cocaine for the first time. Some people cannot metabolize the drug, and this can lead to an overdose from small quantities. The "Casey Jones" reaction immortalized in a song by the Grateful Dead can result in failure of the body's major systems, leading to convulsions and death within a few minutes.

These deaths occur because cocaine has dramatic stimulatory effects on electrical and chemical activity in the brain; this leads to increases in heart rate, blood pressure, and breathing. It is difficult to predict the precise effects cocaine may have on any given individual because these effects depend on the dose of cocaine, its purity, the individual's personal physical makeup, and the mode of administration.

There are three basic ways that cocaine is used: it can be "snorted," injected, or smoked. Snorting, or sniffing, cocaine into the nose is the most-common method. Users often form a line of cocaine on a mirror and snort it through a straw or a rolled-up dollar bill. Cocaine that is snorted produces its effects within three minutes after snorting.

Shooting up, or injecting, cocaine by needle is a riskier method because you can introduce impurities and infection directly into your bloodstream. These impurities damage the heart valve, allowing infection to occur. The result, endocarditis, is 100 percent fatal unless treated by intravenous antibiotics for four to six weeks in a hospital. Even if you survive, this can lead to chronic heart damage or strokes. In addition, shared needles are currently causing an epidemic spread of AIDS and hepatitis among intravenous drug users.

The third method of administration is smoking; the fastest way to get cocaine to the brain is by smoking it in a free-base form such as "crack," or "rock." Smoking produces addiction just as quickly as injection. Cocaine can result in mild to life-threatening symptoms in the respiratory system.

Any of the following four symptoms are grounds for an immediate trip to the hospital emergency room:

- *Gasping for breath*
- *Irregular breathing*
- *Accumulation of fluid in the lungs*
- *Failure to breathe*

Free-basing also leads to symptoms usually associated with smoking cigarettes: bronchitis, hoarseness, and coughing. Asthma, chronic respiratory infections, rhinitis (clogged, inflamed, swollen, runny, and bleeding nose), and damage to the vessels or septum of the nose are frequently experienced by users who snort cocaine.

Cocaine's effects on the cardiovascular system also run the gamut from uncomfortable to deadly. Heart rate, blood pressure, and pulse rate increases are all part of the initial "rush." Extremely high increases in these vital signs may lead to heart damage, internal bleeding, or heart failure.

Any of the following four symptoms require emergency medical attention:

- *Irregular heart rates*
- *Sudden, rapid falls in blood pressure*
- *Weak or irregular pulse*
- *Blue or gray skin color resulting from lack of oxygen*

Smoking and injecting cocaine pose the greatest dangers to the heart. Injection is associated with endocarditis, pulmonary edema, blood clots, and hepatitis. All of these side effects represent serious medical conditions. Of the various methods of administering cocaine, free-basing is the one that most often results in heart attacks.

Malnutrition and severe vitamin deficiency are common in chronic cocaine users. These conditions will lower your resistance and open you to infection and disease from any of the organisms that are commonly found in the environment. Sleep disorders, digestive disorders, severe weight loss, hallucinations, convulsions, and seizures are all disturbing symptoms frequently reported by cocaine users.[6]

## Mood and Personality Changes

Since cocaine can have such dangerous consequences, the question remains as to why the drug has become so popular. Most users are attracted by the initial "rush": feelings of well-being, confidence, euphoria, competence, energy, power, and control. Many cocaine users feel that the drug helps them to perform better socially and on the job. Unfortunately, these "high" feelings are short-lived: they last from fifteen to thirty minutes.

The major problem is the "crash" that users experience as the drug effects wear off: depression, fatigue, paranoia, hallucinations. These negative feelings then prompt the many compulsive users to abuse the drug. The "low" is so bad, especially compared to the high they have just experienced, that users have to turn right around and use any means to get high again. This results in cocaine's vicious cycle of abuse. Cocaine does give people additional energy, but the feelings of greater competence that users report are mostly illusory, particularly at higher levels of cocaine.

And most cocaine users do go on to higher levels. While everyone who uses the drug does not become an addict, few individuals can control a cocaine habit for long. The brief high is followed by a severe slump, and users feel that the only way out of that depression is another dose. Larger and larger doses are required to reach the high, and the time between doses becomes shorter and shorter. Although experts are still debating whether cocaine is physically addictive, these debates may be largely academic because we have more than enough evidence that cocaine can gain a stranglehold on users despite the disastrous effects it has on their lives. Many users become so dependent on the drug that their lives become centered around it and they cannot function without it. It is horrifying to read reports, from successful individuals in every age group, that describe how cocaine has taken over these individuals' lives. Chronic use leads to persistent mood and personality changes and paranoia.

Successful doctors, students, engineers, athletes, business executives, songwriters, and lawyers have all reported the same result: cocaine has destroyed their lives. It is a powerfully addictive drug, and they are not able to give it up. They have lost their families, their careers, their fortunes, their self-respect, and the values that formed the foundations of their lives.

Major personality changes occur as highly motivated individuals lose all interest in their work; loving parents, husbands, and children become alienated from their families; formerly honest workers and students become willing to lie, steal, cheat, sell drugs, and prostitute themselves. They do these things in order to acquire the money they need to finance a habit that grows more and more expensive until it consumes their lives and the lives of their loved ones. Promising careers, satisfying family relationships, physical and psychological health are all sacrificed to an obsessive need to recapture the "high."

The "Test Yourself for Addiction" questionnaire in the following exercise was developed by Dr. Mark Gold, director of the National Cocaine Hotline. If you answer "Yes" to as few as ten of the questions, you may be bordering on an addiction to cocaine. If you answer "Yes" to more than ten items, you have a problem. Get help as soon as possible from a counselor. Cocaine has destroyed the lives of many individuals who thought they were strong enough to fight the addiction on their own. Do not let it destroy your life or college career.

The counseling center at your college has professionals who can help you unravel the problems that cocaine is causing in your life. You can also get advice by calling national hot lines at 1-800-COCAINE, 1-800-662-HELP, or your local community mental health center. Self-help groups like Cocaine Anonymous (CA) and Narcotics Anonymous (NA) are listed in your telephone directory. These groups can provide you with long-term support from others who are struggling with similar problems. Coke Anon and Nar-Anon are self-help groups that can help the family members of an addict through the difficult times ahead.

**EXERCISE:
TESTING
YOURSELF FOR
ADDICTION**

Yes        No

_____    _____    1. Do you have to use larger doses of cocaine to get the high you once experienced with smaller doses?
                        (This means you have developed a tolerance to the drug, that is, that you need more of it by a more-direct route to achieve the same effect.)

_____    _____    2. Do you use cocaine almost continually until your supply is exhausted?

_____    _____    3. Is the cost of cocaine the major factor limiting your use, and do you wish you could afford more?
                        (Your internal controls are virtually gone. The drug is in charge, and you will find yourself doing anything to get it.)

_____    _____    4. Do you use cocaine two or more times per week?
                        (If you do, you are in the highest-risk group for addiction.)

_____    _____    5. Do you have three or more of the following physical symptoms? Sleep problems, nose bleeds, headaches, sinus problems, voice problems, difficulty swallowing, sexual performance problems, nausea or vomiting, trouble breathing or shortness of breath, constant sniffling or rubbing your nose, irregular heartbeats, epileptic seizures, or convulsions?
                        (Three or more of these indicate severe loss of bodily function related to coke abuse-addiction.)

_____    _____    6. Do you have three or more of the following psychological symptoms? Jitteriness, anxiety, depression, panic, irritability, suspiciousness, paranoia, problems concentrating, hallucinations (seeing things that are not there), hearing voices when there are none, loss of interest in friends, hobbies, sports, or other noncocaine activities, memory problems, thoughts about suicide, attempted suicide, compulsive, repetitive acts like combing the hair, straightening of clothes or ties, tapping the feet for no reason?
                        (Cocaine abuse is causing psychological problems that are not within the individual's capacity to control.)

_____    _____    7. Have any or all of the problems specified in the previous two questions caused you to stop using cocaine for a period ranging from two weeks to six months or longer?
                        (If not, the acquired disabilities are not strong enough to overcome the addiction.)

_____    _____    8. Do you find that you must take other drugs or alcohol to calm down following cocaine use?
                        (You are trying to medicate yourself so as to maintain your cocaine habit without suffering the terrible side effects of addiction. You are, of course, flirting with becoming addicted to a second drug.)

_____    _____    9. Are you afraid that if you stop using cocaine, your work will suffer?
                        (You are psychologically dependent on the drug.)

Yes        No
_____  _____  10. Are you afraid that if you stop using cocaine you will be too depressed or unmotivated or without sufficient energy to function at your present level?
(You are addicted and afraid of the withdrawal symptoms.)

_____  _____  11. Do you find that you cannot turn down cocaine when it is offered?
(Use is out of your control.)

_____  _____  12. Do you think about limiting your use of cocaine?
(You are on the verge of addiction and are trying to ration use of the drug.)

_____  _____  13. Do you dream about cocaine?
(This is related to compulsive use and the total domination of the drug.)

_____  _____  14. Do you think about cocaine at work?
(This is also a part of the obsession with the drug.)

_____  _____  15. Do you think about cocaine when you are talking or interacting with a loved one?
(Obsession with the drug dominates all aspects of living.)

_____  _____  16. Are you unable to stop using the drug for one month?

_____  _____  17. Have you lost or discarded your precocaine friends?
(You are stacking the deck in favor of cocaine by reducing negative feedback.)

_____  _____  18. Have you noticed that you have lost your precocaine values: that is, that you don't care about your job or career, your home and family, or that you will lie and steal to get coke?
(Addiction causes slow but steady changes in personality and the approach to life to reduce intrapsychic conflict.)

_____  _____  19. Do you feel the urge to use cocaine when you see your pipe or mirror or other paraphernalia? Or taste it when you are not using it? Or feel the urge to use it when you see it or talk about it?
(This is called conditioning and occurs after long-term, heavy use.)

_____  _____  20. Do you usually use cocaine alone?
(When addiction sets in, this is the pattern. Social usage ceases.)

_____  _____  21. Do you borrow heavily to support your cocaine habit?
(You can be pretty sure you're addicted if you are willing to live so far above your means to get the drug.)

_____  _____  22. Do you prefer cocaine to family activities, food, or sex?
(This is a sure sign of addiction. Cocaine need overrides fundamental human needs for food, sex, social interaction.)

_____  _____  23. Do you deal or distribute cocaine to others?
(This kind of change in behavior signals addiction because it is an accommodation to the need for the drug.)

_____  _____  24. Are you afraid of being found out to be a cocaine user?
(Addicts usually live a double life, preferring not to choose one or another alternative.)

_____  _____  25. When you stop using the drug, do you get depressed or crash?
(This is a sign of withdrawal—a symptom of addiction.)

| Yes | No | |
|-----|-----|---|
| _____ | _____ | 26. Do you miss work, or reschedule appointments, or fail to meet important obligations because of your cocaine use?<br>(The drug has taken over your life.) |
| _____ | _____ | 27. Is your cocaine use a threat to your career or personal goals? Has your cocaine use caused you to lose interest in your career? Has cocaine caused you job problems? Has the drug caused you to lose your job? Has your cocaine use caused you to lose interest in or to have violent quarrels with people you love? Has your cocaine use caused you to lose your spouse or loved one?<br>(You would hardly sacrifice so much if you were not addicted.) |
| _____ | _____ | 28. Do people keep telling you that you are different or have changed in a significant way?<br>(Addicted people are indeed different from the way they were pre-cocaine. Such comments are a clue to addiction.) |
| _____ | _____ | 29. Have you used more than 50 percent of your savings for cocaine? Has your cocaine use bankrupted you and caused you to incur large debts? Have you committed a crime to support yourself and your cocaine habit? Have you stolen from work and/or family and friends?<br>(If you are not addicted, would cocaine be worth these problems?) |
| _____ | _____ | 30. Do you believe that cocaine use has some medicinal value in treating a problem you have with energy, motivation, confidence, depression, or sex?<br>(Users who believe this are the most likely to develop addiction.) |
| _____ | _____ | 31. Do you think you have had withdrawal symptoms when you stopped using cocaine?<br>(Only addicted persons experience withdrawal.) |
| _____ | _____ | 32. If you had $100 to spend would you spend it on cocaine rather than on something for your house or apartment, on a gift for someone you love, on theater, records, movies, going out with friends or family?<br>(Addicts become so fixated on their drug they can think of nothing else, no one else, and no other form of entertainment.) |
| _____ | _____ | 33. Do you think that you are addicted?<br>(If you think so, you probably are.) |
| _____ | _____ | 34. Do you use cocaine compulsively despite your recognition that the drug is a very real threat to your physical and psychological well-being, relationships, family, and job?<br>(This is addiction.) |
| _____ | _____ | 35. Did you ever enter psychiatric treatment or therapy for a cocaine-related problem and not tell the doctor or therapist about your cocaine use or how current or recent it is? |
| _____ | _____ | 36. Did you have a cocaine problem that was cured either through your own efforts alone or with the help of friends or with professional treatment?<br>(The critical word is "cured." No addict is really cured—rather, he has a remission of a chronic disease that can recur should he become a user of cocaine again.) |
| _____ | _____ | 37. Have you ever used cocaine and had hallucinations, a convulsion or seizure, angina (severe pain around the heart), loss of consciousness, the impulse to kill yourself or others? And when any of these side effects passed, did you figure that you would use less next time or use a purer quality of the drug? |

Yes        No

(These side effects are related to addictive use, but the addict prefers to ascribe them to overdose or to the adulterants used to make the drug go further. He then can continue to use the drug under the illusion that it will be okay the next time.)

_____ _____ 38. Do you leave paraphernalia or a supply of cocaine at work?
(This may be a call for help by a person who feels that his life is out of his control. It is like a suicide note left so that people will find it and prevent the act.)

_____ _____ 39. Do you sometimes wish that you would be discovered as a user by someone who would see to it that you got into treatment and recovered?
(If so, you know you need help and want it.)

_____ _____ 40. Do you use cocaine three times a week or even more often, and still try to maintain an interest in diet, health, exercise, and fitness?
(The interest may be there, but the fact is that such heavy use of the drug makes it virtually impossible to act on the interest. There is too great a conflict in values.)

_____ _____ 41. Have you switched from intranasal use to freebasing or intravenous use?
(This usually means that tolerance to the drug has developed, and it is very likely that you will binge and become addicted in short order.)

_____ _____ 42. Have you been using cocaine more than once a week for three or more years?
(With this much use, any stress, or change in your life, can turn you into a daily user with a high probability of addiction resulting.)

_____ _____ 43. Do you find yourself choosing friends or lovers because of their access to cocaine or their cocaine use?
(This kind of behavior usually indicates a life out of control.)

_____ _____ 44. Do you wake up in the morning and wonder how you could have let cocaine gain control over your life?
(You are addicted if you have these thoughts.)

_____ _____ 45. Do you find it almost impossible to fall asleep without a drink or sleeping pill or tranquilizer?
(You now have a second addiction.)

_____ _____ 46. Since you started using cocaine, have you ever wondered whether you would be able to live without it?
(We find that people who raise this question are generally hooked on the drug.)

_____ _____ 47. Have you wondered whether you would be better off dead than continuing to use cocaine?
(This question usually suggests an addiction so profound that the addict feels himself terminally ill.)

_____ _____ 48. Have you ever wished that you would die of an overdose in your sleep?
(Same as above.)

_____ _____ 49. Do you use cocaine in your car, at work in the bathroom, on airplanes, or in other public places?
(You are so desperate you want to be caught—and helped.)

_____ _____ 50. Do you use cocaine and then drive a car within six hours after use?
(Cocaine has impaired your judgment and you are out of control. Don't wait to get help until after you have impaired or killed a pedestrian.)

# CIGARETTES

The U.S. Census Bureau reports that three out of every ten Americans smoke, which makes tobacco the most-common type of drug dependency in the United States. Many carefully controlled studies in the United States show that the death rate is much higher among smokers at all ages than among nonsmokers. One in three smokers will die as a result of this habit. Experts estimate that each cigarette shortens a smoker's life by fourteen minutes.[7]

Smokers are at greater risk for lung cancer, heart attacks, and emphysema. Former Secretary of Health, Education, and Welfare, James Califano, reported 200,000 deaths from heart disease, 78,000 lung cancer deaths, and 22,000 deaths from other cancers during one year in this country.[8] Mortality rates are directly related to the number of cigarettes smoked: heavy smokers, people who have been smoking longer, and individuals who began smoking at an earlier age have higher death rates. People who smoke less than one pack per day have a death rate four times as high as nonsmokers. Those who smoke more than a pack a day have a death rate that is seven times as high.[9]

Aside from decreasing the smoker's life expectancy, cigarettes contain nicotine, which has a few other unfortunate side effects. By increasing heart rate and constricting blood vessels, nicotine causes smokers to lose their healthy skin color, to age and wrinkle faster, and to have cold hands and feet. Smoking also lowers men's sperm count, affects women's fertility, and lowers the birth weight of their babies, exposing the babies to a whole host of physical and psychological problems. Smoking even increases the risk for car accidents; it is not the nicotine that is responsible for this, but the momentary inattention to the road as you light a cigarette or tap out your ashes. This is the reason that many companies offer lower car insurance rates to nonsmokers.

Nicotine, the active ingredient in cigarettes, seems to be a stimulant in terms of its biochemical action in the body, yet many smokers report that smoking helps them to relax. Part of this relaxing effect may come from relief of the withdrawal symptoms. As is the case with other drugs, the large number of people who are addicted to nicotine develop tolerance and experience uncomfortable withdrawal symptoms when the level of the drug in their bodies falls below the amount they need. These withdrawal symptoms include nervousness, insomnia and drowsiness, irritability, headaches, and an intense craving for nicotine.

Cigarettes also have side effects that affect people's social lives. Smokers smell bad; the odor remains in their breath, clothes, and hair. Their teeth and fingers become stained and yellow. Smokers' skin ages and wrinkles prematurely, and the cigarette tars rot the gums. Cigarettes are expensive! They use money that could be spent on social activities. Smoking decreases respiratory reserve, or "wind," when exercising, so smokers age faster and die sooner.

The withdrawal symptoms and craving make it very difficult to stop smoking. Many ex-heroin users report that they found it easier to give up heroin than cigarettes. This craving may last as long as nine years in the case of some ex-smokers. Cigarettes are not likely to force you to withdraw from college, but they will shorten your life.

There is, however, good news. If you are successful in giving up smoking for one year, you will substantially reduce your risk for heart attack. Ten years after quitting, your risk for heart disease is essentially the same as someone who has never smoked! If you wish to stop smoking, consult a counselor, look up Smoke Enders or a smoking clinic in your phone book, or contact the American Cancer Society for a referral.

## CAFFEINE

Caffeine is a natural stimulant found in coffee, cocoa, chocolate, tea, cola, and other soft drinks. It belongs to a class of drugs known as xanthine stimulants. Although there are some conflicting data, a recent study in *The New England Journal of Medicine* has confirmed earlier research that found the risk for heart disease increased two-and-one-half times for people who drink five or more cups of coffee a day.[10] Caffeine has also been implicated in research on depression, peptic ulcers, ovarian cancer, insomnia, irritability, cardiac irregularities, migraine headaches, and persistent, low-grade fever. If you are feeling anxious or depressed, try to avoid caffeine, because it may make your symptoms worse.

There is no question that people acquire tolerance for caffeine (requiring larger doses to achieve the same effects over time) and that withdrawal symptoms occur at the five-cup or more daily dosage level.[11] Headaches, trembling hands, irritability, fatigue, and heart palpitations are some of the symptoms that make it difficult for caffeine addicts to cut back on the amount they consume. At higher doses of five to ten cups a day, the user may suffer from a disorder called caffeinism, which includes unpleasant symptoms of mental disorder, such as confusion, disorientation, restless excitement, fatigue, and insomnia. It is obvious that such symptoms can seriously interfere with your ability to study.

## OTHER DRUGS

Depressants, which include narcotics, barbiturates, and tranquilizers, are a class of drugs that work on your brain to reduce pain, tension, and anxiety. Because they slow down your thinking and coordination, they can interfere with your ability to study. All of them lead to tolerance so that you need larger and larger quantities of the drug as time goes on, and all of them cause withdrawal symptoms when the level of the drug in the body drops so that you feel very uncomfortable. Withdrawal from any depressant is a dangerous business, and it should be supervised by a physician. Life-threatening seizures are common, and you may die without medical attention. All drugs in this class are fatal at high doses because they slow down vital functions such as breathing.

### Heroin

Heroin, first cousin to morphine and opium, is a narcotic that comes from the poppy plant. There are approximately one-half-million heroin addicts in this country. Heroin users usually inject the drug under their skin (''skin popping'') or directly into their veins (''mainlining''). They experience a rush that lasts about five to fifteen minutes and then a high for three to five hours. The withdrawal symptoms are miserable, resulting in anxiety, hot and cold flashes, headaches, cramps, sweating, diarrhea, and sometimes, hallucinations. Because of this discomfort, addicts eventually spend most of their time and energy making sure that they can secure their next dose. This leaves little time for study or social relationships. If withdrawal is carried out under a doctor's supervision, the doctor will prescribe medication that reduces the discomfort of the withdrawal symptoms.

### Barbiturates and Tranquilizers

Sedatives or barbiturates include drugs like Seconal, Valium, and Nembutal (''downers''). The pills are prescribed by doctors in order to help patients relax and fall asleep. Unfortunately, they are habit-forming and can result in worse sleep problems so that the person gets into a vicious cycle of taking more and more pills until he or she is addicted. Sleep problems often become worse, causing exhaustion and irritability. This can certainly interfere with a college career, not to mention any other aspects of a sane life.

These pills often result in death when the person drinks alcohol in addition to taking the pill. (This situation occurred in the deaths of Marilyn Monroe and Judy Garland.) Taking the two drugs together magnifies the effect four times over the effect of taking either alcohol or barbiturates alone. They have similar psychological effects to alcohol: released inhibitions, relaxation, and distorted judgment and coordination. It is, therefore, dangerous to drive if you have taken any of these pills, and your ability to study will also be impaired. Withdrawal symptoms are very unpleasant and can easily lead to seizures or death. Withdrawal should be supervised by a physician.

Tranquilizers like Librium and Valium are rarely abused by young people because they do not really produce a high. They are habit-forming, however, and have become addictive to many people who use them to decrease anxiety. Since their side effects include drowsiness and poor coordination, they should not be taken if you are going to drive. They are likely to interfere with your ability to work effectively in college because of these side effects.

## Amphetamines

Stimulants are a class of drugs that make users feel energetic, alert, and self-confident. We have already discussed cocaine, caffeine, and nicotine, which belong to this group. Amphetamines such as Benzedrine, Dexedrine, and Methedrine ("speed") are other members of this group that are abused. In addition to their energizing effects, they decrease appetite; for this reason, they are sometimes abused by dieters. They improve coordination, so they are popular with some athletes. They hold off the effects of sleeplessness, so they tend to be misused by students who are cramming for exams late at night. (It is not true, as some students believe, that amphetamines help you think better.)

Amphetamines produce tolerance so that users go on to higher levels, and at high levels they can be quite dangerous. "Speed freaks" can carry on for several days at high-energy levels without eating or sleeping. They are likely, however, to literally "go crazy," becoming suspicious and violent when they lose touch with reality. Paranoia, chronic psychosis, and brain damage are all common in amphetamine abusers. None of these symptoms is conducive to becoming a straight *A* student.

## Hallucinogens

Hallucinogens such as lysergic acid diethylamide (LSD), phencyclidene (PCP), dimethyltryptamine (DMT), and mescaline distort your perceptions. Use of these drugs can lead to fantastic images and new awarenesses or it can lead to a "bad trip" involving terror and panic. Some people have suffered long-term mental illness and hospitalization because of the distorted images and perceptions they experienced during a trip that went bad. Users also sometimes experience frightening flashbacks in which they are suddenly on a "trip" even though they have not taken the drug for days, weeks, and even years. A hallucinatory flashback can happen long after a user has stopped taking the drug, and it can create problems in functioning on a day-to-day basis.

These drugs do lead to tolerance, although they do not seem to be physically addictive. There are no particular withdrawal symptoms. PCP, or "angel dust," received a bad reputation in the 1970s because of its poisonous and frequent overdoses. Users often ended up hurting themselves or others because their perceptions were so distorted, and they became suspicious of others. Many users have become "vegetables" in mental hospitals or nursing homes because of extensive damage to their brains.

Marijuana ("pot," "dope," "grass") and hashish ("bhang," "dope," "weed") are classified as minor hallucinogens because their effects are not as dramatic as those of drugs such as LSD and PCP. One in three Americans has tried marijuana or hashish, which makes them the most-common illegal drugs in the country. Marijuana, made by crushing the dried leaves of the cannabis plant, is usually smoked in cigarette form ("joints"), while the stronger hashish, made from the resin of the plant, is usually smoked in a pipe. Either form can also be eaten.

The active ingredient in marijuana, delta 9, tetrahydrocannabinol (THC), increases heart rate and turns the whites of the eyes red. It also slows down reaction time and judgment of time and distance. For these reasons you should not drive if you have smoked marijuana. These effects go away as the drug wears off. Low doses lead to relaxed feelings, more vivid sensations, and a mild high. Higher doses result in a "spaced out" feeling. Occasionally users experience a "bad trip," in which feelings of anxiety, depression, or separation from the self are magnified.

There is some argument among researchers about the long-term effects of marijuana. It is clear that the drug leads to lung cancer and other respiratory illnesses. It has 50 percent more of the same carcinogenic substances that result in lung cancer from tobacco, and chronic users show the beginnings of the same lung diseases that affect tobacco smokers.

What is not clear is marijuana's effects on the male hormone testosterone and on the body's immune system. Researchers have found lowered testosterone levels in men who use the drug regularly over a long period of time, but it is not clear whether this lower hormone level affects their sexual behavior or sexual characteristics. Similarly, studies have showed that part of the immune system that normally fights off disease and illness is damaged by chronic marijuana use, but there is no evidence at the present time to indicate that marijuana smokers suffer from more illnesses or infections than nonusers.

Figure 29 presents an overview of the effects associated with many of the drugs that are abused today. Most of them can ruin your college career by interfering directly with your ability to concentrate, causing you to lose interest in your future and your studies, ruining your health so that you are unable to study, or bringing you into conflict with disciplinary rules and the legal system so that you are suspended from college.

## EXERCISE: RECOGNIZING YOUR PATTERNS OF DRUG USE

This exercise is meant to encourage you to think about your patterns of drug use, to share your thoughts with your peers, and to evaluate your own use of drugs. Remember that the word *drugs* includes alcohol, tobacco, and caffeine, as well as other drugs that are illegal.

Break into small groups of four and discuss the following questions. After your discussion, regroup as a class and share your group's reflections with the whole class. Do not identify any group members' personal habits in the class discussion or in any remarks you make outside of class. Be especially careful not to identify anyone's use of an illegal drug.

1. If you drink or use drugs, when did you start using them?

2. Why did you first try alcohol or other drugs?

3. If you continue to use alcohol or other drugs, what encourages you to use them at this point in your life?

**SATIATION**

| Drug | Street Names | Effects | Withdrawal Symptoms | Adverse/Overdose Reactions |
|---|---|---|---|---|
| *Narcotics:* | | Apathy, difficulty in concentration, slowed speech, decreased physical activity, drooling, itching, euphoria, nausea | Anxiety, vomiting, sneezing, diarrhea, lower back pain, watery eyes, runny nose, yawning, irritability, tremors, panic, chills and sweating, cramps | Depressed levels of consciousness, low blood pressure, rapid heart rate, shallow breathing, convulsions, coma, possible death |
| Heroin | H, hombre, junk, smack, dope, horse, crap | | | |
| Morphine | Drugstore dope, cube, first line, mud | | | |
| Codeine | | | | |
| Percodan | Perks | | | |
| Demerol | | | | |
| Methadone | Meth | | | |
| *Sedative Hypnotics:* | | Impulsiveness, dramatic mood swings, bizarre thoughts, suicidal behavior, slurred speech, disorientation, slowed mental and physical functioning, limited attention span | Weakness, restlessness, nausea and vomiting, headache, nightmares, irritability, depression, acute anxiety, hallucinations, seizures, possible death | Confusion, decreased response to pain, shallow respiration, dilated pupils, weak and rapid pulse, coma, possible death |
| Nembutal | Yellow jackets, yellows | | | |
| Seconal | Reds | | | |
| Tuinal | Tueys | | | |
| Phenobarbital | | | | |
| Quaaludes | Ludes, 714's | | | |
| Valium | V's | | | |
| Librium | | | | |
| Equanil | | | | |

**AROUSAL**

| Drug | Street Names | Effects | Withdrawal Symptoms | Adverse/Overdose Reactions |
|---|---|---|---|---|
| Benzedrine | Speed | Increased confidence, mood elevation, sense of energy and alertness, decreased appetite, anxiety, irritability, insomnia, transient drowsiness, delayed orgasm | Apathy, general fatigue, prolonged sleep, depression, disorientation, suicidal thoughts, agitated motor activity, irritability, bizarre dreams | Elevated blood pressure, increase in body temperature, face-picking, suspiciousness, bizarre and repetitious behavior, vivid hallucinations, convulsions, possible death |
| Dexedrine | Speed | | | |
| Desoxyn | Speed, crystal methedrine | | | |
| Biphetamine | Black beauties, speed | | | |
| Ritalin | | | | |
| Preludin | | | | |
| Cocaine | Coke, blow, toot, snow, lady | | | |

203

FANTASY

| Drug | Street Names | Effects | Withdrawal Symptoms | Adverse/Overdose Reactions |
|------|--------------|---------|---------------------|----------------------------|
| *Hallucinogens:* LSD | Electricity, acid, quasey, blotter acid, microdot, white lightning, purple barrels | Fascination with ordinary objects, heightened esthetic responses to color, texture, spatial arrangements, contours, music, vision and depth distortion, hear colors, see music, slowing of time, heightened sensitivity to faces, gestures, magnified feelings of love, lust, hate, joy, anger, pain, terror, despair, etc., paranoia, panic, euphoria, bliss, impairment of short-term memory, projection of self into dreamlike images | Not reported | Nausea, chills, increased pulse, temperature, and blood pressure, trembling, slow deep breathing, loss of appetite, insomnia, longer, more intense "trips", bizarre, dangerous behavior possibly leading to injury or death |
| Mescaline | Peyote buttons, (natural form) | Similar to LSD but more sensual and perceptual, fewer changes in thought, mood, and sense of self | Not reported | Resemble LSD, but more bodily sensations, vomiting |

204

| | | | | |
|---|---|---|---|---|
| Psilocybin | Mushrooms, shrooms, rooms | Similar to LSD but more visual and less intense, more euphoria, fewer panic reactions | Not reported | Resemble LSD, but less severe |
| *Cannabis* Marijuana Hashish Hash Oil | Bhang, kif, ganja, dope, grass, pot, smoke, hemp, joint, weed, bone, Mary Jane, herb, tea | Euphoria, relaxed inhibitions, increased appetite, disoriented behavior | Hyperactivity, insomnia, decreased appetite, anxiety | Severe reactions are rare, but include panic, paranoia, fatigue, bizarre and dangerous behavior |
| Phencyclidine | PCP, angel dust, hog, rocket fuel, superweed, peace pill, elephant tranquilizer, dust, bad pizza | Increased blood pressure and heart rate, sweating, nausea, numbness, floating sensation, slowed reflexes, altered body image, altered perception of time and space, impaired immediate and recent memory, decreased concentration, paranoid thoughts and delusions | Not reported | Highly variable and possibly dose-related, disorientation, loss of recent memory, lethargy/stupor, bizarre and violent behavior, rigidity and immobility, mutism, staring, hallucinations and delusions, coma |

FIGURE 29. A LISTING OF FACTS ON DRUGS[12]

4. If you do not use alcohol or other drugs, why have you avoided them or stopped using them?

5. How much of the drug do you use (number of cigarettes, number of drinks, number of times you get high per week)?

6. Do you feel that the drug is causing problems for you (interfering with your work or social life, damaging your health)? If it is causing problems, what type of problems are they?

7. Do you drive after you have taken a drug (alcohol, cocaine, barbiturates, marijuana, or other hallucinogens)?

8. How do you feel about people who drive after they have taken a drug? What can you do about these feelings?

9. Do you experience any of the warning signs of a drinking or cocaine problem?

10. Do any members of your family have a drinking problem? (Check with your parents about this question. Often there is or was a family member who had a problem, but this person is not discussed. Tell your parents why you are asking about grandparents, cousins, uncles, etc.)

11. If you feel that you would like to decrease the amount of drug that you use, where can you go for help in cutting back?

## Answers to "Testing Your Alcohol IQ"

| | | |
|---|---|---|
| 1. d | 6. false | 11. c |
| 2. d | 7. true | 12. d |
| 3. a | 8. false | 13. c |
| 4. d | 9. true | 14. a |
| 5. false | 10. d | 15. false |
| | | 16. true |

## NOTES

1. D. Ellis, *Becoming a Master Student* (Rapid City, S.D.: College Survival, Inc., 1985).

2. "The Facts: Impaired Driving by Youth," *MADD in Action* 8 (MADD [Mothers Against Drunk Driving], 1988), 1:3.

3. J. E. Brody, "Personal Health," *New York Times,* 19 August 1987.

4. R. H. Price and S. J. Lynn, *Abnormal Psychology* (Chicago: Dorsey Press, 1986).

5. R. G. Schlaadt and P. T. Shannon, *Drugs of Choice* (Englewood Cliffs, N.J.: Prentice-Hall, 1982).

6. M. S. Gold, *800-COCAINE* (New York: Bantam Books, 1985).

7. R. M. Julien, *A Primer of Drug Action,* 3rd ed. (San Francisco: W. H. Freeman, 1981).

8. R. D. Lyons, "Califano in Drive to End Smoking; Calls Habit 'Slow Motion Suicide,'" *New York Times* 12 January 1978, p. 14a.

9. "Prevalence of Selected Chronic Respiratory Conditions," *Vital Health Statistics* Series 10, No. 84 (U.S. Department of Health, Education, and Welfare, 1970).

10. A. Z. LaCroix et al., "Coffee Consumption and the Incidence of Coronary Heart Disease," *New England Journal of Medicine* 315 (1986): 977–982.

11. *Licit and Illicit Drugs* (Mt. Vernon, N.Y.: Consumers Union, 1972).

12. "Contemporary Drugs of Choice," *Psychology Today* 17 (1983), 10:40–41.

# Chapter 15

## Stress

### STRESS AND STRESSORS

Stress consists of challenges from the environment: both physical challenges, such as hunger, cold, and viral infection, and psychological challenges, such as transferring to a new school, feeling pressured to accomplish too much in too little time, and facing a difficult exam. Stress occurs each time the environment presents you with problems that require solution.

**EXERCISE: MEASURING THE STRESS IN YOUR LIFE**

Complete the following checklist, and estimate how much stress you are experiencing. These events have been selected from several popular stress inventories.[1,2] You may be surprised to find that the list includes pleasant changes, like a vacation, in addition to unpleasant changes, like the death of a close family member. Both positive and negative changes require adjustment, and adjustment involves stress.

The following listed events are grouped into four categories from most stressful (Category A) to least stressful (Category D). Check the events that have occurred in your life within the past year. If an event has occurred twice, count it two times.

The categories from the stressors exercise can serve as a rough guide to the levels of stress in your life. If you have experienced moderate or severe stress, you may wish to consult a counselor to find ways to lower your stress level. Each of us differs somewhat in what we find stressful and in how we respond to stress. Some people will find a change of school to be a refreshing challenge; others will dread the adjustments they have to face under the same circumstances. Some people thrive under pressure, others find it difficult to function when they are hard-pressed. If you have any concerns about the stress in your life, you should consult a professional at the college counseling center.

## Life Stressors Checklist

CATEGORY A

_____ Death of a close family member

_____ Personal injury or illness

_____ Marriage

_____ Change in health of a family member

_____ Divorce of parents

_____ Pregnancy

_____ Placement on academic probation

CATEGORY B

_____ Financial problems (e.g., not having sufficient money to continue with school)

_____ Death of a close friend

_____ Taking out a major loan

_____ Dismissal from dormitory or other residence

_____ Beginning a new school experience at a higher level (e.g., going from high school into college)

_____ Change in living conditions

_____ Failing a course

CATEGORY C

_____ Fired at work

_____ Transferring to a new school at the same level (e.g., transferring from one college to another)

_____ Change in residence

_____ Change in church activities

_____ Joining a fraternity or sorority

_____ Change in social activities

_____ Change in work hours or conditions

_____ Failing an important exam

CATEGORY D

_____ Change in sleeping habits

_____ Change in eating habits

_____ Change in major program at college

_____ Dropping a course

_____ Vacation

_____ Christmas

_____ Minor violation of the law

## Estimating Your Stress Level

_Little Stress:_ Even if you have experienced all the events in Category D, you are probably feeling relatively little stress.

_Mild Stress:_ If you have experienced all the items in Category C plus one item from any other category, you may be experiencing mild stress. If you have experienced most of the items from Category C and several items from other categories, you may also be feeling mild stress.

_Moderate Stress:_ If you have experienced all items from Category C and Category D, you may be undergoing moderate stress. Three items from each of Categories A, B, and C might also indicate moderate stress.

*Major Stress:* If you have experienced four events from Categories A and B, you may be experiencing major stress.

Circle the category that best describes the level of stress you have experienced during this year.

Little Stress

Mild Stress

Moderate Stress

Major Stress

## Reactions to Stress

Stress also refers to the pattern of responses that you make when a stimulus challenges your ability to cope. This pattern of responses involves major physical changes in your hormonal system, autonomic nervous system, and brain: increases in rate of breathing, heart rate, and blood pressure and in the discharge of steroids and adrenaline. All of these complicated physical changes are involved in preparing your body for "flight or fight"; your body becomes physically prepared to face the danger and fight or to turn around and run from the danger.

You are probably more familiar, however, with the psychological reactions to stress such as anxiety, depression, anger, burnout, irritation, and difficulty in concentrating or making decisions. People respond to stress differently; what reactions do you notice in yourself when you are under stress?

**EXERCISE: DETERMINING YOUR REACTIONS TO STRESS**

1. This exercise will help you become aware of your responses to stress. Often people are not aware that they are under stress until they take an inventory of their responses to recent stressors. The following lists contain examples of psychological and physical reactions to stress. What reactions do you notice in yourself when you are under stress?

PSYCHOLOGICAL REACTIONS TO STRESS          PHYSIOLOGICAL REACTIONS TO STRESS

Irritability                                               Upset stomach
Inability to concentrate                                   Sweaty palms
Depression                                                 Headache

2. List the reactions you experience when you are stressed, and compare your observations with those of your classmates. You may discover additional reactions in yourself that you had overlooked before. When you become aware of your responses to stress, you can more easily tell when you are experiencing stress. Once you are aware of stress, you can take steps to cope with it.

PSYCHOLOGICAL REACTIONS TO STRESS          PHYSICAL REACTIONS TO STRESS

_____          _____

_____          _____

_____          _____

_____          _____

## STRESS AND ILLNESS

Stress has been implicated in many illnesses from colds to heart attacks, asthma, ulcers, and possibly even cancer. People who are under chronic stress seem to become ill more frequently than those who experience stress less frequently. Psychologists have identified people with certain personality traits who seem to be constantly stressed. Type A personalities put pressure on themselves continuously. They are hard-driving, aggressive, competitive, always-in-a-rush individuals who try to juggle two or three activities at the same time. Many studies have found a high correlation between these personality characteristics and the occurrence of heart disease, even when other correlates of heart disease, such as diet, smoking, and genetic history are factored out.[3,4]

Heart disease, for example, is twice as frequent among Type A businessmen as among men in the general population. The Type A personality pattern is still relatively rare in nonindustrialized societies. It seems to be spreading, however, among individuals in high-pressure professions of our society. It is also becoming increasingly evident in college, high school, and even elementary school students in our country. The number of women who show this personality pattern is also increasing, as women attempt to juggle careers, child rearing, and household maintenance all at the same time.

You may wish to consider the extent to which your behavior fits the Type A pattern. Our society does seem to reward this type of behavior to a large extent. Are the costs in damaged health and frayed nerves worth the rewards? Is it possible to be successful without taking on the Type A personality?

## SOURCES OF STRESS

It may be worthwhile to evaluate which areas of your life are particularly stressful. Consider the academic, interpersonal, and vocational areas. For example, if you work, the list of job stressors might include pressure from your boss, commuting hassles, inconvenient work hours, or unreasonable demands. An examination of academic stress might result in a list that includes difficulty in passing a course required for your major, an instructor who consistently gives surprise quizzes, the inability to enroll in the courses you need at registration, or a course in which assignments are not clear.

**EXERCISE: DETERMINING YOUR SOURCES OF STRESS**

This exercise concerning the sources of stress will give you the opportunity to take stock of the different types of stress in your life. By sharing this list with your class, you may discover common sources of stress or additional sources that did not originally occur to you. You may later wish to consider whether any of these areas is causing you enough stress to warrant some change. What types of stress do you experience from school, from your interpersonal relationships, or from your job?

Break into small discussion groups of four individuals. If you hold a paying job, you should be in a group with at least one other person who also does. For each of the three major areas in your life, list and share with your group members any specific item or event that results in stress for you.

Some typical sources of stress are

*Academic:* Failing an important course

*Social:* Quarreling with a friend

*Job-related:* Asking for a raise

You will probably discover that you have many sources of stress in common with your peers. Do any of them cause enough stress so that you should consider taking some type of action?

| Academic Stressors | Social Stressors | Job Stressors |
|---|---|---|
| _____ | _____ | _____ |
| _____ | _____ | _____ |
| _____ | _____ | _____ |
| _____ | _____ | _____ |
| _____ | _____ | _____ |
| _____ | _____ | _____ |
| _____ | _____ | _____ |
| _____ | _____ | _____ |
| _____ | _____ | _____ |
| _____ | _____ | _____ |
| _____ | _____ | _____ |
| _____ | _____ | _____ |
| _____ | _____ | _____ |
| _____ | _____ | _____ |
| _____ | _____ | _____ |
| _____ | _____ | _____ |
| _____ | _____ | _____ |

## Individual Approaches to Stress

People vary in their responses to stress. They also vary in their interpretations of stress. Situations that are stressful for one person may be viewed by another person as challenging or as stimulating growth experiences. Some people thrive on excitement, challenge, and change; they find daily structure and routine boring; they seek out diversions such as roller coaster rides, horror movies, and skydiving in order to increase their level of stimulation. They look for change and seize the opportunity for new jobs, new projects, new routines. Other people function best within familiar environments where the expectations are a known quantity. They prefer lower levels of stimulation and familiar structure; they find high-risk activities unsettling.

## RESISTANCE TO STRESS

Certain attitudes and traits can help you withstand stress. Psychologists have called this constellation of characteristics "hardiness." The items in the exercise below are similar to those used in a professional questionnaire that measures hardiness. This exercise can give you some idea of how well you might resist stress.

**EXERCISE: MEASURING YOUR RESISTANCE TO STRESS**

**Measure Your Resistance to Stress**

Write in how much you agree or disagree with each statement. Use the following scale:

0 = *Strongly disagree*      2 = *Mildly agree*

1 = *Mildly disagree*     3 = *Strongly agree*

_____ A. Trying my best at work makes a difference.

_____ B. Trusting to fate is sometimes all I can do in a relationship.

_____ C. I often wake up eager to start on the day's projects.

_____ D. Thinking of myself as a free person leads to great frustration and difficulty.

_____ E. I would be willing to sacrifice financial security in my life if something really challenging came along.

_____ F. It bothers me when I have to deviate from the routine or schedule I've set for myself.

_____ G. An average citizen can have an impact on politics.

_____ H. Without the right breaks, it is hard to be successful in my field.

_____ I. I know why I am doing what I am doing at work (or at school).

_____ J. Getting close to people puts me at risk of being obligated to them.

_____ K. Encountering new situations is an important priority in my life.

_____ L. I really don't mind when I have nothing to do.

**Calculate Your Score**

These questions measure three dimensions of hardiness: control, commitment, and challenge. For half the questions, a high score indicates hardiness; for the other half, a low score indicates hardiness. Thus you must do a combination of addition and subtraction to get your score on each dimension. Fill in the following blanks to calculate your score.

Control score = ___ + ___ − ___ − ___ = ___
               A      G      B      H

Commitment score = ___ + ___ − ___ − ___ = ___
               C      I      D      J

Challenge score = ___ + ___ − ___ − ___ = ___
              E      K      F      L

                                                 ___

Control score + Commitment score + Challenge score = Total hardiness score

*Total Score Interpretation*

10–18 = Hardy personality
 0–9  = Moderate hardiness
Below 0 = Low hardiness

_____

This exercise is reprinted with permission from S. O. Kobasa, "How much stress can you survive?" *American Health Magazine* © 1984, p. 66.

*Eustress* is good stress, a level of stress that feels comfortable and invigorating. Eustress leads to growth and development. Without change or challenge in our lives we become bored, and boredom is itself a stressful stimulus. It is useful for each of us to know the level of stimulation that works best for us when the time comes to make decisions about careers, relationships, and leisure activities.

## TECHNIQUES FOR COPING WITH STRESS

It is also useful to know how to reduce stress levels when we are feeling overwhelmed. We all use a variety of techniques to ease tension when the going gets tough. Do your coping mechanisms include any techniques from the list shown in figure 30?

**EXERCISE: DECREASING STRESS WITH COPING TECHNIQUES**

1. List several of the methods you use to cope with stress. Include the techniques that you think are successful in addition to the ones that you would like to change.

_____

_____

_____

_____

_____

2. Many individuals engage in maladaptive techniques (abusing drugs or alcohol, having a nervous breakdown, overeating, dropping out of school, procrastinating, and so on) in order to relieve stress. Such mechanisms may reduce stress temporarily; they do, however, have important disadvantages. What are they?

_____

_____

_____

_____

1. Using relaxation or meditation exercises.
2. Getting physical exercise.
3. Finding emotional support from friends or relatives.
4. Seeking help from a professional.
5. Practicing better time management.
6. Prioritizing tasks. Taking care of the most important items first and letting the others wait.
7. Redefining your goals; setting more realistic standards.
8. Taking control of your life and systematically reducing some of the sources of stress.
9. Trying to see your problem in a different light that makes it more bearable.
10. Distracting yourself; not thinking about the problem; engaging in some other activity.

**FIGURE 30. COMMON COPING MECHANISMS**

3. Break into small discussion groups, and share your coping techniques with group members. You may discover new techniques that work for you. Have each group present its coping mechanisms to the class so that you can construct a master list on the board. Discuss the advantages and disadvantages of the various techniques.

Successful Coping Techniques

_____
_____
_____
_____
_____
_____
_____
_____

Unsuccessful Coping Techniques

_____
_____
_____
_____
_____
_____
_____

## Relaxation Training

Learning to relax is a coping technique that many people have found helpful in dealing with stress. It is normal to feel nervous and tense when you are facing a challenge such as an important exam. Not only is this anxiety normal, it is also helpful! If you feel totally calm and collected during a test, you may not perform as well as you could. A small amount of anxiety is helpful in activating all your systems so that you are motivated to do your best.

On the other hand, too much anxiety is disruptive; it interferes with your concentration. If you are distracted by your pumping heart, churning stomach, or sweaty palms, you will not be focusing on the test. Psychologists have developed very successful techniques for lowering anxiety. Two of the most successful ones are relaxation training and systematic desensitization.

If you believe that you are experiencing too much anxiety, try the following exercises. If anxiety really gets in your way, however, you may wish to consult a therapist at the college counseling center. Many people find these techniques much more successful when they tackle this problem if they are supervised by a counselor rather than working on their own.

Muscle relaxation and autogenic training were developed by therapists in the 1930s to help patients relax. Since that time, both techniques have been used extensively by psychologists to help clients cope with various discomforts and anxieties. If you learn to recognize tension in your muscles and to practice reducing it, your whole body will feel more relaxed. The key is to recognize and catch the tension before it builds up. Once you have learned how to relax your body, you will find that your mind relaxes as well. You can then condition yourself so that deep breathing and certain phrases will automatically trigger a more-relaxed state when you wish to relax.

One caution before you begin: relaxation is a learned skill. The more you practice it, the more deeply you will be able to relax. Ten minutes of practice once or twice a day over a period of several weeks should enable you to reduce anxiety during situations that cause moderate tension. Continued practice, along with the desensitization exercises, should allow you to handle more difficult situations. These exercises are an abbreviated version of those that a therapist might use. If you find that they are not helping you to reduce anxiety, consult a therapist at the counseling center.

## EXERCISE: DECREASING STRESS WITH DEEP MUSCLE RELAXATION

Find a quiet place where you will not be disturbed for ten or fifteen minutes. A reclining chair that supports your head and legs is the best tool for practicing deep muscle relaxation; however, the exercises may also be done on a carpeted floor. You will find it helpful to have a friend record the relaxation instructions on tape so that you can listen to the recording when you are first learning the exercises. A slow, monotone narration in someone else's voice is most effective at the beginning. As you get better at the exercises, you will discover that saying the instructions in your head or just saying the word *relax* to yourself will result in decreased tension.

Sit or lie down, and make yourself as comfortable as possible. Loosen any clothing that is restricting you (a belt, a collar, a hair clip, a pair of glasses), and close your eyes. Begin breathing deeply and regularly. Continue breathing slowly and deeply, allowing the air to flow in and out at a comfortable rate. Allow your body to begin relaxing. Allow the chair or the floor to take the weight of your arms and legs. Become aware of the point where your buttock sinks into the chair. Allow your shoulders to sink back against the floor or chair. Let the floor take all the weight of your body so that your muscles are free to relax, to let go, and to release their tension. Just continue breathing deeply and regularly.

Now make fists with your hands. Curl your fingers, tense the muscles of your hands, and allow your mind to focus on that tension. Experience the sensation of tension in the fingers of your hands. Remember how it feels. And then relax your hands. Allow the fingers to uncurl. Allow the muscles to release the tension. Allow your hands to rest comfortably and naturally on the chair or on the floor. Notice how different those muscles feel; notice the difference between tension and relaxation in the muscles of your right hands.

Now do that same exercise with the muscles in your arms, neck, and shoulders. Tense all the muscles in your hands and arms; hunch your shoulders up toward your ears. Experience the strain and tension in your hands, arms, neck, and shoulders. Remember that sensation, and then relax. Release the tension. Allow your fingers to uncurl. Allow your hands to relax. Allow the muscles in your arms to go limp. Allow your shoulders to come back down to a comfortable position. As you release the tension, notice how different all of those muscles feel. Remember the different sensations of tension and relaxation in the muscles of your arms, neck, and shoulders.

As you release the tension, allow the relaxed feelings to spread all through your shoulders, across the top of your back, around the base of your neck, and down through your arms to your hands. As your mind focuses on each group of muscles, allow that muscle group to relax a little more. Just becoming aware of the sensations in a particular group of muscles allows those muscles to release a little more tension. Enjoy those warm, pleasant sensations of relaxation. Allow those sensations to spread and deepen;

allow those muscles to loosen up and let go a little more with each breath outward.

Continue to breathe deeply, and enjoy those pleasant sensations of relaxation as you help to make them deeper and spread them further throughout your body. Each time your mind focuses on a group of muscles, allow them to relax a little more deeply.

Now focus on the muscles in your face. Bring your eyebrows together toward your nose as if you were frowning. Press your lips together and clamp your upper teeth down against your lower teeth. Maintain that tension, and remember how the muscles in your face feel when they are tense. And now relax. Allow those muscles to let go. Allow your eyebrows to drift back to their natural position so that the muscles in your forehead and around your eyes are free to relax. Allow the muscles around your lips and your jaw to loosen up and relax. And notice how differently those muscles feel when they are relaxed. Focus on those feelings of relaxation. Allow them to spread and deepen.

Continue breathing deeply and regularly, allowing your mind to focus one by one on the muscle groups in your face: the muscles in your forehead, around your eyes, around your mouth, and in your jaws. Allow them to become more and more deeply relaxed with each breath outward. Allow the relaxation to spread upward from your mouth to your forehead, down your neck, across your shoulders, and into your arms and hands. Loosen up, let go, become more and more deeply relaxed with each breath outward.

Now you are ready to focus on the muscles of your chest and stomach. Take a deep breath, and hold the air in your lungs. At the same time, suck in the muscles of your stomach as though you are trying to avoid a hard punch. As you hold your breath, you will experience tension spreading through all the muscles of your chest and stomach. Remember that uncomfortable feeling, and then relax. Release the tension and continue breathing regularly. Notice how much more comfortable the muscles of your chest and stomach are when they have released that tension. Focus on the feelings of relaxation in these muscle groups. Remember how it feels. Continue breathing deeply and regularly, and notice how you can spread relaxation all through your body with each breath. It's the exhalation phase of your breathing that allows you to send those pleasant feelings of relaxation to all your other muscle groups. Use those exhalations to help yourself relax more deeply.

Now bring your attention to the muscle groups in your legs. Tense the muscles of your legs by lifting them and pointing your toes toward your face. Experience the tension in your feet, in your calves, behind your knees, and in your thighs. Remember those feelings of tension, and then relax. Release the tension. Allow your legs to come down. Allow the chair or floor to take all the weight of your legs so that your muscles are free to relax. Allow them to release the tension, allow them to let go, and note the difference between tension and relaxation throughout the muscles of your feet and legs.

Allow the relaxed feelings to spread upward from your left leg into your groin and stomach. Allow those feelings to pool there, feeling warm and comfortable. Then allow them to descend into your right leg, from your thigh into your calf and down into your foot and toes. Then turn the wave of relaxation around, and allow it to go back up through your legs into your stomach. Allow all of those muscles to feel warmer, more and more comfortable, and more and more deeply relaxed with each breath outward. Continue guiding the warm pool of relaxation up from your stomach into the muscles of your chest, spreading it outward and then upward into the muscles of your neck and face.

Allow your mouth and jaw muscles to become more and more deeply relaxed. Allow the muscles around your cheeks and nose, the muscles around your eyes and in your forehead to loosen up, letting go as the pleasant, relaxed feelings spread upward.

Bring the wave of relaxation over the top of your head and down into the muscles of your neck. From here allow it to spread out along your shoulders and down through your arms. The warm, pleasant sensations descend down through your elbows into your forearms, through your wrists, and all the way down to your hands. Continue breathing deeply and regularly allowing the exhalation phase of your breathing to wash away all traces of tension, allowing the warm, pleasant sensations of relaxation to spread throughout your body.

**EXERCISE: USING IMAGERY TO RELAX**

You can also learn to relax by conditioning yourself with autogenic phrases that suggest feelings of warmth and relaxation. Say each of the following phrases to yourself twice, slowly and rhythmically.

My breathing is deeper and deeper.
My breathing is deeper and deeper.

My arms are warm and heavy.
My arms are warm and heavy.

My legs are warm and heavy.
My legs are warm and heavy.

My arms and my legs are warm and heavy.
My arms and my legs are warm and heavy.

My stomach is warm and relaxed.
My stomach is warm and relaxed.

My entire body is warm and relaxed.
My entire body is warm and relaxed.

My head is clear and tranquil.
My head is clear and tranquil.

My mind is clear and tranquil.
My mind is clear and tranquil.

I feel calmer and calmer.
I feel calmer and calmer.

I feel calm and alert and relaxed.
I feel calm and alert and relaxed.

You should feel relaxed and refreshed after doing the preceding relaxation exercises. You may experience some pins and needles or some feelings of heaviness or drowsiness. Some people experience feelings of lightness or floating. All of these sensations are normal. They are associated with deep feelings of relaxation.

Relaxation exercises have proven helpful with a variety of problems from insomnia to headaches to back pain. Many people have found these exercises helpful in controlling excessive anxiety connected with exams, snakes, driving over a bridge, or giving a speech in front of a large audience.

In order for the exercises to work, you must practice them. Practicing ten minutes once or twice a day should bring you up to a useful level of expertise within two to three weeks. The more you practice, the more effective you will become in reducing your anxiety. Remember that you must catch your tension before it builds. Become adept at quickly checking your major muscle groups or trouble spots and beginning relaxation exercises before the tension increases. As you become more experienced at relaxing, taking just a few deep breaths or saying a few of the autogenic phrases should be enough to relieve the tension. The tensing and relaxing of all the muscle groups will not be necessary once you get beyond the first two to three weeks of learning.

## Systematic Desensitization

Relaxation exercises can help you to feel more comfortable during exams or other problematic situations, if your anxiety level if not too high. If, however, anxiety really interferes with your performance, you may wish to consider a technique called systematic desensitization, through which you actually condition yourself to replace anxiety with relaxation during the situations that are troublesome for you.

Psychologists have demonstrated the effectiveness of systematic desensitization in thousands of studies. This method has proven successful with a wide range of fears from public speaking to snakes to exams. Ordinarily, the technique is conducted with the guidance of a psychologist. There is evidence, however, that individuals can develop effective programs for themselves.

**EXERCISE: DECREASING STRESS WITH SYSTEMATIC DESENSITIZATION**

Exam anxiety can offer a good example of how to set up a program of desensitization. You can, however, tailor a program to fit any inappropriate fear. You will find the exercise "Learning Systematic Desensitization" at the end of Chapter 7. If you are not successful in reducing your anxiety on your own, consult a therapist in your college counseling center for additional guidance.

## EFFECTS OF LONG-TERM STRESS: DEPRESSION AND SUICIDE

Aside from physical illness that may result from prolonged stress, another common reaction to stress involves depression. Depression symptoms vary, of course, in terms of severity, duration, and the degree to which they interfere with our functioning. Most of us have experienced the symptoms of at least the milder forms of depression.

**EXERCISE: RECOGNIZING SIGNS OF DEPRESSION**

1. How do you feel when you are depressed or "down"? What changes do you notice in your behavior or thinking?

_____

_____

_____

_____

_____

_____

_____

2. Common signs of depression include the following. Check off the symptoms that you experience when you are down.

_____    Sleep problems (inability to fall asleep, waking up too early even when tired).

_____    Difficulties in concentration.

_____    Overeating or loss of appetite leading to a decrease in eating.

_____    Irritability, tearfulness.

_____    Apathy, nothing seems to matter.

_____    Loss of energy, constant fatigue.

_____    Inability to enjoy previously enjoyable activities.

_____    Feelings of worthlessness or guilt.

_____    Feelings of pessimism.

_____    Feelings of sadness.

_____    The desire to take one's life.

Usually, when we are "down" or "blue," these feelings go away in a few days. When the blue feelings linger for a long period, however, or when they begin to interfere with your daily functioning, it is time to seek help, from a friend, a family member, or a professional. Often, just talking about your feelings will help you to feel better. At other times, counseling or psychotherapy may be effective. Psychologists have now developed a number of techniques (especially cognitive therapy) that are particularly effective in dealing with depression.

## Suicide and Depression

There is a strong link between depression and suicide, and the suicide rate among young people ages 15 through 19 has tripled in the past thirty years.[5] Depression is an important factor in at least five hundred suicides per year. It seems that at least one-fourth of American college students are depressed at any given point in time and that suicide is 50 percent more frequent among college students than among other young people who are not enrolled in course work. Approximately ten thousand college students attempt suicide each year in the United States, and one thousand succeed.[6]

Since many students will not approach a professional when they are suicidal or seriously depressed, it is worthwhile for all of us to recognize the warning signs of a potential suicide. Check off warning signs of suicide that you may have noticed in a friend. If one of your peers is experiencing any of the symptoms listed in figure 31, convince that friend to see a counselor.

- Feelings of depression, hopelessness, or helplessness.
- Feelings of agitation, restlessness, sleeplessness.
- Giving away prized possessions.
- Recent loss of loved one through death or rejection.
- Recent loss of job; financial difficulties.
- Invention of a suicide plan and the means to carry it out.
- History of one or more suicide attempts or suicide threats. (The majority of suicides are carried out by people who have talked about or attempted suicide previously.)
- Absence of family or friends who are willing to help. Contact with family members has deteriorated or ceased. Family and friends are rejecting or nonsupportive.
- Failing health or presence of chronic illness.
- Deterioration in school performance.
- Abusing alcohol or other drugs. (Many studies show that the majority of suicides are committed when the person is intoxicated.)
- Antisocial behavior. Research is beginning to document the fact that some youths resort to suicide when they have been detained or arrested by police officials for illegal behavior. Youths involved in violent behavior are also more likely to commit suicide.[7,8]

**FIGURE 31. WARNING SIGNS OF SUICIDE**

Most colleges have a counseling center where professionals meet with students who are experiencing difficulties. Some schools also have clergy or peer counselors who can offer support or guidance. If your friend will not consider counseling, contact a residence assistant, a faculty member, or the counseling center about the situation.

- Listen to your friend with concern. Do not ignore your friend; do not put him or her down.
- Share your feelings about a time when you felt badly. Reassure your friend that things got better for you and that things can also get better for him or her.
- Ask your friend if he or she has suicidal thoughts.
- Let your friend know that many people think about suicide but that they do not act on those thoughts.
- Stay with your friend. Talk with him or her or do something together.
- Give your friend a suicide hot line number. Call that number and get advice for your friend if your friend will not do it on his or her own.
- If your friend is suicidal and refuses to get help, notify a responsible person (a counselor, the dormitory manager, an instructor, a minister, etc.).
- Make a date with your friend to see him or her the next day.

**FIGURE 32. WAYS TO HELP A DEPRESSED OR SUICIDAL FRIEND**

Literature about suicide is filled with testimonials from grateful individuals whose plans for suicide were interrupted. When people are depressed, their perspectives are warped; death seems to be the only solution to their problems. Once they have been helped to see other alternatives, they cannot imagine why they ever considered suicide. Consider the steps, listed in figure 32, that you could take to help a suicidal friend.

## NOTES

1. T. H. Holmes and R. H. Rahe, "Social Readjustment Rating Scale," *Journal of Psychosomatic Research* 11 (1967): 213–218.

2. I. G. Sarason, J. H. Johnson, and J. Siegel, "Assessing the Impact of Life Changes: Development of the Life Experience Survey," *Journal of Consulting and Clinical Psychology* 46 (1978): 932–946.

3. R. H. Rosenman et al., "Coronary Heart Disease in the Western Collaborative Group Study: Final Follow-up Experience at 8 1/2 Years," *Journal of the American Medical Association* 233 (1975): 872–877.

4. C. D. Jenkins, S. J. Zyzanski, and R. H. Rosenman, "Risk of New Myocardial Infarction in Middle Age Men with Manifest Coronary Disease," *Circulation* 53 (1976): 342–347.

5. J. E. Brody, "The Haunting Spectre of Teenage Suicide," *New York Times,* 4 March 1984, p. 8E.

6. J. C. Coleman, J. N. Butcher, and R. C. Carson, *Abnormal Psychology and Modern Life* (Glenview, Ill.: Scott, Foresman, 1980).

7. M. Shalfii et al., "Psychological Autopsy of Completed Suicide in Children and Adolescents," *American Journal of Psychiatry* 142 (1985): 1061.

8. L. N. Robins, National Institute of Mental Health 1983 Epidemiological Catchment Study. In "Youth Suicide: New Research Focuses on Growing Social Problem," *Research News,* 22 August 1986, pp. 839–841.

# Chapter 16

---

# Values Clarification

One of the most-important developmental processes involves the acquisition of personal values. *Values* are standards or philosophies for living or behaving. Having values implies living in a way that you consider important, worthwhile, or meaningful. As individuals mature, they learn that there are many different types of value systems.

Growing up involves making choices about which values you will adopt. Setting goals is one way to put your values into action. For recent high school graduates, college may represent the first opportunity to experiment with values that are different from those held by their parents. For students returning to school after years in the world of work or homemaking, college offers the opportunity to reassess their values in the light of new knowledge and perspectives.

## A PYRAMID OF NEEDS

Values are closely related to needs. Some writers believe that people adopt particular values in order to fulfill psychological or physical needs. The humanistic psychologist Abraham Maslow describes human needs and values in terms of a pyramid, as shown in figure 33. At the bottom of the pyramid are basic physiological needs for food, air, water, and sex. Once these basic needs are satisfied, the individual may turn his or her attention to higher needs, thus progressing from one level to the next until he or she reaches the top level where the primary goal is self-actualization.

Other theorists hypothesize that these needs are not hierarchically arranged. You may wish to satisfy any or all of these needs at the same time. But there will be times when you must choose among different needs. A decision to help a friend may satisfy the need for affection and belongingness, but it may conflict with the need to have justice or goodness. A job that satisfies the need for knowledge or beauty will not necessarily meet the need for recognition or security. Making choices among different needs can often involve difficult value judgments.

## Your Personal Needs

To the extent that you know yourself and your value system well, you should be able to make decisions in your life, education, and career with which you

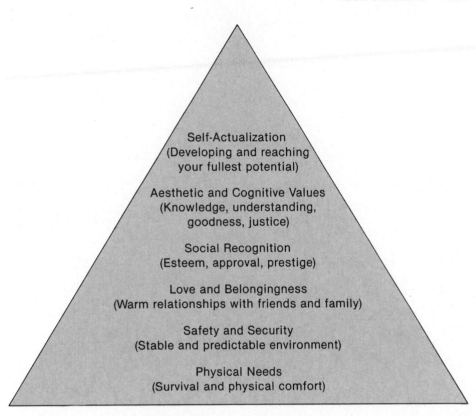

**FIGURE 33. MASLOW'S HIERARCHY OF NEEDS**

can live comfortably. Making decisions requires that you know what you want or what you value. The following exercise will help you identify your personal needs and will give you the opportunity to think about what needs and values are most important to you. Such introspection can help you to define your value system.

**EXERCISE: IDENTIFYING AND SATISFYING PERSONAL NEEDS**

1. Pages 225 through 231 contain cards that you will later remove from the book; these cards list twenty-eight needs commonly identified by adults. People attach different degrees of importance to each of those needs. Look over the cards and become familiar with the needs listed. There are four final cards in which you may record other needs not identified in the twenty-eight preprinted cards.

Choose the cards that currently represent your five most important needs. Write your priority number, on each of the five cards, from most important (1) to fifth in importance (5). Then look through the remaining cards, choose a few that do not seem at all important to you, and mark them with a zero.

It may not be easy for you to identify and rank your needs. You are probably not accustomed to doing this. What's more, you may not feel completely comfortable with some of your choices. The purpose of this exercise is not to judge whether your needs are good or bad or right or wrong, but rather to help you become more aware of what your needs are.

This exercise is excerpted from *Catalyst's Campus Resource: A Guide to Exploring Career and Personal Life Options* copyright by Catalyst 1984. Reproduced by permission of Catalyst, 250 Park Avenue South, New York, NY 10003.

| To feel that I am a good person | To be respected |
| --- | --- |
| To have power | To help others |
| To be physically attractive | To feel competent |
| To be economically secure | To grow and develop |

To be with people I like

To feel needed

To have new experiences

To influence others

To be creative

To feel like an adult

To love and be loved

To feel a part
of something larger
than myself

To have time
for myself alone

To be true to my beliefs

To control my own life

To be famous

To look up to others

To be intellectually
stimulated

To take care of my body

To have aesthetically
pleasing experiences

To achieve something
important

To enjoy life
and have fun

To have stability
in my life

To have wealth
and luxuries

(Another need I have)

(Another need I have)

(Another need I have)

(Another need I have)

2. When class members have finished ranking their needs, your instructor will go around the room and ask each of you to read your most-important need. If you do not feel comfortable responding to this question, just say "Pass," but do pay attention to your peers' responses. Your instructor will list the needs on the board as they are read and will put a check under a need each time a student reads it. You will thus be able to tally the most-popular need.

Your instructor will then repeat this procedure for the needs ranked number 2 and number 3. Which needs appear frequently? How great is the variety of needs that are ranked in the top three priorities by your peers? Do the rankings of the women in the class differ from those of the men?

What are the three most-common needs? Write them here:

1. _____

2. _____

3. _____

3. Your instructor will conduct a class discussion about the three most common needs. Consider the following questions:

- What do you think makes people choose these needs?
  Are they born with them?
  Do they learn them?
  How do they learn them?
  Who teaches them to value those needs?

- (If there are differences between the needs chosen most often by males and females . . . ) Why do you think men (or women) chose this need more often?

- For your first three needs, did you choose those that you are currently satisfying? If so, why? If not, why not?

4. The cards printed on pages 235 through 239 will help you to identify the sources you use to satisfy your needs. On the four final blank cards, write in any other sources of satisfaction that are relevant to you.

Needs I can satisfy best
by having close friends

Needs I can satisfy best by
belonging to an institutionalized
religion (church, synagogue, mosque)

Needs I can satisfy best
by having a career or job

- - - - - - - - - - - - - - - - - - - - - - - - - - - - - - - - -

Needs I can satisfy best
by having a spouse or partner

- - - - - - - - - - - - - - - - - - - - - - - - - - - - - - - - -

Needs I can satisfy best
by having a family or children

- - - - - - - - - - - - - - - - - - - - - - - - - - - - - - - - -

Needs I can satisfy best
by having leisure time

Needs I can satisfy best by

_____

Needs I can satisfy best by

_____

Needs I can satisfy best by

_____

Needs I can satisfy best by

_____

5. After you have finished the number 1 item in this exercise, cut out the cards, along the dotted lines, so that you have a stack of them. Each of these cards should list one of your sources of satisfaction. Now cut out the cards from the previous exercise (pp. 225–231). Each of these cards should list one of your needs.

Spread out the source of satisfaction cards, then go through the need cards, and place each need card on top of a source of satisfaction card. In other words, match your needs with ways of satisfying them.

Look at your stacks and determine which source of satisfaction cards have the most need cards placed on top of them.

Your instructor will ask for a show of hands to find out which source of satisfaction cards have the most needs assigned to them by class members. Write in the three sources of satisfaction cards that satisfy the most needs for members of your class.

a. _____

b. _____

c. _____

6. Participate in a class discussion that addresses the following questions:

- Did you find any needs that you could satisfy through more than one source?

- (If applicable) Why do you think men or women want to satisfy their needs mostly through _____ (most frequently chosen item)?

- Do any of your needs conflict with one another? Do you think that you will have to stifle one need in order to satisfy another? Which needs are in question?

- Do you think it is possible to satisfy all of your needs? Why or why not?

- Do you think the search for satisfaction of your own needs might conflict or interfere with the satisfaction of needs for people who are close to you?

## Sources of Satisfaction

You should realize that the importance you assign to various needs and the way you choose to satisfy them may change over time. Goals that seem very important now may become less pressing in a few years. You may be satisfying some needs through work now whereas you may choose to satisfy those same needs through another avenue in the future.

Perhaps the most important thing to realize is that few people ever completely satisfy all of their needs. By keeping an open mind about what are your possible sources of need satisfaction, you may be more pleased with the results of your search. In that way you can avoid being labeled as workaholic, hooked only on the kids, or fun crazy.

## CAREER AND PERSONAL LIFE CHOICES

In addition to general values that guide your path in education, career, and leisure activities, you will find that values are also important factors in your relationships with other people. The following seven scenarios will help you consider how values affect your career and personal life choices. They will also help you see how priorities change according to circumstances and stages of a person's life. Finally, they will encourage you to find solutions to problems should you find yourself in similar situations.

**EXERCISE: IDENTIFYING VALUES, GOALS, AND PRIORITIES**

Break into small discussion groups of five students. Your instructor will assign three of the following scenarios to each discussion group. Read over the scenario, discuss all the issues, and answer the questions that follow the scenario. Decide how *you* might react in a similar situation.

These scenarios present very difficult conflict situations similar to those in which many people find themselves today. The resolution to these problems is based on individuals' personal value systems. *There are no right or wrong answers.* Decide how you might react in a similar situation. Reaching group consensus about what people in the scenario should do or whether they are right or wrong is not the goal of this exercise. Values, goals, and priorities are highlighted here because they are so rarely discussed and yet are so often at the root of many disputes in life.

---

This exercise is excerpted from *Catalyst's Campus Resource: A Guide to Exploring Career and Personal Life Options,* copyright by Catalyst 1984. Reproduced by permission of Catalyst, 250 Park Avenue South, New York, NY 10003.

**Scenario 1**

Andy, twenty-four, is a sales manager for a midwestern company that makes power tools. His wife, Paula, does not work outside the home and spends her time caring for their six-month-old son. Andy's job involves a lot of traveling; he supervises sales over a large area of the midwest. He drives a great deal every day, calling directly on hardware stores, factories, schools, and the wholesalers who distribute his company's products. Andy often has to travel evenings and weekends to reach his clients who are spread out geographically; in addition, he spends at least two weeks out of every month away from home.

When he travels, he stays in close phone contact with his wife, but he sometimes feels as if his son is growing up without a father. Andy works on salary plus commission; he and Paula both realize that the harder and longer he works, the higher will be his earnings, but neither one is completely happy with the current situation.

QUESTIONS FOR SCENARIO 1

1. Andy and Paula have a traditional relationship. Because there is only one income for the family, the income produced by Andy's job is critical. How do you feel about this relationship? Does it seem satisfactory? Unsatisfactory? Why?

2. Would you suggest that Andy and Paula try to change their situation? If so, why? If not, why?

3. How might you change the situation to give Andy more time with his child (look for a new job, decide/try to live on less money, have Paula work part time so that Andy could work less)?

4. How do you think Andy's job affects Paula's attitude toward him? Toward herself?

5. How do you think Andy's child will be affected by Andy's long periods away from home?

6. If you were in the couple's situation, would you find it acceptable temporarily? For how long? Would it be alright over a long period of time?

7. Could you imagine yourself in a situation similar to the one Andy and Paula have? (If you're a male, you would be in Andy's position; if you're a female, you would be in Paula's position). How might you react?

**Scenario 2**

Anne, now twenty-seven, is a stage actress who has played major roles in community theater and Off-Broadway productions in New York. She and her husband, Vincent, would like to have a child by the time Anne is in her thirties. Anne has had an offer to join a London repertory theater for one year. It is an opportunity to broaden her experience, work with a highly regarded director, and boost her chances for career advancement. When she returns to New York, she hopes to perform on Broadway and join a touring theater company. Eventually, she would like to go to Los Angeles and have an opportunity to work in films.

Vincent teaches history in a small private school in New York City. If Anne takes the London offer, he must decide whether to give up his position to go with her or remain in New York and see Anne only a few times during the year. He is aware that Anne will probably relocate several times because of her career, but the couple never seem to have time to thoroughly discuss their plans or how children and Vincent's career will fit into their future.

QUESTIONS FOR SCENARIO 2

1. In this relationship Anne has the "dominant" career. What do you think about this relationship? Is it workable? If it is, what makes it work? If not, why?

2. If Vincent relocates with Anne what could happen to his career? To their relationship?

3. What do you think will happen to Anne's career if she *doesn't* take the opportunity in London? What will happen to their relationship?

4. How would you suggest that Anne and Vincent work out their possible career conflict?

5. Would you want to be in Vincent's position? How would you feel if Anne asked you to relocate?

6. Would you want a career like Anne's? How would you feel about asking your spouse to relocate?

7. What kind of spouse would *you* have to have (if you were in Anne's position) to make a high-level acting career *and* a stable personal relationship possible?

**Scenario 3**

Joe, who is in his midtwenties, just landed a job with a very important private law firm that employs over one hundred attorneys. Joe graduated with top honors from his law school and his firm has great expectations for him. Right now, Joe is what is called an "associate" and he spends much of his time assisting experienced attorneys with their cases. He has very little contact with clients and instead does a lot of research. But Joe knows that he has to prove himself before he's given more responsibility. He puts in very long days, often working through dinner and sometimes into the early morning hours at the office or in the local law library.

Over the next few years, Joe hopes to prove himself so that his responsibility for clients and cases will steadily increase, and the firm will offer him a partnership. Not many of the associates "make partner" and the competition is fierce. For the moment, he keeps working conscientiously anyway, hoping that it will pay off, but his profession is leaving him with little time for anything but work. In fact, he can't remember the last time he spent an evening "just relaxing." He's single but would like to have a family "someday"; he just doesn't know when he'll find the time.

QUESTIONS FOR SCENARIO 3

1. What do you think of Joe's job? What do you like about it? Dislike about it?

2. If you were in Joe's position, would you stay in the job at the law firm?

3. If Joe were a single parent with custody of his children, would you feel differently about the job? Why?

4. If Joe were a single woman with no children, would you feel differently about the job?

5. How do you feel about the fact that Joe's job gives him little contact with people?

6. How do you feel about a high-pressure, competitive job with the possibility of substantial rewards at the top?

7. How do you feel about the fact that these rewards are uncertain in the case of this job?

**Scenario 4**

Dorothy is a vice president at a large oil company. She is thirty-three and returned to work three months ago after having her first child (a daughter) and taking a two-month maternity leave. She had hoped to take a longer leave, but her office was in the midst of negotiating an important contract for which her services were needed. Her husband, Lee, requested a brief paternity leave from the hospital where he practices psychiatry, but it was denied because hospital policy does not give men parental leaves.

Both Dorothy and Lee worked hard to attain their current career levels and do not wish to leave their jobs. So they decided to hire a daytime caretaker for their daughter and alternate taking time off from work when the baby or the caretaker is sick. They had thought about maintaining this type of arrangement until their child is about two years old. At that time the couple expects to enroll her in the hospital's child care center.

Dorothy and Lee work long hours. Although their schedules are less hectic than they once were, each of their positions demands at least nine or ten hours of work per day. They are beginning to worry that neither of them has the time or energy to be the kind of parents they had hoped to be. They are also worried about the quality of their own relationship, which has suffered since the baby was born.

QUESTIONS FOR SCENARIO 4

1. Do you think it was wise for Dorothy and Lee to have a child at this point in their careers? Why or why not?

2. How do you feel about Dorothy and Lee leaving their baby with a hired caretaker all day, every day? Under the same circumstances, what would you do?

3. Imagine you are Dorothy's boss. How do you think you would respond if she asked you for additional time off to care for her child, even if it was without pay? How long would you guarantee to hold her full-time job open? How would you respond if she asked for a part-time position? What are some of the problems either of these arrangements (more leave, part-time work) might cause?

4. How do you feel about Lee wanting to take a leave to care for his baby? (*For women*) Would you want your spouse to take such a leave? Why or why not? (*For men*) Would you be willing to take such a leave? Why or why not?

5. If you were Dorothy, and you decided to quit your job to care for your child, what would be the most difficult part of leaving? What might be some of the advantages?

6. If you were Lee, and you decided to quit your job, what would be the most difficult part of leaving? What might be some of the advantages?

7. Picture yourself as a policy maker in an organization, institution, or company. Do you think it would be your responsibility to provide paternity leaves? If so, why? If not, why?

## Scenario 5

Eleanor recently returned to college as a full-time student. She has spent the last fifteen years raising her three children (ages 8, 10, and 15) and taking responsibility for most of the household chores. She feels as though her personal identity has completely disappeared while caring for her family's needs. She feels the need for some intellectual stimulation and long-range goals. This is her first experience as a student in seventeen years. She hopes to get her degree and pursue a career in accounting. She feels that time is running out for her. If she does not go to school full time to get her degree, it will soon be too late for her to pursue a meaningful career.

Her husband, Keith, works full time as a manager for the telephone company. He supports her decision to return to school, but is learning the "hard way" how much he took for granted Eleanor's contribution to managing the household.

Eleanor is also experiencing problems with the transition; sometimes she is too tired at night to be a patient mother or take full responsibility for household tasks. In fact, one night Eleanor yelled at Keith for buying the wrong kind of steak for dinner. On several occasions, she could not study adequately for important exams or complete research in time for class papers because of time she spent on housework and child care.

All family members are aware of the upheaval that the change in Eleanor's life caused in their routines, but they haven't really talked as a family about how to cope with these new arrangements.

### QUESTIONS FOR SCENARIO 5

1. How do you feel about Eleanor's decision to return to school?

2. Do you feel that she should have returned to school sooner?

3. Do you feel she should have postponed her plans for school until the children were older?

4. Do you think she has an obligation to stay in the homemaker role permanently since that was the role she chose when she got married?

5. Would you take time from your husband's (or wife's) and children's needs to get a degree and make a meaningful life for yourself?

6. Would you take time from your husband's (or wife's) and children's needs to get a degree if it meant that you could improve their lives by earning (more) money in the long run?

7. What suggestions can you offer Eleanor, her husband, and her children that might ease tensions in their household?

### Scenario 6

Vivian is a graduate student in history. She shares an off-campus apartment with Chris, who is an advanced undergraduate engineering student. They have been friends since they were in high school. This year Chris has to buy a personal computer to do her course work, or her grades will suffer. Chris lives on a fixed income from her family and has no extra money to contribute to the purchase. Vivian lives on a small teaching fellowship and has a loan from her parents. Both women share the apartment expenses equally.

Vivian is considering paying for the computer. She remembers that, when they graduated from high school, Chris paid for Vivian to accompany her on a three-month trip to Europe. In order to buy the computer for Chris, Vivian would need to use her parents' loan, take an additional part-time job, and delay completion of her thesis. She must decide soon.

### QUESTIONS FOR SCENARIO 6

1. If you were in Vivian's situation, what personal values might you consider in making this decision?

2. If you had to prioritize these values, which one(s) would be most important? Least important?

3. What external factors, or influences, might affect her decision? Which is the strongest factor? Which is the weakest?

4. If you were Chris, how would you feel if Vivian decided against buying the computer? What would you do?

5. Do you think it would be wise for Vivian to delay her educational/career goals? What might be the advantages? What might be the disadvantages?

6. If you were Vivian, what kinds of feelings might you have if you decided to buy the computer? How would you feel if you decided against it?

**Scenario 7**

Jose, twenty-six, is a computer technician for a large computer company. He and his wife, Luisa, who is twenty-six also, have been married for four years. They have both been working full time, and are thinking about starting a family within a year. Jose's job pays well, but there is very little room for advancement in his department. He is also on call at night and on weekends, a schedule he doesn't want to maintain when he has children.

Recently, he took some aptitude tests at a local government employment agency and learned that he might do very well as a computer systems designer. If he decided to move into that field, he would need to return to school full time for three or four years. The company will not pay for his training or give him a leave of absence or a part-time position. Jose would have to quit *this* job to go back to school.

Luisa understands and supports Jose's ambitions, but is very anxious to have children, and knows that if she becomes the sole wage-earner and contributes to Jose's tuition, they will have to delay having children for at least five years. Although their finances will be better then, and their schedules will be less demanding, Luisa will be thirty-one years old, and she's worried about starting a family at that age.

QUESTIONS FOR SCENARIO 7

1. Do you think Jose should leave his present position and return to school? Why or why not?

2. If Jose returns to school now, how might it affect Luisa's and Jose's relationship?

3. Which spouse do you think must make the most sacrifices if Jose returns to school? If he stays in his current job? Why?

4. If you were Luisa, how would you feel when Jose told you about his plans to leave his job? How would you respond?

5. How would you feel if you were the one asking Luisa to make this sacrifice? How could you deal with her feelings about the decision?

6. If Luisa were the one who wanted to return to school instead of Jose, do you think the same conflicts would exist? Why or why not?

7. Putting off childbearing for four or five years would make Luisa thirty or thirty-one years old when she tries to start a family. How do you feel about the idea of starting a family at that age? Do you think these feelings would be different for Luisa than for Jose? Why or why not?

8. Do you see any alternatives for resolving this conflict?

# RELATING TO OTHERS

Values enter into your personal relationships in other ways, too. You might experience a conflict if you find that a friend has cheated on an exam in your class. Would you report him or her? Would you lecture your friend about honesty? What would you do if you found that a roommate was selling drugs? How would you react if your boyfriend or girlfriend made a habit of drinking at parties and then driving while intoxicated?

Now that you are on your own in college, you may find that some of your values about what is right and wrong conflict with other values about loyalty, honesty, and security. The following exercise will give you practice in confronting and thinking about some of the difficult questions that arise in the area of values and human relationships.

1. For this exercise, break into small discussion groups of five. Read the following scenario.

**EXERCISE:**
**IDENTIFYING**
**INTERPERSONAL**
**VALUES**

### The Scenario

Susan came from a small town in Pennsylvania where her widowed father was an evangelical Christian minister. He raised her very strictly, and it was only with great reluctance that he allowed Susan to go to the University of Pittsburgh. He feared that the big city would corrupt her morals. As Susan boarded the bus, he warned her "If I ever find out that you've been fooling around with boys or using alcohol or drugs, I'll cut you off from all financial support and never let you enter my home again."

Susan had always obeyed her father and intended to do so while at college. She did stay away from drugs and alcohol, but in October she began dating Larry, a fellow student in her religion class. By December they were sleeping together. When she returned from Christmas vacation, Susan discovered that she was pregnant. Since neither her father nor the private church-affiliated schools she had attended ever mentioned birth control, she had not taken the proper precautions.

Larry did not want to get married. He said, "I'm sorry, but you should have been more careful." He then added, "Besides, how do I know that it's mine?" Rejected by Larry, Susan decided to turn to her father for help. Susan called her father and explained her situation. He said, "I warned you, and you know how I feel. From this day on, you are no longer my daughter," he added before hanging up on her.

Panic-stricken, Susan decided to have an abortion. Susan saw an article that an agency had placed in the *Pitt News* advertising help for unwanted pregnancies. The article said the cost for an abortion would be $400.00. Susan went to her best friend Allison for the money. "I don't approve of abortions," Allison said. "I can't lend you money to destroy a life." Susan then decided to call the agency. The agency head, after finding out that Susan did not have the money, referred her to the Department of Public Assistance. The social worker at the Department of Public Assistance told Susan that she was still the responsibility of her father. The clerk stated coldly, "If the Department of Public Assistance gave money to every irresponsible girl who got pregnant, there would be no money for people who really need it."

In desperation, Susan approached Dorothy. Dorothy was a popular, upperclass student in her dorm, who appeared to be very knowledgeable. "Sure, I've got a concoction that will make you miscarry—no charge," said Dorothy.

After taking the mixture, Susan did miscarry, but in the process, she hemorrhaged severely and died.

---

This exercise is reprinted with permission of Professor Ina R. Hark, University of South Carolina, author of the "Modern Drawbridge Exercise."

2. Discuss the scenario with your group members, and try to reach a consensus in which you rate each of the characters, according to how much he or she appeals to the group, from most appealing (1) to least appealing (6). Compare your group's ratings with the ratings of other groups in the class.

Susan _____    Larry _____    Social worker _____

Susan's father _____    Dorothy _____    Allison _____

3. Participate in a class discussion that addresses the following questions:

• What do you think your rankings reveal about your values?
• How do you feel about the following topics in relation to college students?

  Premarital sex

  Birth control

  Abortion

  Becoming parents before completing college

• Describe the obligations or responsibilities that you feel the characters in Susan's story owe to each other.

  Susan's father to Susan

  Susan to her father

  Larry to Susan

  Susan to Larry

  Allison to Susan

  Susan to Allison

  Dorothy to Susan

  The social worker to Susan

In this chapter you have identified some of your values and considered how they might affect your decisions in relationships, personal choices, and careers. Chapter 19, "Careers," will present additional exercises to help you determine which of your values might give you a sound basis for making career choices.

# Chapter 17

# Racial and Ethnic Minority Groups

## OUR MULTICULTURAL SOCIETY

The United States has been called the melting pot of the world. It is a country where people of varying races, religions, and ethnic backgrounds have come to work together and build a better society. Although our country is made up of people from various backgrounds, many of us come from communities and schools where we have experienced little in the way of diversity.

Your college experience may represent the first time that you will share a dormitory room with someone from a different race or work on a course project with someone from a different country. This may be the first time that you find yourself in classes with students who communicate by sign language or commute by wheelchair. Some students may be twenty years older than you are, with taste in music, politics, clothes, and food that is radically different from your own. It is through your interactions with different types of students that some of the most important learning experiences at college take place. As you come into contact with different ideas, values, and customs, you will reflect upon, evaluate, and forge your own ideals. When you learn to communicate and work with individuals from varied backgrounds, you prepare yourself to function in the real world.

"Workforce 2000," a study commissioned by the U.S. Department of Labor from the Hudson Institute, reports that the work force of the 1990s will be changing as women, minorities, and recent immigrants add 19 million new workers to the American economy by the year 2000. White males will make up less than 10 percent of the new workers, so that managers will be trying to accommodate different gender, ethnic, and cultural work styles to meet the needs of the changing work force.

The increased diversity in the American work force will be fueled by federal legislation and equal opportunity laws and by good business sense. The economy will need workers from new sectors as the generation after the baby boom will yield only two-thirds as many new workers as entered the work force in the 1970s. Many companies are already beginning to experience the increased competition for workers in their entry-level positions. Corporations will also be reaching out to minority workers so that they can tap the diverse American marketplace; exclusively white male management teams will not be able to come up with the most competitive and creative ways to reach this diversified market.

All predictions point to the fact that the workplace will consist of more women, more African-Americans, and more ethnic minorities. If you wish to succeed in this type of work environment, you will have to learn to work effectively with people from a variety of backgrounds. The college campus is a good place to undertake this kind of learning.

Although learning to work with people from diverse backgrounds can be exciting and fascinating, it is not always a smooth process. You may experience emotions such as anxiety, anger, embarrassment, or guilt as you begin to learn about and appreciate perspectives that differ from your own. It is worth persevering in the effort because you will broaden your experience and learn skills that you will need as you enter the more diverse world of the twenty-first century.

It is also worth persevering because learning to appreciate and tolerate other cultures can help maintain peace on the college campus. Many students have been suspended or disciplined because of racial incidents on campus. Some have even gone to jail. Knowledge and understanding can go a long way to ease tensions and build a cooperative community.

A good place to begin this multicultural education is with a look at some of the problems minority groups have confronted in our society. This chapter will examine racial and ethnic issues. Chapter 18 will deal with gender issues and with challenged and nontraditional students.

## AFRICAN-AMERICANS

African-Americans constitute the largest disadvantaged minority in the United States. The 30 million African-Americans currently living in the United States make up 12 percent of the population. This population has been growing at a faster rate than the white population, and African-American growth will continue to outstrip white growth through the year 2000. The Census Bureau estimates that this minority's population will grow almost 13 percent between 1990 and 2000 whereas white growth will only increase by 5 percent.[1]

African-Americans constitute a disadvantaged minority when we look at standard economic, educational, and political indicators such as average income, number of years of education completed, numbers represented in the professions, numbers holding political office, and number of families living below the poverty level. Many of these figures are directly related to discrimination experienced by this group. A brief look at the African-American experience in this country will explain some of the gaps between African-American and white standards of living.

### History

The first African-Americans to enter the colonies arrived as slaves in 1619. Most whites also arrived as slaves (indentured servants), but their period of slavery was limited to a specific number of years while they worked to pay off their passage to the colonies. Although African-Americans were freed from slavery after the Civil War, they continue to face segregation and discrimination in education, employment, housing, and public services.

The Civil Rights Act of 1964 and the Voting Rights Act of 1965 guaranteed African-Americans access to public accommodations (like restaurants and hotels), voting booths, and jobs. Other federal laws followed that led to the active recruitment of African-Americans into businesses and colleges. These developments resulted in a growing African-American middle class. Despite continued discrimination, African-Americans made important gains in political representation, level of education, and economic status.

## Politics

Examples of political gains included the overwhelming reelection of African-American mayors in Detroit and Los Angeles to fourth terms of office. African-Americans were appointed to the jobs of ambassador to the United Nations, associate justice of the Supreme Court, and secretary of the Department of Housing and Urban Development. In 1984 and 1988, an African-American was considered a serious candidate for the Democratic presidential nomination. By 1985, African-Americans held 6,000 elective offices (sixty times as many as in 1954), including 20 members of the House of Representatives, 2 lieutenant governors, and 247 mayors. There were also 325 African-American judges.[2]

## Education

In the eighteenth and nineteenth centuries, the legislatures of some states actually outlawed education for blacks. When African-American children *were* allowed to go to public school, they were forced to attend poorly funded schools where they received an inferior education. On 17 May 1954, the Supreme Court ruled that racial segregation in the schools violated the equal protection clause of the Fourteenth Amendment to the Constitution.

By 1973, 46 percent of southern African-American children attended schools where the majority of students were white. The children of parents who were not themselves educated did not perform as well in school, but the schools continued to promote these students for social and financial reasons even though they had not learned the basics in earlier grades. Educational standards in these schools began to drop and white parents began to put their children into private schools or moved to segregated communities. As African-Americans became the majority population in inner city and rural public schools, many taxpayers became less willing to give adequate financial support to these public schools.[3] The quality of education in many urban public schools across the nation began to decline.

Despite these limitations, African-Americans made impressive progress in raising their level of education. The percentage of African-Americans, ages 25 or over, who completed high school, increased from 13 percent to 59 percent between 1950 and 1984.[4] By 1986, more than 62 percent of African-Americans over the age of 25 years had completed four years or more of high school, while the percentage of whites with four years of high school education or more was 76 percent.[5] In addition, African-American college enrollment multiplied more than five times between 1960 and 1982.[6] By 1986, more than 26 percent of African-Americans over the age of 25 had completed one or more years of college, while the comparable figure for whites was 37 percent.[7]

Some of this progress has since begun to erode. The American Council on Education reports that the number of African-American males enrolled in college has dropped 7.2 percent since its peak in 1980.[8] This erosion is creating an educational gap between African-American men and African-American women that worries a number of social policy analysts. The pool of eligible African-American mates is becoming smaller for African-American women as they move up the educational and career ladder.[9]

## Economics

African-Americans have made tremendous strides in the area of economic status, but their standard of living still lags behind that of the white majority. After World War II, the federal government and most state governments passed fair employment statutes that made it illegal to ask questions about race on job applications. These laws made it more difficult for employers to discriminate on the basis of race. In the 1970s, the federal government went further in the battle against racial discrimination by requiring contractors to actually demonstrate that they were not discriminating: contractors were forced to hire a reasonable number of minority workers. Together with improvements in the level of education, these affirmative action employment policies allowed many African-Americans to enter business and the professions; this combination resulted in a growing African-American middle class.

Between 1960 and 1980, the number of African-Americans entering the professions tripled, and the number of businesses owned by African-Americans rose sharply.[10] By 1982, African-Americans held 15 percent of all federal jobs. The percentage of African-American families earning incomes over $25,000 a year increased from 13 to 23 percent between 1970 and 1983. Between 1940 and 1980, African-American income rose from 43 percent of white earnings to 73 percent of white earnings among fully employed African-American males. Unfortunately, the unemployment rate for African-Americans has been double the rate for whites as many farm and industrial jobs traditionally held by African-Americans have disappeared in an increasingly technological and service-oriented American economy.

Increased public assistance programs, the construction of subsidized housing, school lunch programs, Head Start programs, and Medicaid health insurance programs for the poor have raised the standard of living for many African-Americans living in poverty. African-American infant mortality was cut in half between 1960 and 1982. The life expectancy for African-Americans, during the same period, increased by five years to age 69.[11] The percentage of African-American families living below the poverty level fell from 55 percent in 1959 to 28 percent in 1986.[12]

Despite these impressive economic gains, African-Americans are still more likely to suffer serious health problems, receive public assistance, be victims of crime, rent rather than own their residences, and be convicted of crime. Many researchers even fear that the gap between African-Americans and whites may widen.

Almost 60 percent of African-American children born in 1983 were born to unwed mothers, and this alarming tendency for African-American children to live in households without fathers is continuing. Households headed by women tend to be poorer than households that are headed by men. Seventy percent of the African-American children living in female-headed households are being born and raised in poverty.[13] These children are more likely to suffer from a variety of childhood illnesses and disturbances, to drop out of school, to be unemployed, and to become involved in crime and drug abuse.

Many researchers blame public assistance programs for encouraging African-American fathers to abandon their families. Twenty-five states still have laws that withhold public assistance from families with an able-bodied male living with them, regardless of that man's earning capacity. The only way that many unemployed African-American men can assure financial aid for their families is to abandon them. The number of fatherless African-American households rose from 27 percent in 1956 to 44 percent in 1985.[14] Although the percentage of African-American families living below the poverty line fell to 28 percent in

1986, this figure is still much greater than the 8.6 percent figure that represents the percentage of white families living in poverty.

## African-Americans on Campus

Despite the impressive gains made by African-Americans, problems of discrimination continue to keep them in a subordinate position. Such problems are evident even in the nation's colleges and universities. In the past two years, several incidents have been reported. A white student at Brown University tossed glass bottles at a group of African-American students returning to their dorms from a party. At the University of Alabama, a wooden cross was burned outside a building that was being considered as the location for an African-American sorority chapter. At the University of Michigan, a white disc jockey told crude racial jokes on the air of the campus radio station. At the Citadel, an African-American student withdrew from the academy after five white students dressed in Ku Klux Klan costumes broke into his room and burned a wooden cross. Additional racial incidents have been reported at other campuses across the country.[15]

Although such blatant examples of racism are becoming less frequent on campuses these days, more subtle forms of discrimination seem to continue. A 1985 survey by the National Study of Black College Students reported that 80 percent of African-American respondents experienced some form of racial discrimination during their college years.[16]

**EXERCISE: IDENTIFYING SUBTLE RACISM**

Place a check next to the examples of prejudice against African-Americans that you have witnessed. Write in any additional examples that you may have seen on your campus. Your instructor will go around the room and ask you to volunteer examples. Compile a class list of the many forms that racial prejudice may take.

_____ African-Americans are often chosen last as laboratory partners.

_____ Students frequently lean across a black student to ask a white student what the professor said, implying that the African-American would not have understood the point.

_____ White students rarely ask to borrow the notes of African-American students.

_____ African-Americans are often left out of informal study groups organized by whites.

_____ Professors and students frequently show surprise when African-American students answer correctly in class or do well on exams.

_____ Many white professors and students avoid contact with African-American students and are less likely to know them on a personal basis.

_____

_____

_____

_____

_____

The Department of Education's Center for Statistics reports that more than 80 percent of the nation's African-Americans attend colleges where the majority of students are white.[17] Research by Dr. Jaqueline Fleming, a psychology professor at Barnard University, indicates that African-Americans attending white colleges have a more difficult time than African-Americans who attend predominantly African-American schools. These students do not feel accepted on white campuses; they are often resented; they are frequently isolated.

Whites are often jealous of the extra help given to African-Americans through academic assistance and financial aid programs and also through preferential admissions policies. African-Americans attending white schools report more dissatisfaction with their academic and social lives. They are less likely to make strong bonds with faculty members, and they are more likely to lower their vocational goals.

On the other hand, predominantly white colleges offer African-American students access to more academic resources and to a broad social network that can lead to useful contacts for jobs and graduate training. Integrated colleges can also help teach whites to live and work in a multicultural world. Since a diversified cultural experience is useful for both African-Americans and whites, it is worth looking at what we can do to increase the chances for African-American students to succeed on white campuses.

## African-American Success on White Campuses

Special cultural and social programs can help African-Americans to feel less isolated, by reducing mistaken stereotypes and teaching other students more about African-American culture. The more we learn about another culture and its individual representatives, the less likely we are to harbor fears, misconceptions, and anger toward that group.

Harvard University's Foundation for Intercultural and Racial Relations spends approximately $300,000 each year on creative programming to help students appreciate and understand multicultural perspectives. Carribean festivals, appearances by noted members of minority groups such as the Reverend Desmond Tutu of South Africa, performer Debbie Allen, United Nations Secretary General Javier Perez de Cuellar, and boxer Sugar Ray Robinson, help to destroy stereotypes.[18] Once we get past cultural stereotypes, relationships with individuals can form the basis for more productive cooperation on campus and in the workplace.

As a result of segregation and problems in urban public schools, African-Americans often enter college with poor academic preparation. Along with other disadvantaged minorities and poor whites, they may need extra help with basic academic skills, tutoring in various subjects, and orientation to the expectations and structure of the college. Students from poor families may also need information and help in obtaining financial aid. Many colleges have successfully instituted freshman seminar programs that help all students in these areas. Others have experimented with mentor programs where successful juniors or seniors are assigned to incoming students to "show them the ropes."

## Individual Effort

The ideas described above refer to ways that the college community can help African-American students succeed in the college environment, but there are also important steps that each student must take to ensure his or her success. Any student needing help must take responsibility for identifying the necessary resources on campus: academic advisors, successful advanced students, key administrators, the financial aid office, the counseling center, or the academic support center, which may offer tutoring services or remedial courses. African-American students should seek out the necessary resources early, and follow through to make sure they get the help they need.

African-American students should also be wary of assuming that admission to college automatically guarantees success. The dropout rate for African-Americans is high, and this is especially true at predominantly white schools. Every individual must gain the skills and complete the work to achieve those *As* and *Bs*.

Professors will expect African-American students to compete with other students even though the academic preparation of some African-American students may be different. There can be no separate standards for minority students' despite past discrimination or poor high school preparation. If a double standard was established, employers and graduate admissions officers might assume that African-American college graduates are not competitive with white graduates. Disadvantaged African-American students can learn the skills they need to succeed in the world after college, through their own individual efforts and through finding the necessary resources for help.

**EXERCISE: EXAMINING THE MEANING OF DISCRIMINATION**

Look up and write down a dictionary definition of the words in the list below. Give an example of each term from your own experience, or make up some examples that illustrate each term. For each word, indicate how the term applies to racial or ethnic minorities, to women, or to physically challenged individuals.

*Discrimination:*

_____

_____

_____

_____

_____

*Stereotype:*

_____

_____

_____

_____

_____

_____

This exercise is used with the permission of Professor Arnold Jones and Eileen Quaglino of Ramapo College, who developed it.

*Racism:*

_____

_____

_____

_____

_____

*Sexism:*

_____

_____

_____

_____

_____

*Prejudice:*

_____

_____

_____

_____

_____

*Apartheid:*

_____

_____

_____

_____

_____

## EXAMINING THE ROLE OF HISPANICS

Although people who come from Spanish-speaking cultures are not the largest minority group in this country, they do constitute the fastest-growing minority group. There were more than 18 million Hispanics living in the U.S. in 1987, and the Census Bureau was predicting an increase in Hispanic population growth of 27 percent between 1990 and 2000. In comparison, the white population was expected to grow by only 5 percent during those years.[19]

Hispanics make up approximately 21 percent of the population in Texas, 19 percent of the population in California, 16 percent of the population in Arizona, and more than 10 percent of the population in Florida, Colorado, and New York.[20,21] In some cities, such as San Antonio, El Paso, and Miami, Hispanics constitute more than 50 percent of the population. These cities have become bilingual practically overnight! Americans who live in those cities must speak Spanish if they hope to succeed in corporate positions, financial institutions, or business.[22]

## Mexican-Americans

Although Hispanics share a common language and religion, they differ in most other respects. The group that makes up the second largest disadvantaged minority in the United States has emigrated from Mexico. Many lived in the southwest before their lands became part of the United States. Others have been entering the country since the beginning of the twentieth century, seeking jobs and a better standard of living. Since so many workers in Mexico were unemployed, Mexican immigrants were willing to take jobs as migrant farm laborers or as road workers at low wages that most Americans rejected. Many of these immigrants still earn less than the minimum wage at jobs in factories, warehouses, and motels.

Many of the immigrants and their children live in segregated communities and attend segregated schools. Eighty percent live in the southwestern part of the country, mostly in Texas and California. Arizona and New Mexico have elected Mexican-American governors, and some Mexican-Americans have been elected to seats in Congress. Although Mexican-Americans have made economic and political progress in the past years, one-third have incomes below the poverty level, and one-half of their children drop out before graduating from high school.

## Puerto Ricans

The second largest group of Hispanics in the country has emigrated from Puerto Rico. The United States acquired Puerto Rico from Spain after the Spanish-American War in 1898. Puerto Ricans have enjoyed American citizenship and unrestricted immigration into the United States since 1917. Many Puerto Ricans left their island seeking better economic conditions. Most who arrived were poor and uneducated, and they spoke little English. They could get only the lowest-paying jobs, and less than 20 percent of them graduated from high school. Half of them settled in New York City, and 40 percent were living below the poverty level in 1983, with an average income lower than that for African-Americans.[23] Although many Puerto Ricans have improved their status, others have returned to Puerto Rico in sufficient numbers to tip the scales into a "reverse migration" pattern.

## Cubans

The third largest group of Hispanics entering the country came as refugees after Fidel Castro took over the government of Cuba in 1959 and confiscated the property of many Cubans. Since most of the immigrants were educated or professionally trained, they quickly became self-supporting. Although they started out in the lowest-paying jobs, their children did well in school, attended colleges in above-average numbers, established businesses, banks, and construction companies, and raised their average incomes close to the average income for the nation as a whole.

Many Hispanic immigrants continue to enter the United States from other Central and South American countries seeking political freedom and better economic opportunities. Although many Hispanics have made considerable economic progress, the average income of Hispanics as a group still lags behind the national average by $6000. Almost 1 out of 4 Hispanic families lives below the poverty line (compared to only 1 out of 10 white families), and the number of Hispanics who have completed four or more years of high school is almost 29 percent lower than the number for whites.[24]

## OTHER ETHNIC MINORITIES
## AND INTERNATIONAL STUDENTS

African-Americans and Hispanics are by no means the only minorities that have experienced discrimination in this country. Many ethnic, racial, and religious minority groups that have immigrated in large numbers started out at the bottom of the economic ladder and experienced barriers to educational, vocational, and social advancement.

Like African-Americans and Hispanics, these other immigrant groups contributed thousands of gifted individuals who made important contributions to science, technology, literature, and the arts. They have strengthened the American economy by providing needed skills and labor, and they have added to the richness of the American fabric with contributions from their cultures. Immigrants who entered this country contributed their drive, ideals, and motivation to raise American morale. They often worked harder than other Americans in order to succeed economically and strengthen the American economy.

Yet discrimination against immigrant groups continues today. If you are an international student who has come to study in the United States, you may also run into prejudice. At present, large numbers of people are emigrating from Asia. (For example, more than 115,000 people entered the country from Korea, Vietnam, India, and China in 1986.) As many Asians have been particularly successful in American schools, racial incidents have become more numerous. For example, the doors of five dormitory rooms housing Japanese students were spray-painted with the letters of the Ku Klux Klan at Macalester College.[25]

Resentment has been expressed in some quarters that Asian students are succeeding too well in the competition for scholarships and for places in graduate programs (especially in the fields of science and technology) that otherwise would have gone to white students. The economic success of many Asian families has also incurred resentment among some Americans.

It seems that many new groups go through a period of stereotyping and discrimination after arriving, while their members struggle to achieve economic, academic, and social success. As members of the group succeed and become somewhat assimilated into American culture, discrimination seems to decrease. Most of us no longer remember the discrimination and prejudice that greeted early groups of Italians, Irish, Poles, and Germans who entered the country. These people had to work hard to overcome poverty as well as academic and social barriers to success.

These days many politicians are proud to emphasize their ethnic heritage or minority status, but it was not that long ago, in 1960, when many people wondered whether a Catholic (John F. Kennedy) could succeed in being elected president of the United States. More recently, in 1984, a woman (Geraldine Ferraro) ran for the vice presidency for the first time. Even more recently, in 1988, an African-American man (Jesse Jackson) was seriously considered for the presidential slot. Our prejudicial attitudes toward minorities are decreasing somewhat, but we still have a long road to travel before we erase the barriers that keep minority members from contributing to our society as fully and freely as they are able. Figure 34 relates an account of one teacher's efforts to eliminate discrimination.[26]

**EXERCISE: RECOGNIZING THE CONTRIBUTIONS OF MINORITIES**

Choose an ethnic or minority group (e.g., Japanese, Italians, African-American, women, etc.) and research the contributions that two members of that group have made to American society. You may wish to look at contributions in areas such as the arts, theater, sports, entertainment, politics, science, or literature. Write a paragraph about each person you have chosen and share that information in an oral report to your class.

Discrimination is a vicious practice that can seriously wound both the victims and the perpetrators. Jane Elliot, an elementary-schoolteacher in Riceville, Iowa carried out a courageous experiment with her third grade classes for a number of years. She decided to teach her students firsthand what the experience of discrimination felt like.

On one day, all brown-eyed children in the class were the underdogs; they experienced discrimination in hundreds of blatant and subtle ways. They wore collars around their necks so that they could be identified from a distance; they were not allowed to play on the gym set if the blue-eyed children wished to use it. They were the last ones in line to go to recess. They were not allowed to use paper cups at the drinking fountain. They were not allowed to play with their blue-eyed friends.

If a brown-eyed child did not know the answer to a question, Ms. Elliott made disparaging comments about all brown-eyed children who never listened and, therefore, learned more slowly than blue-eyed children. If a brown-eyed child forgot an assignment, she generalized about the fact that all "brown-eyes" were forgetful. If a brown-eyed child did not complete an assignment, she commented on how lazy all "brown-eyes" were. On the following day, roles were reversed, and the blue-eyed children became the underdogs.

After the experiment, the children discussed the anger, resentment, rage, and despair they felt when they were the underdogs. They talked about how hurt they were when their friends would not play with them. They recounted how guilty and embarassed they were when they belonged to the group on top.

One of Ms. Elliot's classes later met for a twenty-year reunion. Even after twenty years, the experience in discrimination had left important marks on the students and had guided many of their actions later in life. This experiment has since been replicated in many settings with adults as well as children. It is a powerful tool that can help us to learn firsthand about the painful emotional wounds that are left by discriminatory practices in our society.

**FIGURE 34. AN EXPERIMENT IN DISCRIMINATION**

You may wish to list five or six persons who interest you most. In that way, your instructor can approve your choice of person or minority group, before you do your research, to avoid duplications or to assure that a good sampling of minority groups and types of contributions are covered.

**Choice of Minority Group**

First Choice:

Second Choice:

Third Choice:

**Choice for Area of Contribution (literature, politics, science, etc.)**

First Choice:

Second Choice:

Third Choice:

**Choice of Famous Person**

First Choice:

Second Choice:

Third Choice:

Fourth Choice:

Fifth Choice:

# A MULTICULTURAL ROLE MODEL

Research shows that students are more likely to succeed in college if they have mentors, or role models, from their culture who are in positions of power at the institution. These mentors can lend a sympathetic ear, can give you survival tips, and can identify resources that help you to resolve problems. These people have come from where you are now and have succeeded in the system. They can identify differences in the expectations between your culture and the culture you are entering. They can give you advice on how to hold onto your cultural identity and still succeed in the majority system.

**EXERCISE: FINDING A MENTOR**

Choose a minority group with which you identify. This may be women, African-Americans, Hispanics, a particular ethnic group, such as Italians or Irish, or a religious group, such as Jews. If you are an international student who comes from a different country, you may wish to study your ethnic group. If you are learning disabled or physically challenged, you may wish to focus on the issues affecting challenged populations. If you are a nontraditional student who is over twenty-five years of age, you may wish to do this project on the issues that affect older students.

The point of this exercise is to realize that all groups experience some degree of culture shock and adjustment in entering a new environment. Find a person, from a group with which you identify, who can help you ease into that adjustment. This person may be a faculty member, an administrator, or a successful upper-level student. If you cannot find someone from your cultural group on campus, look off campus for a person who has succeeded in the system and who may be sensitive to the differences between your culture and the one you are entering. This person can be a professional, a community leader, or a successful business person. You may wish to do this exercise with more than one interviewee. An upper-level student from your own generation may be able to give you different insights from those of a faculty member or a community leader. Both may be able to share support and helpful information.

Make an appointment to interview that person. The questions listed on the following pages are suggestions, but you may wish to add others that occur to you. Take the questions with you to the interview; record the answers you receive so that you can share them with your peers, in a class discussion, or with your instructor, through a written assignment.

INTERVIEW QUESTIONS

1. Is the relationship between faculty and students at this college different from what we might expect in our culture? How do students typically address faculty (Doctor, Professor, Mr. or Ms., by first name)? Are relationships more formal or less formal? Are faculty likely to discriminate against our cultural group?

_____

_____

_____

_____

_____

_____

_____

_____

_____

2. What type of contact do faculty and students have outside of class? Is there social contact? Are faculty available to help students with personal or academic problems that are unrelated to the course?

_____

_____

_____

_____

_____

_____

_____

_____

_____

_____

3. How can I get to know faculty better and work with them more closely?

_____

_____

_____

_____

_____

_____

_____

_____

4.  Do you have any cautions or suggestions for me that would help me to succeed in establishing good relationships with faculty?

_____

_____

_____

_____

_____

_____

_____

_____

_____

5.  How do relationships among students differ at this college from those among students in our culture? Are they more formal or less formal?

_____

_____

_____

_____

_____

_____

_____

_____

_____

6.  What types of social activities do students share? What types of academic activities do they share?

_____

_____

_____

_____

_____

_____

_____

_____

_____

7. Is there anything I should know about differences in relationships between men and women? Are relationships in the majority culture different from those in our culture?

_____

_____

_____

_____

_____

_____

_____

_____

_____

8. What is the best way to meet other students and make friends?

_____

_____

_____

_____

_____

_____

_____

_____

_____

9. Do you have any precautions or suggestions for me that would help me to succeed in establishing good relationships with other students?

_____

_____

_____

_____

_____

_____

_____

_____

_____

10. What types of problems or frustrations have you encountered because you have come from a different background and tried to adjust to this culture? How have you coped with those problems?

_____
_____
_____
_____
_____
_____
_____
_____

11. What have you found to be the expectations for work at college? How much work is necessary to succeed?

_____
_____
_____
_____
_____
_____
_____
_____
_____

12. Are there differences in how the work must be presented (format, mechanics, appearance, etc.)? Must the work be submitted on time? How should I approach the work (through research, personal experience, summaries, or critiques)?

_____
_____
_____
_____
_____
_____
_____
_____

13. Are there particular behaviors, beliefs, or values among people in our culture that will lead to problems with the majority culture at this college (e.g., differences in dress, assertiveness, eye contact, formality of relations, punctuality, etc.)?

_____

_____

_____

_____

_____

_____

_____

_____

_____

_____

14. Where might I find other people from my culture who have succeeded on this campus?

_____

_____

_____

_____

_____

_____

_____

_____

_____

_____

15. Are there any clubs, organizations, or activities that you recommend I join in order to help me become more comfortable in this culture?

_____

_____

_____

_____

_____

_____

_____

_____

_____

_____

_____

16. Are there any other people or resources that might be helpful to me in adjusting to this culture?

_____

_____

_____

_____

_____

_____

_____

_____

_____

# NOTES

1. *Statistical Abstracts of the United States 1988* (Washington, D.C.: U.S. Department of Commerce, Bureau of the Census, 1987), p. 15.

2. W. M. Bagby, *Introduction to Social Science* (Chicago: Nelson-Hall, 1987), p. 35.

3. Ibid., pp. 25–27, 31–38.

4. Ibid., p. 36.

5. *Statistical Abstracts of the United States 1988* (Washington, D.C.: U.S. Department of Commerce, Bureau of the Census, 1987), p. 125.

6. W. M. Bagby, *Introduction to Social Science,* p. 36.

7. *Statistical Abstracts of the United States 1988* (Washington, D.C.: U.S. Department of Commerce, Bureau of the Census, 1987), p. 125.

8. J. P. Daniels, "Experts Foresee a Social Gap Between Sexes Among Blacks," *New York Times,* 5 May 1989, pp. 1, 30.

9. J. Ladner in ibid., p. 30.

10. W. M. Bagby, *Introduction to Social Science,* p. 37.

11. Ibid., p. 38.

12. *Statistical Abstracts of the United States 1988* (Washington, D.C.: U.S. Department of Commerce, Bureau of the Census, 1987), p. 436.

13. R. Benenson, "Black America: Long March for Equality," in *Editorial Research Reports, vol. II,* ed. H. Gimlin, R. Worsnop, M. Gottron (Washington, D.C.: Congressional Quarterly, Inc., 1985), pp. 863–884.

14. W. M. Bagby, *Introduction to Social Science,* p. 38.

15. J. C. Simpson, "Campus Barrier? Black College Students are Viewed as Victims of a Subtle Racism," *Wall Street Journal,* 3 April 1987.

16. Ibid.

17. G. Evans, "Black Students who Attend White Colleges Face Contradictions in Their Campus Life," *Chronicle of Higher Education,* 30 April 1986.

18. E. T. Louis, "Black and Blue on Campus," *Essence,* August 1986, pp. 67, 68, 132, 134.

19. *Statistical Abstracts of the United States 1988* (Washington, D.C.: U.S. Department of Commerce, Bureau of the Census, 1987), pp. 14, 15.

20. J. Schmalz, "Hispanic Influx Spurs Step to Bolster English," *New York Times,* 26 October 1988, pp. 1, B8.

21. W. M. Bagby, *Introduction to Social Science,* pp. 25–27, 31–38.

22. J. Schmalz, "Hispanic Influx," pp. 1, B8.

23. W. M. Bagby, *Introduction to Social Science,* p. 25.

24. *Statistical Abstracts of the United States 1988* (Washington, D.C.: U.S. Department of Commerce, Bureau of the Census, 1987), pp. 422, 436.

25. G. Evans, "Black Students Who Attend White Colleges."

26. This experiment was powerfully recorded in a CBS documentary entitled "A Class Divided." The video is available from Public Broadcasting Services, Alexandria, Va., 800-424-7963.

# Chapter 18

# Women, Challenged Students, and Nontraditional Students

## EXAMINING THE ROLE OF WOMEN

Many people are surprised when they hear a reference to women as a "minority." Women are not a minority in the statistical sense, but they have been treated like a minority group in many ways.

### Sex Stereotypes

In our society many people have very fixed ideas about masculinity and femininity. Men are expected to behave in masculine ways, while women are supposed to respond in feminine ways. These expectations are rigid enough so that many researchers refer to them as sex stereotypes: fixed traits or patterns of behavior that are ascribed to each of the sexes. Stereotypes are important because they influence our perceptions of ourselves, our perceptions of others, and how we actually behave.

If a girl believes that little girls are supposed to be relatively quiet and follow the rules, she may often try to meet her own and others' expectations for subdued behavior and submissiveness. If a little boy knows, on the other hand, that boys are supposed to roughhouse and engage in aggressive behavior, he may also live up to those expectations and unleash his exuberance in physical activities.

Girls and boys are treated differently from the moment they are born. What is the first question that proud, new parents are asked? Right! "Is it a boy or a girl?" From that moment on, female babies are dressed in different colors and clothes so that everyone will immediately recognize their sex and know how to treat them. They receive different toys. They are assigned different chores in the household.

Boys receive more roughhousing when they play with their parents. They are given more praise and more punishment. Their chores involve more outside work. Their clothes are sturdier and allow them more freedom. Fewer restrictions are placed on their behavior, and they are encouraged to explore independently. They also receive more parental pressure to achieve in school and careers. Figure 35 presents some of the categories in which girls and boys are raised differently.

Eventually, the different expectations and stereotypes can have important consequences for the way men and women behave in social relationships, the types of education they choose, the careers they pursue, the amount of money they earn, and how they feel about themselves.

Many researchers believe that stereotypes restrict both sexes and make it difficult for men as well as women to achieve their full human potential. To the extent that you try to live up to certain idealized expectations for men or women in general, you may put pressure on yourself to achieve certain goals that do not truly reflect your needs. You may limit the way you express yourself in personal and professional relationships, and you may restrict the range of hobbies and interests you pursue.

**EXERCISE: RECOGNIZING STEREOTYPES AND IDENTIFYING IDEAL CHARACTERISTICS**

1. Look at the list of personality characteristics and interests on page 274. In the first column, list the items that you believe are more characteristic of men in general, and in the second column, list the items you believe apply more to women. Are the items for men and women different? Are there any characteristics that you feel both sexes share?
2. Now that you have noted some of the general characteristics that are often ascribed to women and men, go over these characteristics again and list those items that you would find desirable in the ideal woman and the ideal man on page 275. Are the two lists different?

| Girls | | Boys |
|---|---|---|
| Wear pinks and pastels. | *Colors* | Wear blues and primaries. |
| Wear fragile, delicate clothes (dresses and skirts) that encourage subdued behavior. | *Clothes* | Wear sturdy clothes (pants) that allow freedom and encourage action. |
| Play with dolls and domestic equipment (dish sets, stoves, etc.). | *Toys* | Play with trucks, sports and action equipment, work equipment (Tools, science kits). |
| Set the table and wash dishes. | *Chores* | Take out garbage and do outdoor, yard work. |
| Behaves quietly, in a dependent, submissive manner; makes marriage and family life goals. | *Expectations* | Behaves in an independent, assertive manner; makes school achievement and career life goals. |
| Behaves "properly" and "safely." | *Restrictions* | Bends rules of etiquette; has later curfews; goes out unescorted. |

**FIGURE 35. CATEGORIES IN WHICH GIRLS AND BOYS ARE RAISED DIFFERENTLY**

|  | More Characteristic of Men | More Characteristic of Women |
|---|---|---|
| Aggressive | _____ | _____ |
| Independent | _____ | _____ |
| Emotional | _____ | _____ |
| Easily influenced | _____ | _____ |
| Active | _____ | _____ |
| Submissive | _____ | _____ |
| Competitive | _____ | _____ |
| Logical | _____ | _____ |
| Manipulative | _____ | _____ |
| Passive | _____ | _____ |
| Easily hurt | _____ | _____ |
| Weak | _____ | _____ |
| Adventurous | _____ | _____ |
| Tough | _____ | _____ |
| Self-confident | _____ | _____ |
| Gentle | _____ | _____ |
| Shows leadership | _____ | _____ |
| Sneaky/devious | _____ | _____ |
| Ambitious | _____ | _____ |
| Dependent | _____ | _____ |
| Talkative | _____ | _____ |
| Quiet | _____ | _____ |
| Sensitive to others | _____ | _____ |
| Sloppy | _____ | _____ |
| Decisive | _____ | _____ |
| Strong | _____ | _____ |
| Compassionate | _____ | _____ |
| Neat in personal habits | _____ | _____ |
| Interested in literature | _____ | _____ |
| Enjoys sports | _____ | _____ |
| Interested in math and science | _____ | _____ |
| Enjoys art | _____ | _____ |
| Other traits | _____ | _____ |

| | More Characteristic of the Ideal Man | More Characteristic of the Ideal Woman |
|---|---|---|
| Aggressive | | |
| Independent | | |
| Emotional | | |
| Easily influenced | | |
| Active | | |
| Submissive | | |
| Competitive | | |
| Logical | | |
| Manipulative | | |
| Passive | | |
| Easily hurt | | |
| Weak | | |
| Adventurous | | |
| Tough | | |
| Self-confident | | |
| Gentle | | |
| Shows leadership | | |
| Sneaky/devious | | |
| Ambitious | | |
| Dependent | | |
| Talkative | | |
| Quiet | | |
| Sensitive to others | | |
| Sloppy | | |
| Decisive | | |
| Strong | | |
| Compassionate | | |
| Neat in personal habits | | |
| Interested in literature | | |
| Enjoys sports | | |
| Interested in math and science | | |
| Enjoys art | | |
| Other traits | | |

3. Bring the exercise lists to class so that your instructor can tally the number of students who listed given traits or interests for men or women. Discuss the following questions with your classmates:

- Is there general agreement among class members about which traits are more characteristic of men or women?

- Do your perceptions agree with those of your classmates?

- Do you believe that the lists you have compiled reflect true differences between men and women? Do you know men or women whose personalities or interests do not fit the stereotypes?

- Which lists, the ones for men or the ones for women include traits that are more highly valued in our society?

- Are there differences between the traits seen as desirable for the ideal woman and those seen as desirable for the ideal man?

Many research studies have shown surprising consistency about interests and characteristics that are judged masculine and feminine by college students, but such stereotypes tend to be oversimplifications. There is little evidence to support generalized differences between the sexes. Where differences do exist, they may be the result of past experience and training.

As women enter the world of sports, for example, they are catching up in many of the areas where men have traditionally excelled. (The best female performance in the marathon run improved by more than 20 percent between 1970 and 1982; the best male performance improved by only 0.1 percent. Hall and Lee's study of girls who had spent a year or more in a coeducational physical fitness program found that they performed at similar levels to boys on most physical fitness items.) In any event, strength and size do not carry as much importance in our technological society where much of the work that was previously done with brute strength is now accomplished by the press of a button.

The traditional stereotypes are simply not accurate about the two sexes on the whole, and they are certainly likely to be wrong about any given individual. You certainly know some women who are stronger or more aggressive or more decisive than some of the men that you know. You also undoubtedly know men who are more sensitive, more easily influenced, and more compassionate than some of the women that you know.

Many professionals believe that the list of traits for the ideal man and the ideal woman is the same. There is one list of traits for what constitutes the ideal mature adult, and this list includes the best traits that are traditionally ascribed to both males and females. When this view is adopted, men need no longer fit the "strong, silent" stereotype. They become free to express their emotions as fully as women so that they can experience the satisfactions of intimate relations with their lovers, children, and friends. They need no longer live with the stress of pretending that they are never afraid and never depressed. When this happens, they need no longer feel pressured to always take charge, to always have the answers, to be the sole supporters of their families.

In order for men to be freed from the restrictions of sex stereotyping, however, women must also be released from false generalizations about what they can and cannot do. They must be allowed to show their strength and competence to achieve in their careers. They must receive help with household duties and child care so that they are not required to shoulder the sole responsibility for the domestic sphere at the same time that they are trying to advance professionally. They must be allowed to participate in decisions and take the initiative in important projects. Men and women will be free to pursue their full potential only when we are able to let go of some of the false stereotypes about what constitutes masculine and feminine behavior.

Recent research indicates that changes may be occurring in some of the traditional sex stereotypes. As the traditional stereotypes become looser, there does seem to be some movement towards androgeny: combining the best traits associated with each of the sexes into a single individual. Thus it may become acceptable for one person, male or female, to be warm, compassionate, and affectionate and also independent, assertive, and self-reliant.

**EXERCISE: IMAGINING YOUR IDEAL SPOUSE OR PARTNER**

This exercise will help you become aware of your own values in the area of sex roles. Many of us are not conscious of the biases we carry and bring to our relationships.

1. In the following space, write a short paragraph describing your concept of the ideal spouse or partner. List the characteristics, values, and strengths *you* (not your friends, parents, or society) would look for in that person. The Merriam-Webster dictionary defines the word *ideal* as existing only in the mind, lacking practicality, or relating to perfection. So, let your imagination fly, think about the best of all possible situations, and be as honest as you can.

You might want to consider the following questions about the ideal spouse or partner:

- Would your partner work?
- What would he or she do?
- What attitudes or beliefs would your partner hold?
- What would his or her personality be like?
- Would your partner be older or younger than you?
- What kind of family would he or she come from?
- What physical or sexual characteristics would your partner have?
- Would you be your partner's first "real" love?
- What kinds of things would you enjoy doing together?
- What intellectual interests would your partner have?
- What beliefs and goals would be important to your partner?

_____

_____

_____

_____

_____

_____

_____

_____

_____

2. Does your ideal partner reflect any of the stereotyped male or female characteristics you listed above? Why do you think the characteristics you chose might be attractive or important to you?

_____

_____

_____

_____

_____

_____

_____

_____

3. If you are married, living with a partner, or dating someone special, you might want to consider how close that person comes to the stereotyped ideal for males or females? How close does your partner come to the ideal you described? Remember that few people ever find a perfect match. How close do you think you might be to your partner's ideal?

_____

_____

_____

_____

_____

_____

_____

_____

_____

## Discrimination in the Classroom

Although some of the stereotypes may be changing, many of the discriminatory practices based on them still exist. A landmark study by Professors Serbin and O'Leary in 1973 showed that discriminatory practices exist even at the nursery school level, where teachers treat boys and girls very differently. Boys received more attention from the teachers, they were praised more often, and teachers were twice as likely to have extended conversations with them. Teachers were also twice as likely to give boys detailed directions on how to do things for themselves.[1]

A more recent three-year study by Professors Myra and David Sadker showed that the same trends continued through elementary school.[2] The Sadkers evaluated teaching in more than one hundred fourth-, sixth-, and eighth-grade classrooms. Their researchers found that teachers were giving boys more academic help, that they praised boys more than girls, and that they were more likely to accept boys' comments during class discussions.

Teachers responded differently, for example, when boys and girls called out answers. If girls called out answers, they were reprimanded with comments such as, "In this class we don't shout out answers, we raise our hands." When boys called out answers, teachers were much more likely to accept their answers. It is no wonder that boys are eight times more likely to call out in class than girls![3]

Although many people believe that sexism in the classroom died out in the 1970s, clearly it still exists. The Sadkers's study showed that boys were encouraged to dominate the class. Although the teachers thought that girls were talking more, detailed counts of classroom interactions showed that boys were outtalking the girls by a ratio of three to one![4] The teachers were unconsciously giving boys a superior learning experience. This was true in all subject areas, at all grade levels, and in all communities. Sexual stereotypes can affect our perceptions and behaviors even though we are not aware of them.

Sex stereotypes also influence instruction at higher levels of the educational system. Sociologist Safilios-Rothschild found similar results in her study of sex desegregation at the Coast Guard Academy to those found in nursery and elementary schools.[5] Teachers tended to give detailed instructions to male students on how to complete an assignment; when female students needed help, the instructors did the job or operated the equipment for them.

Roberta Hall and Bernice Sandler[6] have reported that many prominent colleges and universities are conducting research to measure the extent to which their female students are facing discrimination in the educational environment. Women are still reporting differences, such as those listed in the following exercise, in the ways they are treated by their instructors.

**EXERCISE: RECOGNIZING SEXIST BEHAVIOR IN THE CLASSROOM**

Hold a group discussion and compare notes with your classmates. To what extent have you noticed any of the following practices in your classes? Give examples from your experience. How might such practices make it difficult for female students to receive an education equal to that of male students?

Some discussion questions about sexist behavior in the classroom are as follows:

• Are faculty more likely to call on male students?

• Do instructors tend to ask the same types of questions of both male and female students?

• Do female students receive the same encouragement as male students to think for themselves?

• Do female students receive as much praise, encouragement, and feedback as male students on their academic work?

• Are female students interrupted more frequently than male students?

• Do professors make eye contact with male students more when they are asking a question of the class? (This would encourage male students to participate more in class discussion.)

• Are some instructors more likely to remember the names of male rather than female students?

• Are instructors equally likely to choose female students as they are to choose male students for research assistants and to give them the same types of responsibilities?

• Do advisors discourage female students from enrolling in traditionally masculine or "hard" majors?

- Do some teachers use sexist humor to liven up their classes?
- Do some instructors make discriminatory or disparaging remarks about female students or their abilities in their courses?
- Are advisors more likely to contact male rather than female students for job openings or other professional opportunities?

As a result of such discriminatory practices, universities are finding that many female undergraduates feel less confident about their preparation for graduate school than do the male students in their classes. Female students continue to avoid many fields (e.g., math and science) that have been traditionally identified as masculine, and they lower their academic and career goals during their college years.

Women continue to be viewed as less capable by both men and women in our society. A series of studies have been done where two groups of people were asked to evaluate items such as articles, resumés, paintings, etc. One group was led to believe that the work was associated with a woman, while the second group of evaluators believed that the identical work belonged to a man. Regardless of the items, when they were ascribed to a man, identical items were rated higher than when the evaluators thought they belonged to a woman.

## Discrimination in the Workplace

Such prejudicial attitudes towards women and their work have followed women into the workplace. Women have entered the labor force in record numbers. Sixty-three percent of the women between the ages of 18 and 64 are employed, and they constitute 43 percent of the work force. They have taken two-thirds of the new jobs in the American economy over the past five years. The rate of female employment has grown by 2.4 percent a year compared to the male increase of only 0.9 percent per year. Yet despite passage of the Equal Pay Act of 1963 and Title VII of the Civil Rights Act of 1972, which prohibits sex discrimination in employment, women are still earning only 64 cents for every dollar earned by men![7]

This difference in salaries for males and females is not based on years of education, type of occupation, years of experience, or any other relevant variables. Men earn more money than women, even when all of these factors are taken into account.

For example, a woman with four years of college earns 62 cents for every dollar earned by a man with a similar level of education. A female executive earns 61 cents for every dollar earned by a male executive. Part-time female workers earn 47 percent of the salaries paid to part-time male workers. People often assume that a man needs to earn more because he is supporting a family, but the number of households headed by women rose to almost ten million in 1986, and the numbers continue to rise steeply. More than half of these female-headed families live below the federal poverty line. In addition, many women continue to work because their families cannot live on their husband's salaries alone.

The major explanation for the discrepancy between male and female earnings seems to lie in the fact that women and men have different occupations and that female-dominated occupations are paid less than male-dominated occupations. One-fourth of the women in the work force are concentrated in five occupations: secretary, bookkeeper, elementary school teacher, waitress, and retail sales clerk. Men's occupations are spread over a wider range of categories, and the occupations that they dominate are more highly paid than the occupations dominated by women.

A man who dropped out of high school may well earn a salary similar to a woman college graduate because he is more likely to be a union worker or craftsman whereas she is more likely to be a nurse or a teacher. Women constitute 99 percent of the secretaries, 93 percent of the bank tellers, telephone operators, and registered nurses, 84 percent of the elementary school teachers, but only 0.5 percent of the plumbers and auto mechanics, 2 percent of the carpenters, 4.5 percent of the dentists and engineers, 14 percent of the lawyers and judges, 17 percent of the stock brokers, and 35 percent of college and university teachers.[8]

Unless women begin to enter the male-dominated occupations in larger numbers or unless female-dominated occupations are reevaluated so that they are compensated on a similar basis to male-dominated occupations, women will continue to be second-class citizens with regard to power, property, and prestige. Until the traditional sex stereotypes are reevaluated, both men and women will continue to suffer, as members of neither sex will be able to develop to their fullest human potential.

## EXAMINING THE ROLE OF CHALLENGED STUDENTS

The Constitution of the United States guarantees equal opportunity for all Americans. For 36 million physically challenged Americans, this guarantee has proved elusive. Members of this minority group are undereducated, underemployed, unable to socialize as much as other Americans, and unable to develop their fullest potential.

A physical challenge is a health-related condition that prevents a person from participating fully in work, school, or other normal activities. A recent Harris poll reports that the majority of physically challenged Americans feel that life has gotten much better for them over the past ten years; many, however, are still not happy with the quality of the lives they lead.[9] Life for the physically challenged is less satisfying and more restricting than for the general population; the physically challenged often feel shut out of mainstream American society.

Physically challenged Americans are unable, for example, to socialize as much as other Americans. More than one-half of them report that their physical challenge keeps them from getting out to socialize or to attend cultural and sports events. Almost two-thirds of the physically challenged individuals surveyed did not go to the movies even once in the past year (as compared to only 22 percent of the general American population who missed out on movies). Almost two-thirds failed to attend any sports events (compared to one-half of the general American population). Public transportation is either unavailable or inaccessible for many of our physically challenged citizens.

### Employment and Income

One of the most important areas where the physically challenged experience a disadvantage is in work. Two-thirds of physically challenged Americans are not working. This unemployment rate is higher than for any other minority group in the country. Two-thirds of the physically challenged individuals who are not working say they would like to work. Those who work are better educated, have more money, and are more satisfied with their lives.[10]

Many physically challenged Americans report that they have experienced job discrimination. Almost one-half say that they are not able to work because employers will not believe that they can do the job. Others feel that they do not have the necessary education, the marketable skills, or the access to transportation necessary to get a job.

Physically challenged workers have demonstrated their productivity and ability to work in the past. During World War II, when the country's labor pool was drained of potential workers, many businesses realized that those who had traditionally been excluded from the work force made excellent workers. Large numbers of physically challenged workers (as well as women and minority group members) pitched in to maintain the production that helped us win the war.

Now America is facing competition in a global economy and the end of the postwar baby boom, and many corporations are again beginning to face labor shortages. Companies are finding that skilled physically challenged workers make excellent employees. E. I. du Pont de Nemours is one company that has recruited large numbers of physically challenged workers. Although this policy is good for public relations, representatives of the company point out that it makes even more sense for economic reasons.

One of the company's regular productivity reports stated, for example, that 92 percent of almost three thousand physically challenged workers received ratings of average or above average in job performance, compared to 91 percent for workers who were not physically challenged. The physically challenged workers also compared favorably in the areas of safety and attendance on the job. Du Pont's experience with physically challenged workers and the experiences of many other corporations have been positive and have destroyed some of the myths and stereotypes about physically challenged workers and productivity.[11]

Federal legislation has joined with economic pressures to open employment opportunities for the physically challenged. The Rehabilitation Act of 1973 requires employers that have federal government contracts for more than $2,500 to hire qualified physically challenged employees if they can do the job given "reasonable accommodation." About three million companies, half the businesses in the country, are covered by this law, and many are finding that making the reasonable accommodations that allow physically challenged employees to work makes good economic sense.[12]

Some companies have cut the legs on drafting tables to make them accessible to workers in wheelchairs; other companies have installed inexpensive ramps for wheelchairs or dog walks for Seeing Eye dogs. Many companies are taking advantage of advances in computer technology that allow physically challenged (and other) workers to transfer work performed at home to the company's terminals. More than one-third of the physically challenged people surveyed in a recent Harris poll said that they have been able to find work because employers have made special accommodations for their specific physical challenge.[13] These accommodations often save employers money as workers who have become physically challenged can be rehired in order to reduce the costs of training new workers. Such measures also reduce the high costs of disability payments. Physically challenged workers who are employed more than make up for the cost of their rehabilitation by paying income taxes and lowering the cost of support payments.

There is, of course, a close relationship between unemployment and income. More than one-third of the physically challenged people under the age of 65 must rely on government or insurance payments for some part of their income; physically challenged Americans are poorer than other groups. Only 12 percent of the physically challenged reported incomes of $35,000 or more at a time when 27 percent of Americans in general earned this amount of money. Poverty is especially widespread among older physically challenged individuals: almost one-third of this group reported incomes of $7,500 or less.[14]

# Education

One of the important factors that affects employment and income is education. As a group, the physically challenged are undereducated in comparison to other Americans. Forty percent have not completed high school. That rate is almost three times as high as the figure for Americans in general! Less than 30 percent of the physically challenged have had some college course work; in comparison, 48 percent of Americans in general have completed some college work.[15]

Progress is occurring in this area, once again, due to federal legislation. We are beginning to see more physically challenged students on campus. The Rehabilitation Act of 1973 first guaranteed, to physically challenged children, an appropriate education in the public schools. Section 504 of that law further stipulates that all colleges and universities that receive federal funding must be accessible to qualified students who have physical challenges. Before this law was passed, most schools were not accessible to physically challenged students because of attitudes and policies that did not allow them to get past the admissions process or because of physical barriers that made it impossible for them to negotiate their way around the campus.

Many administrators believed, for example, that physically challenged students could not become teachers because they would not be able to handle their classes during a fire drill. Others closed off careers in engineering and science to blind or deaf students because they believed that their physical challenge would be dangerous around specialized scientific equipment. Campuses were constructed so that students in wheelchairs could not get into classrooms or bathrooms. Textbooks were not available in braille or on taped cassettes. Interpreters who translated lectures into sign language were not available on campus. Recorders were not available to help learning challenged students write their exams.

The government's equal opportunity laws have literally opened the doors of higher education to physically challenged students. In 1978, less than 3 percent of the freshmen enrolled full time in college reported that they had a physical challenge. By 1987, the number had almost reached 7 percent, and some researchers are estimating that as many as 10 percent of college students may have some type of physical challenge.[16,17,18]

## Success for Physically Challenged Students

As physically challenged students enter college in larger numbers, institutions and instructors must provide services that will give these students an equal opportunity to obtain a college education. Electric doors, ramps, elevators, and special parking areas may be needed so that students in wheelchairs are able to get around the campus. Some allowances must be made for physically challenged students. Some of these students may occasionally arrive late to class because it is difficult to commute by wheelchair, negotiate icy walks with a cane, or wait for assistance with dressing or personal hygiene.

Visually impaired, or blind, students may require tape-recorded textbooks or classmates who take duplicate sets of notes with carbon paper. Deaf students may need to attend class with an interpreter, and students with hand-function impairments may require a recorder or a computer to write exams. Learning challenged students may need extra time to read or type assignments due to their specific learning challenges.

The attitudes of the students on campus can also make a tremendous difference in the success of physically challenged students. If you tend to avoid eye contact with physically challenged students because you feel awkward, they may begin to feel isolated. Try saying "hello," and start a conversation instead. If you are with a physically challenged person and do not know whether or how to help in a particular situation, ask him or her. If you automatically cut up food or push a wheelchair for a physically challenged person, the student may feel that you are taking away his or her independence. If you make decisions for a physically challenged person about what that person may or may not want to do, he or she will feel excluded. Some physically challenged students, for example, may be just as interested in sports or dancing as you are. A double amputee "ran" the New York marathon (on his hands) and another amputee competed in Olympic-level pole vaulting events (on one leg). If you are going jogging or bowling, ask your physically challenged friend to come along.

Physically challenged students, on the other hand, must take responsibility for explaining their needs to their peers and instructors. I remember one student whose physical challenge was not obvious. He took an exam along with the rest of the class because he did not want to ask for special favors due to his physical challenge. Unfortunately, it was only after he failed the exam that he told me that his visual impairment had made it difficult for him to complete the exam during the time allotted by the class period. It would have been much more appropriate for him to tell me about his physical challenge before the exam, so that we could have made arrangements for a reader or for extra time. Instead, he had to ask me to give him a make-up exam after failing the first test.

EXERCISE:
SIMULATING A
PHYSICAL
CHALLENGE

One way to appreciate some of the difficulties that physically challenged students experience on a daily basis is to simulate a physical challenge for a few hours or for a day. If your campus has extra wheelchairs, try borrowing one and experience the challenge of getting around campus without the use of your legs for a class period. Or wear earplugs and see how well you can lip read the contents of a lecture, a discussion, or a conversation. You might simulate blindness by having a friend act as your guide while you go around campus for a few hours blindfolded.

As you go through your simulation, try to focus on the feelings you are experiencing: frustration, anger, humiliation, embarrassment, anxiety, jealousy, exhaustion, irritation, or confusion. Come back to class and discuss the simulation and your feelings with your classmates. You may now be in a better position to identify with physically challenged students who experience these stresses and humiliations on a daily basis.

EXERCISE:
SIMULATING A
LEARNING
CHALLENGE

You are probably familiar with the game of Simple Simon, in which you follow the leader's instructions as long as he or she says, "Simple Simon says . . . " If the leader does not say "Simple Simon says . . . " you should not do what he or she says or does.

This particular version of Simple Simon is a bit more challenging: we are going to reverse left and right because many learning challenged people have to concentrate carefully in order to avoid reversing left and right. A learning challenged student may often read the word *bad* as *dab* or transpose material from the right-hand side of the board to the left-hand side of his or her paper.

So now, if your leader says, "Raise your right foot," what are you going to do? I hope that you all said "Nothing," because you should remember

This exercise is adapted from "Simulations Approximating Learning Disabilities" by D. Raschke and C. Dedrick, *TEACHING Exceptional Children,* Summer, 1986, pp. 266–271. Copyright 1986 by the Council for Exceptional Children. Reprinted with permission.

not to do anything unless "Simple Simon says" you should do it. Now, what would you do if Simple Simon says, "Raise your right foot"? Right! Raise your *left* foot.

We are also going to reverse the directions for the words *over* and *under,* to show you how frustrating many learning challenged students find it when they have to process teachers' instructions and class materials through information channels that do not come easily to them. If your leader says, "Simple Simon says put your left hand over your right elbow," what are you going to do? Think about this now. I hope that you will put your *right* hand *under* your *left* elbow. Now that you have practiced with the rules a bit, we are ready to begin our "simple" game. Some sample instructions might include the following:

- Put your right hand over your left ankle. Ah ha! Did some of you forget about "Simple Simon says"?
- Simple Simon says, "Hold your right elbow and touch your index finger to your right eye." Did we lose some of our students there?
- Simple Simon says, "Hop on your left foot."
- Simple Simon says, "Hold your right hand."
- Hold your left hand.
- Touch your head with your right hand.
- Simple Simon says, "Put your right hand over your chin."
- Simple Simon says, "Touch your head with your left hand."
- Put your left hand under your right ankle.
- Simple Simon says, "Hold your left ankle and touch your eye with your right hand."
- Simple Simon says, "Touch your right hip."
- Touch your left hip.

It seems that many of you are making mistakes or responding very slowly. I cannot understand why you are having difficulty with such an easy game! If you are having trouble following directions, come to the front of the room where the teacher can give you extra help (and where the other students can see just how much trouble you are having following "simple" instructions). (Learning challenged students are often singled out and ridiculed in this way.)

How do you feel after ten minutes of this game? Are you experiencing some confusion or frustration? Do you feel overwhelmed or embarrassed? How would you feel if this were not just a game, but some type of assignment where success was important to you? Might you become irritable? Would you lose your temper or give up because it was so difficult to learn what everyone else was doing with ease?

If your college has a program or service for physically challenged students, ask whether a speaker might come to your class to talk about the difficulties physically challenged students experience on campus. The speaker will be able to answer questions about some of the ways you might help these students cope with campus barriers. As more and more physically challenged people enter the mainstream on campuses and workplaces, all of us will benefit from learning to work comfortably and competently with them. In the process, you will also undoubtedly learn that you share more similarities than differences with your physically challenged friends.

# EXAMINING THE ROLE OF NONTRADITIONAL STUDENTS

An increasing number of students is coming to the campus after several years in the workplace or the home. A number of analysts predict that by the year 2000, more than one-third of the students in college will be more than twenty-five years old. Indeed, several of the courses I teach regularly already enroll one-third nontraditional students. In many evening and Saturday programs, nontraditional students make up more than 80 percent of the class.

Nontraditional students form a very diverse group. Some are returning to college after retiring from a career; others are enrolling in a few courses in order to gain advancement or promotion in their professions; still others, who needed a break from school after high school graduation, are returning because they are not satisfied with the limited opportunities available to them in the work world. Some of these students are coming when their children grow older, when they are freed from the burdens of child care. Others are enrolling as they go through divorce, knowing that they will have to support themselves for the first time through work outside the home. Some of these students are enrolling because they feel the need for intellectual stimulation or for a worthwhile goal around which to structure their lives.

## Assets of the Nontraditional Student

Whatever the reasons for nontraditional students to enroll, many instructors welcome them into the classroom. These students usually bring with them a high level of motivation with which to succeed in college. (Instructors enjoy teaching students who are eager to learn.) Nontraditional students often have a specific purpose for enrolling in college, and they are willing to work hard to achieve their goals. They bring a wealth of life experiences that enrich class discussions, and they contribute the perspectives of later stages in life development that lend a more-balanced view to a variety of topics.

Unfortunately, most nontraditional students also bring a high level of anxiety to class. They worry about competing with younger students who may be faster or brighter or more up-to-date in academic subjects. They worry that their academic skills are rusty. They fear that they will not remember as much or as well as they used to. They worry that their energy levels are not high enough. They are concerned that family obligations or responsibilities at work will not allow them enough time to succeed in college. They are afraid that their grades will not be as good as the ones they received in years gone by. They fear they will be embarrassed because they are too old to be in school.

Some of these fears are justified. It *is* much harder to juggle course work at the same time that you are responsible for child care or for running a household. Demands at work *can* indeed compete with demands in class. Study skills that have not been used for many years *may* need to be polished.

In general, nontraditional students tend to do as well as, if not better than, traditional age students. One of the main reasons for this is their motivation: nontraditional students work harder. Another factor is the skills they have perfected during the years they were managing a home or an office: time management, organization, assertiveness, and verbal and written communication.

There is greater acceptance for nontraditional students on campus as people realize that our complex and rapidly changing society makes continuing education a necessity for many people. There is also greater acceptance as the census figures underscore the declining number of traditional age students who can fill the seats in college classrooms.

## Anxiety Coping Techniques

If you are a nontraditional student, recognize your anxiety for what it is. Anxiety is a signal from your body that says you are facing a new challenge; to do your best, you need the extra energy that anxiety provides. Channel that anxiety constructively to help you try a little harder and work a little longer. If you find that your anxiety becomes uncomfortably high, check off techniques you might use to reduce it:

**EXERCISE:
IDENTIFYING
TECHNIQUES TO
DECREASE
ANXIETY**

_____ Enroll in school part time; take fewer courses until you have adapted to the campus environment and reassured yourself about your ability to succeed in college.

_____ Enroll in courses in which you can brush up on academic skills. Many colleges offer noncredit courses in how to study, how to write research papers, how to use the library, and so on.

_____ Use the academic services available on your campus to review skills in math or writing that form the basis for college course work. Many schools offer review courses, tutoring, or laboratories in basic skills.

_____ Make friends with other nontraditional students. You may meet them in your classes, in orientation programs, in a Women's Center, in peer support groups, or in courses designed specifically for nontraditional students. Find out which of these are available on your campus. You can receive support and learn a great deal from people who are experiencing similar challenges.

_____ Find a good advisor or faculty mentor who knows the system and is willing to help you find your way through it. There are many services and many tricks that can make your life on campus much easier. There is no reason to go through four years of college before you discover them.

_____ If you live with others, hold a planning session with the members of your household (spouse, children, partner, parents, etc.) early in the semester. Find out how these people feel about your return to school. Are they willing to support you so that you may succeed in college? This support can become crucial at "crunch" times during the semester when you have three exams or two papers due at the same time. Plan ahead for those times. Delegate responsibility. Decide what chores can wait for a less hectic time in your schedule.

_____ Evaluate your expectations realistically. Do you really have to be a straight A student? Must you really earn that degree in four years or less? Is it necessary to complete every optional reading assignment?

_____ Practice the relaxation exercises described in Chapter 15, "Stress."

_____ Adapt the desensitization exercises described in Chapter 7, "Examinations" which deals with exam anxiety to your particular fears.

_____ Seek help at the college's counseling center. A few sessions with a friendly, trained counselor can give you a clearer perspective on how to deal with your problem.

Above all, believe in yourself and allow yourself to enjoy the challenge and fulfillment your college career brings.

## NOTES

1. L. A. Serbin et al., "A Comparison of Teacher Response to Preacademic and Problem Behavior of Boys and Girls," *Child Development* 44 (1973): 769–804.

2. M. Sadker and D. Sadker, "Sexism in the Schoolroom of the '80s," *Psychology Today,* March 1985, pp. 54–55.

3. Ibid.

4. Ibid.

5. Safilios-Rothschild, in ibid.

6. R. Hall with B. Sandler, "The Classroom Climate: A Chilly One for Women?" *Project on the Status of and Education of Women* (Washington, D.C.: Association of American Colleges, 1982).

7. M. Mason, "The Equality Trap," *Working Mother,* September 1988, pp. 38–42.

8. *Statistical Abstracts of the United States 1986* (Washington, D.C.: U.S. Department of Commerce, Bureau of the Census, 1985), p. 154.

9. H. Taylor, M. R. Kagay, and S. Leichenko, *The ICD International Center for the Disabled) Survey of Disabled Americans: A Nationwide Survey of 1000 Disabled People* (New York: Louis Harris & Associates, Inc., 1986).

10. Ibid.

11. J. Sarno, "Disabled Workers: Nation's Untapped Resource," *Bergen County N.J. Record,* 15 June 1986.

12. Ibid.

13. Taylor et al., *The ICD Survey.*

14. Ibid.

15. Ibid.

16. P. Hippolitus, *College Freshmen with Disabilities: Preparing for Employment.* (Washington, D.C.: Committee on Youth Development of President's Commission on Employment of the Handicapped and American Council of Education, 1987).

17. National Clearinghouse on Postsecondary Education for Handicapped Individuals. Personal communication, 1988.

18. *American Freshman: National Norms for 1987* (Washington, D.C.: American Council on Education, 1988).

# Chapter 19

## Careers

### CAREER GOALS AND PLANNING

The latest edition of *The Dictionary of Occupational Titles* describes more than 20,000 occupations. Choosing among these options and then preparing for your choices can present quite a challenge! Studies by the Carnegie Foundation and the American Council on Education indicate that today's freshmen are more concerned about job prospects and financial security than freshmen in previous years. Although a college education is not meant to prepare you for a particular job, many institutions of higher education are responding to student concerns by committing increasing resources to guiding students in career options.

*Career planning should begin during your first year of college and continue through each succeeding year.* The Four-Year Career Guide presented at the end of this chapter guides you through a check-off list of steps you should take throughout each of your four years at college. Doing this will help you achieve your career goals.

### CAREER GUIDANCE
### AND PLACEMENT OFFICES

Most colleges have career guidance or placement offices that are stocked with a wealth of information about current trends in employment: what fields are growing and have the largest number of openings, what salary ranges are like, what types of education are needed for various careers, what parts of the country (or world) are opening up new career opportunities, and so on.

These offices also offer vocational testing that can help you discover careers in which you might be interested and also help you evaluate the skills necessary to succeed in those careers. In addition to paper-and-pencil tests, an increasingly popular form of vocational testing is a computer-based interactive guidance system. The computer asks you questions about your interests, values, and abilities, analyzes your answers, and makes recommendations about career paths you might explore. Sigi is one example of a systematic, comprehensive program that takes you through three hours' worth of exploration and then offers individualized career recommendations.

Services at career offices often include individual and group counseling sessions with career advisors, workshops with alumni who are employed in various fields, and job fairs where you can meet and question representatives from a number of corporations. All of these activities are aimed at helping you to explore and decide on career options.

In addition to helping you with long-range career planning, these offices frequently offer placement services for part-time and summer jobs where you can earn money, try out a career that interests you, and gain valuable work experience while you are still enrolled in college. Internships may also be available through cooperative education programs or through practicum courses associated with various majors. Some of these fieldwork placements offer a salary in addition to the opportunity to explore career options before you graduate. The hands-on work experience you gain through a practicum course, a summer job, or part-time work can be very valuable in helping you to land that first job after college.

Besides offering information and services related to jobs, career planning offices are often the place to go for information about graduate school and professional training programs. Some of the careers that interest you may require advanced educational degrees. The career planning office or graduate school advisory office is where you will go to find directories that describe the types of graduate programs there are, where these programs are located, what the admissions requirements are, how much they cost, and how long they take to complete. If you are thinking about going to graduate school or pursuing professional training after college, you should set up an appointment for postgraduate counseling in your sophomore or junior year. Many of the programs require that you complete particular course sequences and take certain admissions exams while you are still enrolled in college.

It is useful for you to begin thinking about career possibilities early so that you can coordinate your vocational interests with your academic program and explore as many options as possible while you are still attending college. It doesn't make sense to program yourself for a certain type of career all through your college years, only to discover after you graduate that that type of work does not suit you.

## WORK VALUES

The following exercise concerning work values will help you to think about what job-related satisfactions are most important to you. Salary should not be the major consideration in choosing a career. People who enjoy their work tend to put in the time and effort that help them succeed in their careers. Hard work is necessary for any career and so is a commitment of time, usually several years, to learn the skills needed in that area. Job dissatisfaction will limit your commitment. It can also spread to the other areas of your life and have negative effects on your relationships and leisure time. Since your values will change over time, you might want to complete this exercise again in a year or two.

**EXERCISE:
IDENTIFYING
YOUR WORK
VALUES**

1. The following list describes a variety of satisfactions that people obtain from their jobs. Look over the definitions of these satisfactions, and using the following scale, rate how important each satisfaction is for you.

1 = *Not important at all*      3 = *Reasonably important*

2 = *Not very important*       4 = *Very important in my choice of career*

_____ *Help Society:* Do something to contribute to the betterment of the world I live in.

_____ *Help Others:* Be involved in helping other people in a direct way, either individually or in small groups.

_____ *Public Contact:* Have a lot of day-to-day contact with people.

_____ *Work with Others:* Have close working relationships with a group; work as a team toward common goals.

_____ *Affiliation:* Be recognized as a member of a particular organization.

_____ *Friendships:* Develop close personal relationships with people as a result of my work activities.

_____ *Competition:* Engage in activities which pit my abilities against others where there are clear win-and-lose outcomes.

_____ *Make Decisions:* Have the power to decide courses of action, policies, etc.

_____ *Work under Pressure:* Work in situations where time pressure is prevalent and/or the quality of my work is judged critically by supervisors, customers or others.

_____ *Power and Authority:* Control the work activities or (partially) the destinies of other people.

_____ *Influence People:* Be in a position to change attitudes or opinions of other people.

_____ *Work Alone:* Do projects by myself, without any significant amount of contact with others.

_____ *Knowledge:* Engage myself in the pursuit of knowledge, truth and understanding.

_____ *Intellectual Status:* Be regarded as a person of high intellectual prowess or as one who is an acknowledged "expert" in a given field.

_____ *Artistic Creativity:* Engage in creative work in any of several art forms.

_____ *Creativity (general):* Create new ideas, programs, organizational structures or anything else not following a format previously developed by others.

_____

This exercise is reprinted by permission from H. E. Figler, (1979). *PATH: A Career Workbook for Liberal Arts Students.* Cranston, RI: The Carroll Press, pp. 77–79.

_____ *Aesthetics:* Be involved in studying or appreciating the beauty of things, ideas, etc.

_____ *Supervision:* Have a job in which I am directly responsible for the work done by others.

_____ *Change and Variety:* Have work responsibilities which frequently change in their content and setting.

_____ *Precision Work:* Work in situations where there is very little tolerance for error.

_____ *Stability:* Have a work routine and job duties that are largely predictable and not likely to change over a long period of time.

_____ *Security:* Be assured of keeping my job and a reasonable financial reward.

_____ *Fast Pace:* Work in circumstances where there is a high pace of activity, work must be done rapidly.

_____ *Recognition:* Be recognized for the quality of my work in some visible or public way.

_____ *Excitement:* Experience a high degree of (or frequent) excitement in the course of my work.

_____ *Adventure:* Have work duties which involve frequent risk-taking.

_____ *Profit, Gain:* Have a strong likelihood of accumulating large amounts of money or other material gain.

_____ *Independence:* Be able to determine the nature of my work without significant direction from others; not have to do what others tell me to.

_____ *Moral Fulfillment:* Feel that my work is contributing significantly to a set of moral standards which I feel are very important.

_____ *Location:* Find a place to live (town, geographical area) which is conducive to my life-style and affords me the opportunity to do the things I enjoy most.

_____ *Community:* Live in a town or city where I can get involved in community affairs.

_____ *Physical Challenge:* Have a job that makes physical demands which I would find rewarding.

_____ *Time Freedom:* Have work responsibilities which I can work at according to my own time schedule; no specific working hours required.

2. Now choose five of the above work values that are most important to you and write them on the following blanks. If you can think of any other values or satisfactions you would like from your work that were not included in the previous list, add them to the five values you have listed.

*Example*
1. Help Others
2. Security
3. Power and Authority
4. Creativity
5. Adventure

**Work Values**

1. _____

2. _____

3. _____

4. _____

5. _____

When you are considering a career or a job, ask yourself whether it will give you the satisfactions you have rated as most important for yourself. When you are interviewing people who hold various types of jobs, ask them what they like about their jobs so that you can judge whether those jobs would satisfy you.

**EXERCISE: ASSESSING YOUR ABILITIES**

1. In addition to considering work values and satisfactions, another factor that is likely to influence your success in a particular career is ability. Do you have the skills that are needed to do the job? The following list will help you to evaluate your abilities and identify skills that are needed in various types of jobs. Think about how well you typically perform on different tasks. What types of grades have you received on assignments that require these skills? Have you had much success on tasks where you must use these abilities? Evaluate yourself on each of the abilities categories according to the following scale:

1 = *No ability here at all*       3 = *Some ability*

2 = *Enough ability to get by*      4 = *Strong ability in this area*
    *with help from others*

*Self-Rating*          VERBAL-PERSUASIVE

_____ *Writing:* Express myself well in written forms of communication.

_____ *Talking:* Relate easily with people in ordinary conversational settings.

_____ *Speaking:* Able to deliver a talk or address to an audience.

_____ *Persuading:* Able to convince others to believe something that I hold to be true.

_____ *Selling:* Able to convince others to buy a product that I am selling.

_____ *Dramatic:* Able to portray ideas or stories in a dramatic format.

_____ *Negotiation:* Able to bargain or discuss with a view toward reaching agreement.

SOCIAL

_____ *Social ease:* Relate easily in situations which are primarily social in nature; i.e., parties, receptions, etc.

---

This exercise is reprinted with permission from Figler, H. E. (1979). *PATH: A Career Workbook for Liberal Arts Students.* Cranston, RI: The Carroll Press, pp. 94–97.

_____ *Deal with public:* Relate on a continual basis with people who come to an establishment for information, service or help, including a broad cross section of people.

_____ *Good appearance:* Dress presentably and appropriately for a variety of interpersonal situations or group occasions.

_____ *Deal with negative feedback:* Able to cope with criticism.

### NUMERICAL

_____ *Computational speed:* Able to manipulate numerical data rapidly without the aid of a mechanical device, demonstrating considerable accuracy in the process.

_____ *Work with numerical data:* Comfortable with large amounts of quantitative data, compiling, interpreting, presenting such data.

_____ *Solve quantitative problems:* Able to reason quantitatively so that problems having numerical solutions can be solved without the aid of a computer or other mechanical equipment.

_____ *Computer use:* Able to use electronic computers to solve quantitative problems; knowledge of programming, computer capabilities, etc.

### INVESTIGATE

_____ *Scientific curiosity:* Ability to learn scientific phenomena and investigate events which may lead to such learning.

_____ *Research:* Gather information in a systematic way for a particular field of knowledge in order to establish certain facts or principles.

_____ *Technical work:* Work easily with practical, mechanical or industrial aspects of a particular science, profession or craft.

### MANUAL-PHYSICAL

_____ *Mechanical reasoning:* Able to understand the ways that machinery or tools operate and the relationships between mechanical operations.

_____ *Manual dexterity:* Skill in using one's hands or body.

_____ *Spatial perception:* Able to judge the relationships of objects in space, to judge sizes and shapes, manipulate them mentally and visualize the effects of putting them together or of turning them over or around.[3]

_____ *Physical stamina:* Physical resistance to fatigue, hardship and illness.

_____ *Outdoor work:* Familiar with the outdoors, ability to work outdoors without encountering obstacles or knowledge deficiencies.

### CREATIVE

_____ *Artistic:* Keenly sensitive to aesthetic values, able to create works of art.

_____   *Imaginative with things:* Able to create new ideas and forms with various physical objects.

_____   *Imaginative with ideas:* Able to create new ideas and programs through conceiving existing elements of behavior in new ways; able to merge abstract ideas in new ways.

### WORKING WITH OTHERS

_____   *Supervising:* Able to oversee, manage or direct work of others.

_____   *Teaching:* Able to help others learn how to do or understand something; able to provide knowledge or insight.

_____   *Coaching:* Able to instruct or train an individual to improve his or her performance in a specific subject area.

_____   *Counseling:* Able to engage in a direct helping relationship with another individual in situations where the person's concern is not solvable through direct information giving or advice.

### MANAGERIAL

_____   *Organization and planning:* Able to develop a program project to set of ideas through systematic preparation and arrangement of tasks, coordinating the people and resources necessary to put a plan into effect.

_____   *Orderliness:* Able to arrange items in a systematic, regular fashion so that such items or information can be readily used or retrieved with a minimum of difficulty.

_____   *Handle details:* Able to work with a great variety and/or volume of information without losing track of any items in the total situation; comfortable with small informational tasks that are part of the larger project responsibility.

_____   *Make decisions:* Comfortable in making judgments or reaching conclusions about matters which require specific action; able to accept the responsibility for the consequences of such actions.

2. Look back over the abilities you have rated, and in the following space write down the areas in which you are strongest:

**Abilities**

_____

_____

_____

_____

_____

_____

When you are researching careers, see which ones require abilities that you have rated 3 or 4 in yourself. When you interview job holders, ask them what skills helped them to succeed in their careers. You will eventually have to consider your strengths and weaknesses when you make a decision about career paths. Reevaluate your abilities from time to time. You may find yourself improving in certain skills as you progress through your college years.

## INTERNSHIPS AND SUMMER JOBS

It will be helpful if you begin exploration of career options through internships and summer jobs while you are still enrolled in college. Such experiences give you concrete bases for making decisions about whether a particular career is right for you. They also provide work experience that you may list on a résumé and a source of recommendations (from supervisors) who can commend your sterling abilities to future employers. Many colleges offer courses in your major that include an internship or fieldwork as part of the course work. If your college offers that type of course, take advantage of the experience. Find out whether your college has a cooperative education program. These programs, in which you work for a semester or more at a job related to your major, offer an additional way to gain valuable hands-on experience during your college career.

**EXERCISE: RESEARCHING A CAREER THROUGH AN INTERVIEW**

The freshman year is not too soon to begin some of the research that will help you find a satisfying career. One of the best ways to find out whether a particular career is right for you is to interview people who are working in the field. Choose a field that interests you, and make an appointment to interview someone who works in that area. You might interview someone you know or ask your parents, a faculty member, or a career advisor for suggestions.

The questions on the following pages can guide you in obtaining information that will help you to make decisions about future career paths. Take the questions with you and write down the answers so that you can share the information with your classmates, through an oral presentation, or with your instructor, through a written assignment.

INTERVIEW QUESTIONS

1. What is the nature of the work?

_____

_____

_____

2. What are the major duties of workers in this occupation? (Be aware, however, that although you should be able to determine a general job description, duties are likely to vary somewhat by employer and size of the employing program.)

_____

_____

_____

3. What are the entry-level positions in the field?

_____

_____

_____

4. What is the next rung to which I can aspire?

_____

_____

_____

5. How long should I anticipate it will take to reach that level?

_____

_____

_____

6. What training and other qualifications do I need for entry into this field?

_____

_____

_____

7. Is on-the-job training or a formal training program available?

_____

_____

_____

8. What are the characteristics or traits one should have in order to enter this field?

_____

_____

_____

Excerpted with permission from Tepper, R. (1988). *Career Manual.* Mahwah, NJ: Ramapo College, p. 20.

9. What will I need to do in order to advance?

_____

_____

_____

10. Do you feel it is more beneficial to go to graduate school first or to obtain work experience before entering graduate school?

_____

_____

_____

11. What graduate level program do you feel is best in order to enhance one's ability to advance in this field?

_____

_____

_____

12. What are the criteria on which performance in this field is evaluated?

_____

_____

_____

13. What are the advantages of working for a small rather than large firm or vice versa?

_____

_____

_____

14. What are the entry-level salaries in this field? What can established professionals earn?

_____

_____

_____

15. What are the working conditions like? Are there likely to be long hours, physical demands, etc.?

_____

_____

_____

16. Will I be required to travel or relocate?

_____

_____

_____

17. What do you perceive to be the major rewards in this field? Major frustrations?

_____

_____

_____

18. What are the most frequently recurring problems? What undergraduate experiences do employers in this field find valuable? How can I gain these experiences?

_____

_____

_____

19. Is the field different from what it was in the past? What changes do you anticipate for the future?

_____

_____

_____

20. What is the employment outlook for this field?

_____

_____

_____

21. If you had it do to over again, what would you do differently?

_____

_____

_____

22. Can you give me any tips or suggestions?

_____

_____

_____

23. What professional associations could I join now as a student?

_____

_____

_____

24. Where can I obtain further information about this field?

_____

_____

_____

# THE FOUR-YEAR CAREER PLANNING GUIDE

**EXERCISE:**
**FOLLOWING**
**THROUGH ON THE**
**FOUR-YEAR**
**CAREER**
**PLANNING GUIDE**

The following Four-Year Career Planning Guide offers a year-by-year program of activities that will bring you closer to reaching your career objectives. Make plans now to participate in activities that will keep you moving toward success on your career path. Check off the date you complete each activity, and be sure to look over the entire guide before registering for the semester; this will keep you moving toward your career goals.

## The Freshman Year

*Date*
*Completed*

1. Begin to consider possible career choices through exploratory exercises.

_____ Complete "Identifying Your Work Values" in this chapter (see pages 291–293).

_____ Complete the "Assessing Your Abilities" in this chapter (see pages 293–295).

_____ Complete the "Researching a Career through an Interview" in this chapter (see pages 297–299).

_____ Make an appointment at the career planning office to work with Sigi or another computerized career guidance system that will help you explore your values and interests and give you information about careers that interest you.

2. Visit the career planning office.

_____ Visit the career planning office at your college. Take a look at the library and materials they have available for you. Find out what types of services they offer that will help you explore career and graduate training options.

3. Participate in extracurricular activities.

_____ Attend meetings of several clubs or organizations, and join at least one. Student organizations offer the opportunity to develop career-related skills, make friends, and serve the college community. You can join a club related to your major, participate on an athletic team, or work on the college newspaper, student government, or radio station.

4. Attend workshops given by the career planning office.

_____ Most career planning offices offer workshops during the year on job search methods, résumé writing, interviewing skills, particular career fields, and preparation for graduate school. Attend several of these.

5. Get to know the faculty at your college.

Faculty, administrators, and counselors can advise you about careers. Faculty who really know you and your work can write better letters supporting your applications for jobs or graduate programs. Begin building those relationships now.

_____ Set up appointments with faculty during their office hours to discuss your work and interests.

_____ Ask your professors about opportunities to work with them on research projects.

Adapted with permission from Tepper, R. (1988). *Career Manual.* Mahwah, NJ: Ramapo College, pp. 6–15.

6. Begin to develop communications skills.

   Most employers consistently list writing and speaking skills as most desirable in new employees.

   _____ To improve your speaking skills, take a public speaking course or another course that requires oral presentations.

   _____ Register for courses that require several writing assignments so that you can improve your writing skills.

   _____ Work on the college newspaper, yearbook, or literary magazine to improve your writing skills.

   _____ Work at the college radio station, the student government, or a theater production to improve your speaking skills.

7. Choose your part-time and summer jobs carefully.

   If you need to work while you are attending college, try to find a job on campus that is related to your career goals.

   An on-campus job will cut down on the amount of time you spend commuting. Being a student should be your first priority, since your education is a lifelong investment. Spend as much time as you can on your course work and extracurricular activities. Work only as many hours as is required to meet necessary expenses.

   _____ A job related to your major or career will give you valuable experience that you can list on your résumé or graduate school applications. Use your jobs as opportunities to evaluate your career interests and develop important work skills.

## The Sophomore Year

1. Continue career exploration at the career planning office.

   _____ Look over materials in the career planning office library. *The Encyclopedia of Careers* and *The Occupational Outlook Handbook* can give you basic information on many careers and fields. Other books and pamphlets on particular fields offer information on how to prepare for specific careers and how to find employment in them.

   _____ Make an appointment for vocational testing. Individual testing and meetings with a career counselor can help you zero in on careers that will suit you.

2. Conduct informational interviews.

   _____ Schedule informational interviews with professionals who are working in fields that interest you. Counselors in the career planning office may be able to give you names of people to interview and suggestions for questions to ask.

3. Meet with career advisors or faculty in your major.

   _____ Make appointments to discuss your choice of courses to maximize your career options. Ask about second majors or minors that might enhance your vocational opportunities.

4. Participate in a cooperative education program, if your college has one.

   _____ Cooperative education counselors may be able to place you in a job where you will earn money, college credits, and work experience related to your career. Make an appointment with a counselor as soon as you are eligible for the program.

5. Enroll in internships.

_____ Some of the courses associated with your major may offer a practicum component where you can acquire hands-on experience in your field. Faculty may know of agencies that will give you supervision and job experience in exchange for volunteer work during the semester or over the summer. The career planning office may have books that list corporations offering internships. Explore these options early in the year. Many summer internships have applications deadlines in January.

### The Junior Year

1. Choose your courses carefully.

Many colleges encourage you to explore a variety of areas and to broaden your general knowledge during your first two years of college. General education courses and electives expose you to many different fields and help to make you a more well-rounded individual. By your junior year, however, most colleges expect that you will have chosen a major. The junior and senior years are traditionally the years in which students delve deeper into their majors and strengthen skills and commitment to their area of specialization.

_____ Be certain that you are enrolling in the courses that you will need in order to graduate with a degree in your major. Check the college catalog or other handouts from your department that list required courses.

_____ Meet with an academic advisor in your major to discuss your courses. Many colleges give you a choice in selecting courses that fulfill requirements in your major. Some of these courses may prepare you better than others for a particular graduate program or career.

_____ In addition to taking the courses required by your major program, enroll in electives that will complement or broaden your knowledge in the major. A student specializing in business management may find, for example, that courses like Industrial/Organizational Psychology from the psychology program, Business Ethics from the philosophy program, or Advanced Microcomputer Applications from the computer science program add important career skills to the program in his or her major. A psychology major may find that courses like Sociology of Deviance, Child Welfare, and Cultural Anthropology round out his interests in the major's program. Ask your advisor which courses from other programs at the college best complement your interests and career goals.

_____ Be sure that you are taking courses that will help you develop strong speaking and writing skills.

2. Work as a research assistant.

_____ Find out which faculty members are doing research in areas that interest you. Make appointments to talk to them during their office hours, and ask whether you can work as a research assistant. Graduate admissions officers and employers appreciate the initiative and commitment that such experience shows. They also know that you will have gained valuable hands-on experience and individualized supervision from such work.

3. Join a professional organization.

_____ Many professional programs encourage college students to join by offering reduced student membership rates. State or county organizations like the New Jersey State Psychological Association or the Westchester County Psychological Association may be more accessible to you than national associations like the American Psychological Association.

_____ As a member, you will receive journals or newsletters that will keep you up to date on the newest developments in your field. Read those publications regularly. Ask your academic advisor which organizations might be of the most interest to you.

_____ Attend the conferences of some of the professional organizations in your field. In addition to learning about new trends, some organizations also offer the opportunity to meet with employers at these conferences.

4. Continue your career research.

_____ Be certain that you will be qualified to work in your field. Check the requirements for entry-level skills. Consult career advisors and books in the career planning office library.

_____ Schedule interviews with professionals who are working in your field.

5. Continue to gain work experience related to your field.

_____ Choose your part-time and summer work experiences wisely. Continue to search out cooperative education and internship experiences related to your career interests.

_____ Think about skills you have acquired through job experience, extracurricular activities, or course work that might be of interest to an employer. Organizational ability, leadership skills, and the ability to cooperate or work effectively with different types of people are valuable. Computer skills, fluency in a foreign language, statistical analysis, accounting skills, and research abilities may make you more marketable to many employers. You should be able to talk about such skills during a job interview. You may wish to include some of them on your résumé.

6. Take steps to prepare for graduate school.

_____ Make an appointment to talk with an academic advisor in your field about graduate school. What advantages would graduate or professional training give you? What are your chances of gaining admission to a graduate or professional program?

_____ Check the literature in the graduate advisement office of your college or department to find out about admissions requirements and scholarships.

_____ Many colleges organize a graduate school fair where you can meet admissions officers from a number of schools and programs. Use this opportunity to ask specific questions in addition to picking up general literature about various programs.

_____ Most graduate programs require admissions examinations. Check with the graduate advisement office to see when and where these are scheduled. Take advantage of practice books and practice tests in order to do your best. If you are dissatisfied with your scores, you may be able to take the tests a second time, but both sets of scores (the lower and the higher scores) will be forwarded to the graduate school admissions committees.

_____ Plan to visit graduate schools that interest you while classes are in session. Call ahead and ask whether you can sit in on classes. Talk to students and faculty at the school when you go for an interview or visit. Make a list of questions ahead of time that will help you decide whether you wish to apply for admission to this school.

**The Senior Year**

1. Check your courses against the graduation requirements.

_____ Make an appointment with your academic advisor to be sure that you have completed all the requirements for graduation. April of your senior year is no time to discover that you are missing a required course or credit!

2. Step up your job campaign.

_____   If you have not yet prepared a résumé, meet with a career advisor who can give you pointers on how to write one. The career planning office will also have literature available on content, layout, printing, and so on. This is one of your most-important tools in getting a job. Give it the time and attention it deserves.

_____   Attend a workshop on interview skills. Ask a career advisor about the types of questions that are frequently posed by employers during interviews. Read *Sweaty Palms: The Neglected Art of Being Interviewed* by H. Anthony Medley.

_____   If your college participates in on-campus recruiting programs, make appointments for interviews with companies that interest you. A career advisor may be able to suggest additional appropriate employers for you to contact. Make a list of people you have met who are working in your field. Tell them that you are looking for a job. Give them a copy of your résumé, if that is appropriate.

_____   Always do some research on a company before you go for an interview. Prepare some comments or questions before the interview that will show the employer that you know something about his or her company. This demonstrates both your initiative and sincere interest in the company. Many career planning offices maintain corporate files that include literature and annual reports that can give you information about your prospective employer. Most offices also have directories of employers in specific industries. Do not neglect books like *The 100 Best Companies to Work for in America, The National Job Bank,* and *U.S. Employment Opportunities.*

_____   Attend the job fair, if your college sponsors one. This is a good opportunity to speak to employers about your interests, to ask questions, and to set up interviews. Bring copies of your résumé to the fair, and dress as you would for a job interview.

_____   Make appointments with former employers and faculty members who know your work, to discuss a letter of reference. Give them a copy of your transcript, and highlight the course(s) that you have taken with them. Attach a list of extracurricular activities or other accomplishments that should be mentioned in the letter of recommendation. Ask them to send a copy of the letter to the career planning office so that a copy can be kept in your file for future job applications.

3. Complete the applications process for graduate school if you are planning to continue your education.

_____   Make certain that you have taken the necessary admissions tests, and have the scores mailed to the schools where you are applying.

_____   Send away early in the semester for applications forms from the schools in which you are interested. These forms require considerable time and attention; almost all schools require that you ask faculty to send letters of recommendation, and many ask you to write essays that require some careful thought on your part. Getting your forms in early gives you an advantage at many schools.

_____   If the school suggests that you come in for an interview, take advantage of the opportunity to visit, ask questions, and make a favorable impression. If you have not done so earlier, make an appointment to sit in on classes and talk with students enrolled in the program.

## NOTES

1.   "Identifying Work Values," by H. E. Figler, is reprinted with permission from *Path: A Career Workbook for Liberal Arts Students* (Cranston, R.I.: The Carroll Press, 1979), pp. 77–79.

2. ''Abilities Evaluation,'' by H. E. Figler, is reprinted with permission from *Path: A Career Workbook for Liberal Arts Students* (Cranston, R.I.: The Carroll Press, 1979), pp. 94–97.

3. D. E. Super and J. O. Crites, *Appraising Vocational Fitness,* rev. ed. (New York: Harper Brothers, 1962), p. 287.

# Conclusion

You have come to the end of your first semester at college and are now ready to begin your second. *Congratulations!* You have reached a major survival milestone. I anticipate that the skills you have practiced in this book will make your second semester and the rest of your college experience easier. *Best wishes for a successful college career!*

# Bibliography
# and References

ABELSON, H. I., and MILLER, J. D. "A Decade of Trends in Cocaine Use in the Household Population." *National Institute of Drug Abuse Research Monograph Series* 61 (1985): 35–49.

American Council on Education. "American Freshmen: National Norms for 1987." Washington, D.C.: American Council on Education, 1988.

BAGBY, W. M. *Introduction to Social Science.* Chicago: Nelson-Hall (1987): 25–27, 31–38.

BENENSON, R. "Black America: Long March for Equality," in *Editorial Research Reports.* Vol. 2. Edited by H. Gimlin, R. Worsnop, and M. Gottron. Washington, D.C.: Congressional Quarterly, Inc., 1985.

BRICK, P., and COOPERMAN, C. "Choice and Consequences: Making Decisions About Birth Control." *Positive Images: A New Approach to Contraceptive Education.* Bergen County, N.J.: Planned Parenthood.

BRODY, J. E. "Personal Health." *New York Times,* 19 August 1987.

BRODY, J. E. "The Haunting Spectre of Teenage Suicide." *New York Times,* 4 March 1984, p. 8E.

Catalyst. *Catalyst's Campus Resource: A Guide to Exploring Career and Personal Life Options.* New York: Author, 1984.

Center for Disease Control. "Human Immunodeficiency Virus Infection in the U.S.: A Review of Current Knowledge." *Morbidity and Mortality Weekly Reports* 36, 18 December 1987, pp. 801–804.

CHENEY, L. "Students of Success." *Newsweek,* 1 September 1986, p. 7.

COLEMAN, J. C.; BUTCHER, J. N.; and CARSON, R. C. *Abnormal Psychology and Modern Life.* Glenview, Ill.: Scott, Foresman, 1980.

COMER, J. P. In "Experts Foresee a Social Gap Between Sexes Among Blacks," by L. A. Daniels. *New York Times,* 5 May 1989, p. 30.

Consumers Union. *Licit and Illicit Drugs.* Mount Vernon, N.Y.: Author, 1972.

COREY, G. *I Never Knew I Had a Choice.* 2d ed. Monterey, Calif.: Brooks/Cole Publishing Co., 1986.

COSTANZA, W. V. "The Electronic Text: Learning to Write, Read, and Reason with Computers.'' Englewood Cliffs, N.J.: Englewood Cliffs Publications, New Jersey Educational Technology, forthcoming.

DANIELS, J. P. ''Experts Foresee a Social Gap Between Sexes Among Blacks.'' *New York Times,* 5 May 1989, p. 1.

DeLuca, J. R. *Fourth Special Report to the U.S. Congress on Alcohol and Health.* Washington, D.C.: U.S. Department of Health, Education, and Welfare, January 1980.

DESSLER, G. ''Just Earning College Degree Is Important.'' *Bergen County Record,* 8 September 1986.

DEVINE, T. G. *Teaching Study Skills: A Guide for Teachers.* Boston: Allyn and Bacon, 1987.

DUNPHY, L.; MILLER, T. E.; WOODRUFF, T.; and NELSON, J. E. In *Increasing Retention: Academic and Affairs Administrators in Partnership. New Directions for Higher Education,* no. 60. Edited by M. M. Stodt and W. M. Klepper. San Francisco: Jossey-Bass, 1987.

ECKARDT, M. J.; HARFORD, T. C.; KAELBER, C. T.; PARKER, E. S.; ROSENTHAL, L. S.; RYBACK, R. S.; SALMOIRAGHI, G. C., VANDERVEEN, E.; and WARREN, K. R. ''Health Hazards Associated with Alcohol Consumption.'' *Journal of the American Medical Association* 246 (1981): 648–666.

EL-KAWAS, E., ed. ''Campus Trends, 1984: A Survey of the American Council on Education.'' *Higher Education Report,* no. 65 (1985): 9.

ELLIS, D. *Becoming a Master Student.* Rapid City, S.D.: College Survival, Inc., 1985.

ERICKSON, M. T. *Behavior Disorders of Children and Adolescents.* Englewood Cliffs, N.J.: Prentice Hall, 1987.

EVANS, G. ''Black Students Who Attend White Colleges Face Contradictions in Their Campus Life.'' *Chronicle of Higher Education,* 30 April 1986.

FIDLER, P. P. ''Evidence of Effectiveness of the Freshman Seminar.'' In *Enhancing the Success of the First Year Students: The Freshman Experience.* Edited by J. N. Gardner and M. L. Upcraft. San Francisco: Jossey-Bass, forthcoming.

FIGLER, H. E. *Path: A Career Workbook for the Liberal Arts Student.* Cranston, R.I.: The Carroll Press, 1979.

GOLD, M. S. *800-Cocaine.* New York: Bantam Books, 1986.

GOLD, M. S. *The Facts About Drugs and Alcohol.* New York: Bantam Books, 1986.

GORDON, V. N., and GRITES, T. J. ''The Freshman Seminar Course: Helping Students Succeed.'' *Journal of College Student Personnel,* July 1984, pp. 315–320.

GREENHOUSE, S. ''A New Pill, a Fierce Battle.'' *New York Times,* 12 February 1985, p. 23.

GRIECO, A. ''Cutting the Risks for STDs.'' *Medical Aspects of Human Sexuality,* March 1987, pp. 70–84.

HALL, R., with SANDLER, B. ''The Classroom Climate: A Chilly One for Women?'' *Project on the Status and Education of Women.* Washington, D.C.: Association of American Colleges, 1982.

HATCHER, R. A.; GUEST, F.; STEWART, F.; STEWART, G. K.; TRUSSELL, J.; BOWEN, S. C.; and CATES, W. *Contraceptive Technology 1988–1989.* 14th ed. Atlanta: Printed Matter, Inc.; New York: Irvington Publishers, 1988.

HIPPOLITUS, P. *College Freshmen with Disabilities: Preparing for Employment.* Washington, D.C.: Committee on Youth Development of President's Commission on Employment of the Handicapped and American Council of Education, 1987.

HITCHCOCK, S. T., and BENNER, R. In ''Life after Liberal Arts,'' by W. Raspberry. *Bergen County Record,* 19 June 1986.

HOLMES, T. H., and RAHE, R. H. ''Social Readjustment Rating Scale.'' *Journal of Psychosomatic Research* 11 (1967): 213–218.

HUGHES, T. ''Word Processing: Changes in the Classroom, Changes in the Writer.'' *Conference for Secondary School English Department Chairpersons (CSSEDC) Quarterly* 10, no. 3 (1988): 2–3.

JENKINS, C. D.; ZYZANSKI, S. J.; and ROSENMAN, R. H. ''Risk of New Myocardial Infarction in Middle Age Men with Manifest Coronary Disease.'' *Circulation* 53 (1976): 342–347.

JOHANSEN, C. C.; BALSTER, R. L.; and BONSE, K. ''Self Administration of Psychomotor Stimulant Drugs: The Effects of Unlimited Access." *Psychopharmacology, Biochemistry, and Behavior* 4 (1976): 45–51.

JONES, E. F.; FORREST, J.; GOLDMAN, N.; HENSHAW, S.; LINCOLN, R.; ROSSOFF, J.; WESTOFF, C.; and WUFF, D. "Teenage Pregnancy in Industrialized Countries." In *Contraceptive Technology 1988–1989.* 14 ed. By R. A. Hatcher et al. Atlanta: Printed Matter, Inc.; New York: Irvington Publishers, 1988, p. 51.

JULIEN, R. M. *A Primer of Drug Action.* 3d ed. San Francisco: W. H. Freeman, 1981.

KINNEY, J., and LEIGHTON, G. *Loosening the Grip: A Handbook of Alcohol Information.* 3d ed. St. Louis: C. V. Mosby, 1982.

KOBASA, S. O. "How Much Stress Can You Survive?" *American Health* 66, September 1984.

LACROIX, A. Z.; MEAD, L. A.; LIANG, K. Y.; THOMAS, C. B.; and PEARSON, T. A. "Coffee Consumption and the Incidence of Coronary Heart Disease." *New England Journal of Medicine* 315 (1986): 977–982.

LADNER, J. In "Experts Foresee a Social Gap Between Sexes Among Blacks," by L. A. Daniels. *New York Times,* 5 May 1989, p. 30.

LOUIS, E. T. "Black and Blue on Campus." *Essence,* August 1986, p. 67.

LURIA, A. R. *Mind of a Mnemonist.* Translated by L. Solotaroff. New York: Basic Books, 1968.

LYONS, R. D. "Califano in Drive to End Smoking; Calls Habit 'Slow Motion Suicide.'" *New York Times,* 12 January 1978, p. 14a.

MADD (Mothers Against Drunk Driving). "The Facts: Impaired Driving by Youth." *MADD in Action* 8 (1988): 3.

MASON, M. "The Equality Trap." *Working Mother,* September 1988, pp. 38–42.

MAYER, W. "Alcohol Abuse and Alcoholism: The Psychologist's Role in Prevention, Research, and Treatment." *American Psychologist* 38 (1983): 1116–1121.

MCWHORTER, K. *Study and Thinking Skills in College.* Glenview, Ill.: Scott, Foresman, 1988.

MCWHORTER, K. *College Reading and Study Skills.* Boston: Little Brown, 1982.

Metropolitan Life Insurance Company, Health and Safety Division. *How You Can Control Your Weight.*

National Institute on Drug Abuse. *National Household Survey on Drug Abuse: Population Estimates 1985.* Washington, D.C.: U.S. Department of Health and Human Services, 1987. DHHS Publication No. (ADM) 87-1539.

National Institute on Drug Abuse. *National Trends in Drug Use and Related Factors Among American High School Students and Young Adults, 1975–1986.* Washington, D.C.: U.S. Department of Health and Human Services, 1987. DHHS Publication No. (ADM) 87-1535.

POSTMAN, R. D.; KECKLER, B.; and SCHNECKER, P. *College Reading and Study Skills.* New York: Macmillan Publishing Company, 1985.

President's Committee on Employment of the Handicapped. *The Disabled College Freshman.* Washington, D.C.: Author, 1979.

PRICE, R. H., and LYNN, S. J. *Abnormal Psychology.* Chicago: Dorsey Press, 1986.

PRITCHARD, C. *Avoiding Rape On and Off Campus.* Wenonah, N.J.: State College Publishing Co., 1985.

RASCHKE, D., and DEDRICK, C. "Simulations Approximating Learning Disabilities." *TEACHING Exceptional Children,* Summer 1986, pp. 266–271.

RICHARDSON, L. *The Dynamics of Sex and Gender: A Sociological Perspective.* New York: Harper & Row, 1988.

ROBINS, L. N. National Institute of Mental Health 1983 Epidemiological Catchment Study. In "Youth Suicide: New Research Focuses on Growing Social Problem." *Research News,* 22 August 1986, pp. 839–841.

ROSENMAN, R. H.; BRAND, R. J.; JENKINS, C. D.; FRIEDMAN, M.; STRAUS, R.; and WURM, M. "Coronary Heart Disease in the Western Collaborative Group Study: Final Follow-up Experience at 8½ Years." *Journal of the American Medical Association* 233 (1975): 872–877.

SADKER, M., and SADKER, D. "Sexism in the '80s." *Psychology Today,* March 1985, pp. 54–55.

SAFILIOS-ROTHSCHILD. Reported in M. Sadker and D. Sadker. "Sexism in the '80s." *Psychology Today,* March 1985, pp. 54–55.

SARASON, I. G.; JOHNSON, J. H.; and SIEGEL, J. "Assessing the Impact of Life Changes: Development of the Life Experience Survey." *Journal of Consulting and Clinical Psychology* 46 (1978): 932–946.

SARNO, J. "Disabled Workers: Nation's Untapped Resource." *Bergen County Record,* 15 June 1986.

SCHATZKIN, A. et al. "Alcohol Consumption and Breast Cancer in the Epidemiologic Follow-up Study of the First National Health and Nutrition Examination Survey." *New England Journal of Medicine* 316 (1987): 1169–1173.

SCHLAADT, R. G., and SHANNON, P. T. *Drugs of Choice.* Englewood Cliffs, N.J.: Prentice-Hall, 1982.

SCHMALZ, J. "Hispanic Influx Spurs Step to Bolster English." *New York Times,* 26 October 1988, p. 1.

SEBOLD, A. "Speaking of the Unspeakable." *New York Times Magazine,* 26 February 1989, Sect. 6, p. 16.

SERBIN, L. A.; O'LEARY, K. D.; KENT, R. N.; and TONICK, I. J. "A Comparison of Teacher Response to the Pre-academic and Problem Behavior of Boys and Girls." *Child Development* 44 (1973): 796–804.

SHAFII, M. et al. "Psychological Autopsy of Completed Suicide in Children and Adolescents." *American Journal of Psychiatry* 142 (1985): 1061.

SIMPSON, J. C. "Campus Barrier? Black College Students Are Viewed as Victims of a Subtle Racism." *Wall Street Journal,* 3 April 1987.

SMITH, H. M., and KENNEDY, M. L. *Word Processing for College Writers.* Englewood Cliffs, N.J.: Prentice-Hall, 1989.

"Special Report: Medical Complications of Cocaine Abuse." *New England Journal of Medicine* 315 (1986): 1495–1500.

STARKE, M. C., and BEAR, G. "Grading in Higher Education: A Survey of American Systems and Practices." *Journal of Research and Development in Education* 21, no. 4 (1988): 62–68.

STARKE, M. C. "Retention and Bonding: The Effectiveness of the Freshman Seminar at Ramapo College." Paper presented at the Seventh Annual Conference of the Freshman Year Experience, White Plains, N.Y., April 1988.

STOCKTON, W. "Just How Far, How Fast, for Fitness?" *New York Times,* 16 November 1987, p. C11.

STRICKLAND, J. "The Reluctant Writer and Word Processing." *Conference for Secondary School English Department Chairpersons (CSSEDC) Quarterly* (1988): 4–5.

SUPER, D. E., and CRITES, J. O. *Appraising Vocational Fitness.* Rev. ed. New York: Harper Brothers, 1962.

TAYLOR, H.; KAGAY, M. R.; and LEICHENKO, S. *The ICD (International Center for the Disabled) Survey of Disabled Americans: A Nationwide Survey of 1000 Disabled People.* New York: Louis Harris and Associates, Inc., 1986.

TEPPER, R. *Career Manual.* Mahwah, N.J.: Ramapo College, 1988.

U.S. Department of Commerce, Bureau of the Census. *Statistical Abstracts of the United States 1986,* p. 154. Washington, D.C.: Author, 1985.

U.S. Department of Commerce, Bureau of the Census. "College Enrollment, Degree Credit Only." *Statistical Abstracts of the United States 1986,* p. 149. Washington, D.C.: Author, 1985.

U.S. Department of Commerce, Bureau of the Census. "Median Income of Year-round Full-Time Workers." *Statistical Abstracts of the United States 1986,* table 764, p. 456. Washington, D.C.: Author, 1985.

U.S. Department of Commerce, Bureau of the Census. "Money Income of Households by Educational Attainment of Householder, March 1985." *Statistical Abstracts of the United States 1986,* table 743, p. 446. Washington, D.C.: Author, 1985.

U.S. Department of Commerce, Bureau of the Census. *Statistical Abstracts of the United States 1988,* pp. 11, 14, 15, 20, 26, 125, 422, 423, 436. Washington, D.C.: Author, 1987.

# Index